Contents

SOCIOLOGY

AN INTRODUCTORY COURSE

PAUL COOPER

Senior Lecturer in Sociology
South Downs College of Further Education, Havant

Longman

Acknowledgements

We are grateful to the following for permission to reproduce photographs:

BBC Hulton Picture Library (photo Kurt Hutton), page 51 *left;* Gloria Chalmers, page 51 *right;* Sally and Richard Greenhill, page 183; *The Guardian*, page 114; Scottish Ethnological Archive, National Museums of Scotland, page 11; Tom Steel St Kilda Collection (photo Dr A.M. Cockburn), page 10; Thames Television International, pages 141, 142; Wiener Library, page 22.

COVER: Salford Art Gallery & Museum, Lowry: *Going to Work*

We are also grateful to the following for permission to reproduce cartoons:

Columbus Books *The Extremely Serious Guide to Parenthood* by Keith Ray, pages 3, 24 *above*, 27, 35, 39, 40, 174 *above*, 223, 224, 228, 234; *The Guardian*, pages 147, 159, 176; Ian Kellas/*Oxfam News*, page 179; Leeds Postcards, pages 45, 83, 85, 91, 98, 249; McGraw-Hill Book Co (UK) *Sociology (4th Edn)* by Paul B Horton and Chester L Hunt, page 6, 8, 58; *New Internationalist*, page 251; *Oxfam News*, page 179; *The Sunday People*, Mirror Group Newspapers, page 203; *Portsmouth News*, pages 219, 246; *Private Eye*, pages 37, 73, 100, 174 *below;* *Radio Times*, page 119; *Punch*, pages 23, 24 *below*, 53, 57, 60, 74, 79, 110, 204, 235, 242, 247, 253, 261; *Socialist Worker*, page 237; Sphere Books *The Kids Are All Right* by Tony Husband, pages 13, 15, 30, 41, 47, 70, 86, 106, 109, 117, 121, 230; *The Sun*, page 54; *Sunday Mirror*, page 116; Wildwood House, London, *Sociology 'A' Level Units 8–16* by Penny Henderson, page 201.

We are grateful to the following for permission to reproduce copyright material:

Associated Book Publishers (UK) Ltd for extracts from 'Working Class Youth Cultures' by John Clarke and Tony Jefferson pp 154–156 *Working Class Youth Culture* ed G Mungham and G Pearson (pub Routledge & Kegan Paul plc, 1976) and 'Reactions To Labelling' by David Hargreaves pp 201–202 *The Process of Schooling* ed M Hannersley and P Woods (pub Routledge & Kegan Paul plc); Cambridge University Press for extracts from *Society and The New Technology* by Kenneth Ruthven (1983); Commission For Racial Equality for an extract and table from pp 7, 35 *Overseas Doctors* by Muhammed Anwar and Ameer Ali (1987); the author for extracts from pp 204–205, 206–207 *Human Society* by Professor Kingsley Davis (1948–49); Family Policy Studies Centre for an extract and diagram from *The Family Today* Factsheet 1, September 1985; Gower Publishing Group Ltd for a slightly adapted extract from 'Getting On' by Margaret Attwood and Frances Hatton pp 123–124 *Gender, Class and Work* ed E Gamarnikow et al (1983);

the author's agents for extracts from pp 9, 19 *Black Like Me* by John Howard Griffin © John Howard Griffin 1960, 1961; Guardian Newspapers Ltd for an extract from an article by Robin Lloyd-Jones in *The Guardian* 19/12/86; The Controller of Her Majesty's Stationery Office and The Home Office for extracts and tables from pp 4–6 *Criminal Justice* (1986); the author and BBC Enterprises Ltd for an extract from an article by Nicholas Humphrey p 17 *The Listener* 23/10/86; Hyperion Press for extracts from pp 13, 14 *Women and Power* by Lorraine Culley (1986) Copyright Hyperion Press, Leicester; Macmillan Accounts and Administration for extracts from pp 50–51 *Deciphering Sociological Research* by Gerry Rose (1983) and pp 258–259 *Mastering Social Welfare* by Pat Young (1985); Methuen & Co for an extract from pp 143–145 *The Sociology of Education* by P W Musgrave (1965); The Modern Studies Association for extracts from 'Unemployment and Poverty' by Adrian Sinfield and Neil Fraser pp 41, 43 *The Thatcher Revolution* by The Modern Studies Association (1986); Market & Opinion Research International Ltd and London Weekend Television for extracts and table from *Breadline Britain* (1983) © London Weekend Television, Market & Opinion Research International (MORI) 1983; Thomas Nelson & Sons Ltd for an extract from 'Finding Out' by Ian Shelton pp 38–39 *Perspectives on Society* ed R Meighan, I Shelton and A Marks; New Society for extracts from the articles 'Hooligans, The Forgotten Side' pp 16–17 *New Society* 29/8/86, 'The State of Welfare' by Kenneth O Morgan pp i, iv *New Society* (for Channel Four), 'Society Today' p ii *New Society* 19/11/81; Newspaper Publishing plc for an extract from the article 'The Heartbeat Wales Survey' p 3 *The Independent* 20/2/87; Penguin Books Ltd and Basic Books Inc for extracts from pp 236–237, 382–383 *Sociology: A Biographical Approach* by Peter and Brigitte Berger (Penguin Books, 1976) © Peter and Brigitte Berger 1972, 1976; Pressdram Ltd for an article from *Private Eye* October 1986 © Christopher Logue, Private Eye; The Reader's Digest Association Ltd for extracts from *AA Book of British Birds* (pub Drive Publications Ltd., London 1981); Saturday Review Magazine Co for extracts from the article 'The Double Standard of Ageing' by Susan Sontag in *Saturday Review* 23/9/72 © 1972 Saturday Review Magazine; Times Newspapers Ltd for an extract from *The Times Educational Supplement* 6/2/87; the author, Sylvia Walby and The British Sociological Association for an extract from her article 'Social Inequality: Sociology's Central Issue' from *Exploring Society* ed R Burgess (pub Longman Group Ltd., 1986); Williamson Music Ltd., London and International Music Publications for the lyrics of the song 'Carefully Taught' from *South Pacific* by Richard Rodgers and Oscar Hammerstein II © 1949, 1950 Richard Rodgers and Oscar Hammerstein II, Williamson Music Inc., USA.

Preface

This book could not have been written without the help, direct and indirect, of many people. I should like to thank: my parents; colleagues in the Association for the Teaching of the Social Sciences, at the Associated Examining Board and the Southern Examining Group; teachers and students involved in the Wakeford Community School; and friends, colleagues and students of South Downs College.

Paul Cooper

Introduction

This book aims to provide an introduction to sociology for those students approaching the subject for the first time. It is designed for students taking GCSE Sociology, but should also be useful for students taking GCSE Social Science and Integrated Humanities, as well as those following other introductory courses in sociology.

The sociological approach

What is important about your sociology course is not that you learn a series of facts, dates and names, but that you learn to approach the world in a sociological way. In particular, it is essential to be able to ask the right questions. The sorts of questions you should be asking as you work your way through this book, and indeed when you do any work in sociology, are: 'Who says?', 'What evidence is there for that statement?', and 'How reliable and valid is the evidence?' These, of course, are the very questions we should ask when watching television, reading a newspaper or simply talking with a friend.

In the same way as the historian is interested in what *did* happen rather than what he or she thinks *ought* to have happened, so the sociologist is concerned with the world as it *is*, and should not, as a sociologist, pass moral judgements on what is desirable and undesirable. This is not to say that you should not have your own personal opinions on many of the issues in this book – indeed, you should have – only that those opinions should not colour your sociological judgement.

How to use this book

The real world is not broken up into different topics or themes as this book necessarily is, and it is essential that you are constantly looking for links between the different parts of your sociology course. Many of the extracts, activities and questions have been deliberately chosen to show the links between topics and themes, and it is hoped that by the end of your course you will see how different elements of society affect each other, and that one cannot fully understand any one area of social life without seeing it in the context of the wider society.

Each chapter is organised in a similar way, with the *text* and *extracts* providing an outline of the types of questions sociologists ask in each area. The extracts do vary in difficulty, but all should be accessible to most students. Each extract is followed by several questions, the first one or two usually testing comprehension, and the rest testing more analytical skills. The extracts can either by used as individual written exercises (in which case it is suggested teachers give a mark allocation as they think appropriate) or as a basis for group discussions.

Key terms are highlighted; to a very great extent sociology only makes sense when you fully grasp, and can use confidently, the key terms and concepts, so you should always make sure you understand any new words you come across.

The *activities* are perhaps the most important part of the book. They range from short group exercises to pieces of research which will prove time-consuming. Most, however, require you to find things out for yourself and involve you *doing* sociology, rather than being taught it.

Each chapter has questions which you can use to test your understanding or to practise for the examination. *Review questions* are straightforward questions to test how much you remember of the topic or theme. *Theme-linking questions* are designed to get you thinking about the links between different parts of your course; these might be better used as questions for group work rather than individual written exercises. It is suggested that the *stimulus–response questions*, with marks out of 20, be used as revision exercises. Three essays, in different formats, are set on each topic – you should check which type of essay, if any, you will face in your examination.

There are five suggested projects on every topic, and many of the activities could also provide the basis for a project. Not all suggestions might be suitable and appropriate – your school or college might not have the necessary facilities and resources for some suggestions, for example. You must, therefore, talk over your project with your teacher, and, in any event, all the suggestions need to be developed in some detail to make them manageable and realistic research titles.

If you are studying alone it will obviously be impossible for you to do many of the group-based activities. Try, however, to do as many of the more individual activities as possible; you should find they help your understanding of sociology. Similarly, make sure you think about the answers to the extract questions, even if you do not always write them down.

It is not necessary to study the book in the order of the chapters; indeed, you should try to develop links between topics and themes by frequent cross-chapter reading and activity. It is, however, strongly recommended that you begin with Chapters 1–3 as they provide a necessary foundation for much of the rest of the book.

1

People and Society

Introduction

Societies cannot, of course, exist without people, but, equally, people cannot live without societies. Sociology is about how people create, change and live in societies.

This chapter looks at
> how our behaviour is affected by our biological inheritance and by the particular society in which we live
> how behaviour varies between societies
> how we learn the culture of our society.

Heredity and Environment

One of the dominant themes which runs through much of sociology is the question of how far our behaviour is determined by our biology and how far it is influenced by the society in which we live. Researchers looking at educational achievement, for example, have examined whether some children are born more intelligent than others, or whether educational achievement varies so widely because of the different ways children are brought up and educated. Similarly, sociologists have asked whether violent criminals are genetically different from other people or whether it is social factors which make them as they are. On every such issue opinions differ, and these different views are often referred to as the heredity-environment or nature-nurture debate.

The biological inheritance of humans does place massive restrictions on what we are capable of – however much we practise, for example, we will never be able to fly unaided – but humans are unlike any other species in the way our biology allows us so much choice and freedom.

KEY TERM

instinct an inherited behaviour pattern that does not therefore have to be learnt.

Extract 1 Instinct and Learning in Birds

The study of other species can illustrate the importance of learning in humans. In the following extract, note particularly how, unlike humans, birds have no real choice as to how to behave.

From the moment a bird starts to break its way out of the egg, its behaviour is instinctive. Instinct tells the bird how to take food from its parents, how to fly, how to care for its feathers, how and when to migrate and how to navigate. A bird sings by instinct, pecks at food, threatens rivals and attracts a mate by instinct; it builds its nest by instinct; and, finally, it knows instinctively how to rear its own young.

Instinctive behaviour is inborn, a part of the bird's genetic inheritance; and the bird has no choice but to follow the instincts which it shares with the rest of its species. A great crested grebe, for instance, threatens rivals by adopting a forward posture, with the head and neck low along the water; and it greets its mate by head-shaking, with the neck erect. There is no more a question of an individual grebe suddenly improvising a new movement – for example, scratching its head with its wing instead of its foot – than of its growing an extra wing.

In terms of modern communication, instinctive behaviour has been 'programmed' or 'encoded' into the bird's central nervous system; it is a sort of species-memory, passed on from generation to generation in the genetic material of reproduction.

Even if an individual bird has been reared in isolation from others of its species, it will behave instinctively; a wren, for instance, needs no lessons in singing.

Although instincts generally serve birds well – after all, they are products of natural selection – they do not always serve the best interests of an individual bird. This is because instincts are inflexible.

Instinct tells parent meadow pipits to push food in the wide, vivid gapes of their young; it tells them still more urgently to feed the wider gape of a young cuckoo, even when its own young have been pushed out of the nest and, if still alive, are begging unavailingly for food.

Learning by imitation

As a general rule, young birds do not learn by imitating their parents; and the parents do not deliberately teach their young.

Birds fly by instinct as soon as they leave the nest, and need no teacher other than experience to improve their performance. Instinct does not provide the whole range of skills needed to make a successful landing, and young birds may misjudge distances and crash on their first few landings; but they soon discover how to avoid this. Stories of parent birds teaching their young to

fly – or, in the case of some seabirds, to dive – may be discounted as a misinterpretation, based on the wishful thinking of the observer.

Much of what looks like imitation is, in fact, caused by the transference of mood from one bird to another so that it, too, starts to carry out the same activity. This process, known as social facilitation, may be observed in flocks of birds, when one bird, spotting a predator, flies up and the rest follow; or one starts feeding and the others do the same. The same kind of transference happens with humans when one person starts yawning or looking at his watch in company.

There are some ways, however, in which inexperienced birds do imitate adults. Feeding habits are learnt to the extent that young birds will watch where others feed, and what they feed on; but the actual technique of feeding – the way a thrush hammers open a snail or a nuthatch wedges nuts in the bark of trees before attacking them – is instinctive.

Imitation is probably responsible, too, for sporadic outbreaks of doorstep milk-stealing among blue tits and great tits. One or more birds in a district learn that pecking through the glinting foil of milk-bottle tops will bring a reward of cream, and others follow their example.

Source: *Readers Digest AA Book of British Birds*, Drive Publications, 1981, pp326–28

a What is the major disadvantage of behaviour that is instinctive?
b How can birds improve on their instincts?
c Contrast how birds learn to fly with how babies learn to walk.

Activity 1

Find out which pets (include animals, birds, reptiles, fish and insects) are owned by members of your class.

a Rank the different species in order of intelligence.

b Compare the importance of heredity and learning in the most intelligent and the least intelligent species.

c What are the similarities and differences in the learning processes between your most intelligent species and humans?

d Explain how you decided which species are most intelligent.

'Mummy said that if I wanted proof that we evolved from apes all I had to do was look at you, Dad.'

Humans are, of course, creatures of both nature and nurture. We have biological needs and drives such as food and sex, but how we meet these needs and drives depends upon the particular society and groups in which we live. We are far more flexible than any other species. The kingfisher, for example, will die if there are no fish available; compare this inflexibility with the almost infinite variety of things humans around the world eat. But our flexibility is not total; for example, the protein deficiencies suffered by many African children result in damage to the brain and thus to the very ability to think and perform.

So what does make humans so special and so different from all other species?

Extract 2   *The Ascent of Man*

In *The Ascent of Man* Jacob Bronowski traces our rise both as a species and as moulders of our environment and future. Bronowski here stresses the active nature of humans; unlike other species we do not just respond to our environment. We can, if we wish, change the world we live in.

Man is a singular creature. He has a set of gifts which make him unique among the animals: so that, unlike them, he is not a figure in the landscape – he is a shaper of the landscape. In body and in mind he is the explorer of nature, the ubiquitous animal, who did not find but has made his home in every continent.

It is reported that when the Spaniards arrived overland at the Pacific Ocean in 1769 the California Indians used to say that at full moon the fish came and danced on these beaches. And it is true that there is a local variety of fish, the grunion, that comes up out of the water and lays its eggs above the normal high-tide mark. The females bury themselves tail first in the sand and the males gyrate round them and fertilise the eggs as they are being laid. The full moon is important, because it gives the time needed for the eggs to incubate undisturbed in the sand, nine or ten days, between these very high tides and the next ones that will wash the hatched fish out to sea again.

Every landscape in the world is full of these exact and beautiful adaptations, by which an animal fits into its environment like one cog-wheel into another. The sleeping hedgehog waits for the spring to burst its metabolism into life. The humming-bird beats the air and dips its needle-fine beak into hanging blossoms. Butterflies mimic leaves and even noxious creatures to deceive their predators. The mole plods through the ground as if he had been designed as a mechanical shuttle.

So millions of years of evolution have shaped the grunion to fit and sit exactly with the tides. But nature – that is, biological evolution – has not fitted man to any specific environment. On the contrary, by comparison with the grunion he has a rather crude survival kit; and yet – this is the paradox of the human condition – one that fits him to all environments. Among the multitude of animals which scamper, fly, burrow and swim around us, man is the only one who is not locked into his environment. His imagination, his reason, his emotional subtlety and toughness, make it possible for him not to accept the environment but to change it. And that series of inventions, by which man from age to age has remade his environment, is a different kind of evolution – not biological, but cultural evolution.

GLOSSARY

ubiquitous being everywhere

Source: *The Ascent of Man*, Jacob Bronowski, BBC Publications, 1973, pp19–20

a 1 What does Bronowski mean by 'crude survival kit'?
  2 What is its major advantage?
b Explain the difference between biological and cultural evolution.
c Bronowski is clearly optimistic about what he calls the 'ascent of man'. Write two or three paragraphs, titled 'The Descent of Man', giving a more pessimistic view of human society and social change.

Extract 3 The Human Animal

By definition, every species is different from every other species, but, as Bronowski points out in *Extract 2*, humans are the most unique and distinct of all. In this extract, Richard Leakey outlines, firstly, what is physically unusual about us, and secondly, what is so special about our behaviour.

What are we? To the biologist we are members of a sub-species called *Homo sapiens sapiens*, which represents a division of the species known as *Homo sapiens*. Every species is unique and distinct: that is part of the definition of a species. But what is particularly interesting about our species? For a start, we walk upright on our hindlegs at all times, which is an extremely unusual way of getting around for a mammal. There are also several unusual features about our head, not the least of which is the very large brain it contains. A second unusual feature is our strangely flattened face with its prominent, down-turned nose. Apes and monkeys have faces that protrude forwards as a muzzle and have 'squashed' noses on top of this muzzle. There are many mysteries about human evolution, and the reason for our unusually shaped nose is one of them. Another mystery is our nakedness, or rather *apparent* nakedness. Unlike the apes, we are not covered by a coat of thick hair. Human body hair is very plentiful, but it is extremely fine and short so that, for all practical purposes, we are naked. Very probably this has something to do with the second

interesting feature of our body: the skin is richly covered with millions of microscopic sweat glands. The human ability to sweat is unmatched in the primate world.

So much for our appearance: what about our behaviour? Our forelimbs, being freed from helping us to get about, possess a very high degree of manipulative skills. Part of this skill lies in the anatomical structure of the hands, but the crucial element is, of course, the power of the brain. No matter how suitable the limbs are for detailed manipulation, they are useless in the absence of finely tuned instructions delivered through nerve fibres. The most obvious product of our hands and brains is technology. No other animal manipulates the world in the extensive and arbitrary way that humans do. The termites are capable of constructing intricately structured mounds which create their own 'air-conditioned' environment inside. But the termites cannot choose to build a cathedral instead. Humans are unique because they have the capacity to *choose* what they do.

Communication is a vital thread of all animal life. Social insects such as termites possess a system of com-

munication that is clearly essential for their complex labours: their language is not verbal but is based upon an exchange of chemicals between individuals and on certain sorts of signalling with the body. In many animal groups, such as birds and mammals, communicating by sound is important, and the posture and movement of the body can also transmit messages. The tilting of the head, the staring or averted eyes, the arched back, the bristled hair or feathers: all are part of an extensive repertoire of animal signals. In animals that live in groups, the need to be able to communicate effectively is paramount.

For humans, body language is still very important but the voice has taken over as the main channel of information flow. Unlike any other animal, we have a spoken language which is characterised by a huge vocabulary and a complex grammatical structure. Speech is also an unparalleled medium for exchanging complex information, and it is also an essential part of social interactions in that most social of all creatures, *Homo sapiens sapiens*.

Source: *The Making of Mankind*, Richard E. Leakey, Michael Joseph, 1981, p18–19

a State three physical features which, according to Leakey, make humans unusual.
b What are the main differences between human and animal forms of communication?
c Explain what Leakey means when he calls humans 'that most social of all creatures'.

symbol a word or sign which is generally accepted as representing, or standing for, an object, event or idea.

Language therefore is all-important. We can use words to act as symbols for things we have never seen and feelings and thoughts that do not have a physical appearance. With language, we can study the past and predict the future, and create and share ideas with each other.

Only the human race uses symbols.

Activity 2

a Explain what the following symbolise (i.e. what do they 'tell' you?):
   1 the word 'cat'
   2 double yellow lines by the roadside
   3 standing up while the national anthem is being played.
b What do your answers to the questions tell you about symbols? Explain how and why people sometimes disagree on the meaning of symbols.

Culture

If one striking characteristic of humans is how different we are from all other species, then a second is how we differ from each other. It is these differences between people and societies that sociologists are interested in explaining.

Food is a subject we have different deeply held feelings about, as the following extracts illustrate.

Extract 4 *Attitudes Towards Food*

'I was always interested in unusual food,' said Mr Union Agu, a chef from Chukwak in Nigeria. 'As a child my mother used to heat termites in her pan. They tasted like peanuts. Some people preferred butterflies, but if there were no termites about, we chose cockroaches. They tasted like sardines.
'Nowadays I am serving dog in my restaurant, the Calabar Cross, and it is very popular. Mostly we serve dog stew – corn, alulu spices, and pepper soup, with back-chunks. However, dog dishes are getting special names: Gear Box, for example, means a whole head on a bed of rice with sweet potatoes; Wheels means an order of legs with mixed vegetables; and so forth.'

Source: *Private Eye*, 17 October 1986

I once knew a trader's wife in Arizona who took a somewhat devilish interest in producing a cultural reaction. Guests who came her way were often served delicious sandwiches filled with a meat that seemed to be neither chicken nor tuna fish yet was reminiscent of both. To queries she gave no reply until each had eaten his fill. She then explained that what they had eaten was not chicken, nor tuna fish, but the rich, white flesh of freshly killed rattlesnakes. The response was instantaneous – vomiting, often violent vomiting. A biological process is caught in a cultural web.

Source: *Mirror for Man*, Clyde Kluckhohn, Premier Books, 1963, pp25–26

a What would your reaction be if you went into the Calabar Cross Restaurant for a meal and read the menu? Why do you think you would respond in that way?

b In the second extract, what does the author mean by 'a biological process is caught in a cultural web'?

c What do the two extracts tell us about human societies?

KEY TERM

ethnocentrism the view that one's own culture is superior to that of others.

Most British people reading the first extract would probably think that eating dogs is disgusting, and how morally superior our eating habits are. This tendency to assume that one's own way of life is better than others is known as ethnocentrism.

Ethnocentrism is, of course, widespread, and probably exists in all of us to a greater or lesser extent. We must be particularly careful, however, when doing sociology that we do not regard other societies and groups as in some way inferior, for any bias or prejudice would make it more difficult for us to accurately describe and understand the behaviour of others.

Activity 3

Which of the following statements are ethnocentric?
a It is unnatural to have more than one husband or wife.
b Many people in Africa are not yet civilised.
c Swedes live, on average, longer than Britons.
d I prefer classical to pop music.
e Pop music is rubbish.
The answers are at the end of the chapter.

Ethnocentrism also acts to discourage change.

KEY TERM

culture the way of life of a society, including values and beliefs, attitudes and ideas, customs and patterns of behaviour. Culture has two key characteristics – it is learned and it is shared.

Unlike other species, humans are not born with a blueprint for living; we therefore have to learn the culture of our society before we can participate in it. A word of caution – in everyday language 'culture' usually refers to art, music and literature, but in sociology it has a much broader meaning.

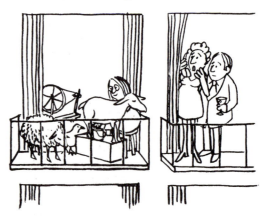

The goodness or badness of a cultural trait depends upon its setting.

If we look at societies other than our own we can immediately see the incredible variety of cultures that have existed and still exist. *Extracts 5* and *6* illustrate the very different views people may have of the world around them.

Extract 5 *Animals in Crime*

Societies vary dramatically in the view their members have of animals. In some cultures certain animals may be worshipped as gods, while in others all animals are seen as mere objects whose sole purpose is to be at the disposal of humans. The following extract may appear hard to believe, but it is worth reflecting on how some pets are treated by their owners at present.

Leafing through some books in Cambridge University Library some months back, Dr Nicholas Humphrey came across a remarkable tome. Published 80 years ago, it was called *The Criminal Prosecution and Capital Punishment of Animals* by E. P. Evans. And no, it was not a joke, as he discovered: 'All over Europe, throughout the Middle Ages and right on into the 19th century, animals were, it seems, tried for human crimes. Dogs, pigs, cows, rats and even flies and caterpillars were arraigned in court on charges ranging from murder to obscenity. The trials were conducted with full ceremony: evidence was heard on both sides, witnesses were called, and in many cases the accused animal was granted a form of legal aid – a lawyer being appointed at the tax-payer's expense to conduct the animals' defence.

'Evans's book details more than 200 such trials: rats being put on trial for having "feloniously eaten up and wantonly destroyed" some local barley; sparrows being prosecuted for chattering in church; a pig executed for stealing a Communion wafer; a cock burnt at the stake for laying an egg. Every case was argued with the utmost ingenuity. Precedents were bandied back and forth, and appeals made to classical and biblical authority.

'In doubtful cases the courts appear, in general, to have been lenient, on the principle of "innocent until proved guilty beyond reasonable doubt". In 1457 a sow was convicted of murder and sentenced to be "hanged by the hind feet from a gallows tree". Her six suckling piglets, being found stained with blood, were included in the indictment as accomplices. But no evidence was offered against them, and on account of their tender age they were acquitted.'

Source: *The Listener*, 23 October 1986, p17

GLOSSARY

arraigned accused
feloniously criminally

As Humphrey goes on to point out, we must be careful not to see the trial of animals as merely the product of irrational minds. It served a purpose – it was in some ways easier to see a pig trampling a child to death through wickedness than as a purely random accident. The trial of animals, in other words, made order out of a world of chaos and accidents.

a Whilst on trial, animals were given human qualities such as wickedness. Explain the ways in which animals, especially pets, are today often treated as if they have human characteristics.
b Using the deaths column of your local newspaper as a source of evidence, explain how some people in Britain today might attempt to 'make sense' of a tragic accident, such as the death of a small child.

Extract 6 *Life on St Kilda*

Sociologists frequently look at small pre-industrial societies in Asia and Africa to illustrate cultural variety. But we should not ignore the differences in lifestyles in Britain, both in the recent past and today.

St Kilda, a group of islands off Scotland's western coast, was for centuries the most remote inhabited part of the British Isles. In 1930 the remaining 36 inhabitants left St Kilda for the Scottish mainland, but until then they had lived a life almost untouched by the rest of Britain. In a harsh climate and with a poor soil, the killing of seabirds was essential to life on St Kilda and was a major economic activity.

Everyone had a part to play in the fulmar harvest which took place every August. Women and children carried the heavy birds down from the top of the cliffs of Conachair to the village.

At the end of each day's killing, the seabirds were shared out equally. Even the old and infirm, who played no part in their slaughter, received a portion. The same night, the birds would be plucked, and then preserved for eating during the long winter months.

The diet of the St Kildans was based on the flesh of these sea birds. Breakfast normally consisted of porridge and milk, with a puffin boiled in with the oats to give flavour. Until the end of the nineteenth century, the people disliked wheaten food and fish, and ate mutton or beef only as a last resort. The main meal of the day, taken at about lunchtime, comprised potatoes and the flesh of the fulmars.

Nearly all food on Hirta had to be boiled or stewed. There were no ovens on the island, save the range that was the proud possession of the minister in the manse. To the outsider, food tasted rather bland, and a lack of proper fuel meant that it was usually undercooked and never served very hot. 'When boiling the fulmar,' wrote John Ross, 'they sometimes pour some oatmeal over the juice and take that as porridge, which they consider very good and wholesome food which I have no doubt it is to a stomach that can manage to digest it.'

The islanders also ate large quantities of eggs, which, one visitor remarked, 'they just eat as the peasantry eat potatoes'. Gathered in the spring months, the eggs were boiled and eaten immediately, or else preserved in barrels. The St Kildans were never too fussy about the freshness of the eggs, often keeping them for six to eight weeks before eating them because, they said, time added to their flavour.

The most important possessions on Hirta, used and maintained by the community as a whole, were the boats. Without them, the St Kildans could hardly have existed. They depended upon being able to make the frequently hazardous journey to Boreray and the great stacs to trap the thousands of sea birds that were their livelihood.

At the end of the seventeenth century, the community owned one boat only sixteen cubits long. It was divided into sections, proportional to the number of families on the island at the time, and every householder was responsible for providing a piece of turf large enough to cover his section of the boat in summer to prevent the hot sun from warping and rotting the precious wooden shell.

Source: *The Life and Death of St Kilda*, Tom Steel, Fontana, 1975, pp58–59

a Explain how the killing of the seabirds served to bring the St Kildans together.

b When the St Kildans moved to the mainland in 1930, many of them found it very difficult to adjust to their new way of life. What problems do you think they would have faced?

Activity 4

a Write a paragraph about three of the following in a society other than Britain:
  1 laws
  2 politics
  3 dress
  4 religion
  5 music
  6 education
  7 eating habits.

You could find out the information you need by using your school/college or public library, watching TV documentaries or videos, or interviewing people who have lived in the society.

b Carry out the same activity for Britain today.

c Compare your paragraphs on Britain with those of your fellow students. What does this comparison tell you about the difficulties of studying and writing about other societies?

KEY TERMS

norm a standard of expected behaviour in a particular situation, e.g. it is a norm to wear clothes to work, but not in the bath.
value a belief in society about what is good and desirable, e.g. a 'good' job, happiness.

KEY TERMS

folkways normal and conventional behaviour, but not norms of fundamental importance. Not obeying a folkway is not considered too serious. For example, it is a folkway to wear dark clothes at a funeral.
mores these are norms the group considers of major importance. Breaking mores will be punished severely. For example, killing someone because you have had an argument is breaking the mores of society.

All cultures contain guidelines or rules of behaviour; without them social life would be impossible. We cannot, for example, choose which side of the road to drive on or take what we want from shops without paying, just as we cannot make up our own rules when playing a sport or game.

Norms and values do not just appear; they are created by people and they can be changed. Precisely where society's norms and values come from is a central concern of sociology.

Activity 5

a Draw up a list of three different norms which guide your behaviour. What happens if you break them?

b Do you think that the different age groups in Britain share the same values?

The line between folkways and mores is rarely clear and straight-forward; it is perhaps best to see norms as more or less important, and distinguish them in terms of how strongly they are enforced.

KEY TERMS

socialisation the process in which an individual learns the culture, i.e. norms, values, beliefs and symbols, of the society or group to which s/he belongs.

primary socialisation takes place in early childhood, mainly within a family, and is when a child learns the basic rules of society and develops a personality of its own.

secondary socialisation takes place after early childhood when we learn, not just from our family, but from such institutions as schools, work and the mass media.

Socialisation

Culture can be seen as what we learn from other people. How we learn, and from whom we learn, thus become key questions of sociology, and this process of learning is known as socialisation.

Secondary socialisation continues until we die; we are constantly learning new ideas and how to behave in situations we have not faced before.

'Young Thomas is very much like his father, isn't he?'

Extract 7 Isolated Children

The case of children brought up without any, or very little, contact with other people illustrates most dramatically the importance of the socialisation process. Scientific experiments which deny babies contact with other people would, of course, be totally immoral, but occasionally children are discovered who have been largely isolated from other people.

Two such cases have been seen by the writer. The first was the case of an illegitimate child called Anna, whose grandfather strongly disapproved of the mother's indiscretion and who therefore caused the child to be kept in an upstairs room. As a result the infant received only enough care to keep her barely alive. She was seldom moved from one position to another. Her clothing and bedding were filthy. She apparently had no instruction, no friendly attention.

When finally found and removed from the room at the age of nearly six years, Anna could not talk, walk, or do anything that showed intelligence. She was in an extremely emaciated and under-nourished condition, with skeleton-like legs and a bloated abdomen. She was completely apathetic, lying in a limp supine position and remaining immobile, expressionless, and indifferent to everything. She was believed to be deaf and possibly blind. She of course could not feed herself or make any move on her own behalf. Here, then, was a human organism which had missed nearly six years of socialisation. Her condition shows how little her purely biological resources, when acting alone, could contribute to making her a complete person.

By the time Anna died of haemorrhagic jaundice approximately four and a half years later, she had made considerable progress as compared with her condition when found. She could follow directions, string beads, identify a few colours, build with blocks, and differentiate between attractive and unattractive pictures. She had a good sense of rhythm and loved a doll. She talked mainly in phrases but would repeat words and try to carry on a conversation. She was clean about clothing. She habitually washed her hands and brushed her teeth. She would try to help other children. She walked well

and could run fairly well, though clumsily. Although easily excited, she had a pleasant disposition. Her improvement showed that socialisation, even when started at the late age of six, could still do a great deal toward making her a person. Even though her development was no more than that of a normal child of two to three years, she had made noteworthy progress.

The other case of extreme isolation, that of Isabelle, helps in the interpretation of Anna. This girl was found at about the same time as Anna under strikingly similar circumstances when approximately six and a half years old. Like Anna, she was an illegitimate child and had been kept in seclusion for that reason. Her mother was a deaf-mute and it appears that she and Isabelle spent most of their time together in a dark room. As a result Isabelle had no chance to develop speech; when she communicated with her mother it was by means of gestures. Lack of sunshine and inadequacy of diet had caused her to become rachitic. Her legs in particular were affected; they 'were so bowed that as she stood erect the soles of her shoes came nearly flat together, and she got about with a skittering gait'. Her behaviour toward strangers, especially men, was almost that of a wild animal, manifesting much fear and hostility. In lieu of speech she made only a strange croaking sound. In many ways she acted like an infant. 'She was apparently unaware of relationships of any kind. When presented with a ball for the first time, she held it in the palm of her hand, then reached out and stroked my face with it. Such behaviour is comparable to that of a child of six months.' At first it was even hard to tell whether or not she could hear, so unused were her senses. Many of her actions resembled those of deaf children.

Once it was established that she could hear, specialists who worked with her pronounced her feebleminded. Even on non-verbal tests her performance was so low as to promise little for the future. 'The general impression was that she was wholly uneducable and that any attempt to teach her to speak, after so long a period of silence, would meet with failure.' Yet the individuals in charge of her launched a systematic and skilful programme of training. The task seemed hopeless at first but gradually she began to respond. After the first few hurdles had at last been overcome, a curious thing happened. She went through the usual stages of learning characteristic of the years from one to six not only in proper succession but far more rapidly than normal. In a little over two months after her first vocalisation she was putting sentences together. Nine months after that she could identify words and sentences on the printed page, could write well, could add to ten, and could retell a story after hearing it. Seven months beyond this point she had a vocabulary of 1,500–2,000 words and was asking complicated questions. Starting from an educational level of between one and three years (depending on what aspect one considers), she had reached a normal level by the time she was eight-and-a-half years old. In short, she covered in two years the stages of learning that ordinarily require six. Or, to put it another way, her IQ trebled in a year and a half. The speed with which she reached the normal level of mental development seems analogous to the recovery of body weight in a growing child after an illness, the recovery being achieved by extra fast growth until restoration of normal weight for the given age. She eventually entered school where she participated in all school activities as normally as other children.

GLOSSARY

emaciated thin
supine face upwards
rachitic having rickets
IQ Intelligence Quotient
anologous similar

Source: *Human Society*, Kingsley Davis, Macmillan, 1948–49, pp204–205

a Why had Anna and Isabelle been isolated?

b What skills that six-year-olds normally possess were Anna and Isabelle unable to perform when discovered?

c What does the case of Isabelle tell us about primary socialisation?

Activity 6

Frederick II, Holy Roman Emperor from 1220 to 1250, wished to discover what language children would speak naturally, if they never heard a single word. He thought it likely such children would speak Hebrew, Greek, Latin or the language of their parents. A group of children were selected and physically cared for by nurses, but they were never spoken to. Unfortunately, all the children died before the truth could be revealed to the Emperor.

a What language would the children have spoken had they lived?

b What false assumption did the Emperor make?

c Had the children lived, what sort of adults would they have become?

'Dad, when are you going to tell me about the facts of life? – unemployment, divorce, crime, drugs, street violence . . .'

The main agencies of socialisation are the family, peer group (people of approximately the same age, usually friends), school, mass media, religion and work.

The different socialising agencies vary widely, both in their power and influence, and how they actually socialise people. A peer group, for example, does not deliberately and consciously set out to socialise its members while a school might have a definite policy on the types of personality characteristics it wishes to instil into its students. The peer group, of course, might well be more influential than the school! Socialisation is a theme that runs through much of sociology; how we learn to behave as we do and how we learn the different roles we play throughout life are questions that are central to many of the issues discussed in this book.

Each of us occupies a variety of different social positions during our lifetime. Even in the course of a single day, for example, we may be a daughter, sister, student, friend, neighbour and employee, and we will probably be expected to behave differently according to the particular position we are filling at any particular time.

KEY TERMS

status a position in society.
ascribed status a position one is born into, e.g. daughter.
achieved status a position one obtains through choice and/or effort, e.g. teacher.

Activity 7

List three ascribed statuses and three achieved statuses you occupy.

In practice it is not always so easy to distinguish between ascribed and achieved statuses as sociologists often suggest. The eldest son of the monarch, for example, has the status of heir to the throne through ascription or birth, not through achievement or effort, but he does not have to become king. Abdication or renouncing his right to the monarchy may be rare, but the heir does have that choice.

As we occupy a new status, so we must learn the new patterns of behaviour expected from us.

KEY TERM

role the pattern of behaviour expected from the occupant of a particular social position.

We expect shop assistants, bus conductors and teachers, for example, to behave in a particular way; social life would be totally chaotic and disorganised if we could not expect people to conform, within certain limits, to our view of a particular role.

Activity 8

What are the roles associated with the following statuses:
a wife
b post office clerk
c vicar
d elderly man?
Compare your answers with your fellow students. Do you all agree?

Your answers to *Activity 8* may well have shown that there are some roles in society on which there is considerable disagreement. This can give rise to personal disagreements and social conflicts, especially when these roles are personally important to us, such as our various family roles.

Extract 8 *Roles and Role Conflict*

There are a variety of terms that sociologists use when looking at roles. In the extract below, Martin Slattery outlines some of the more important ones.

Social roles can be divided into formal (judge, priest, milkman) and informal (father, son, friend), but no individual plays only one role in society. Most of us perform a variety of roles. The local bank manager may also be chairman of the ratepayers' association or the golf club, for instance.

The term role-set is more specific and refers to the way one of these major roles brings an individual into direct relationships with others. A local doctor's role-set would include his relationships with his patients, doctors in the local hospital, fellow doctors in his professional association and so on.

Inevitably, such variety and inter-connection of expected ways of behaving involves the possibility of role conflict either for: the individual – the military chaplain, say, who is both an officer and a priest; or between individuals, in the performance of their expected roles – the engineer and the production manager clashing over quality versus quantity, for example.

As we grow up, we learn roles as part of the socialisation process. We acquire the norms, values and roles expected by society both by observing and imitating adults – especially our parents – and by a system of rewards and punishments. A dutiful son is praised, a naughty pupil is punished.

Equally a doctor who commits misconduct with a patient is struck off, a hard-working manager is promoted. Such sanctions can be quite minor or informal but nevertheless effective – a stern look, 'being sent to Coventry', idle gossip, for example.

Source: *The ABC of Sociology*, Martin Slattery, Macmillan, 1985, p92

a Explain briefly the meaning of:
   1 multiple roles
   2 role-set
   3 role conflict.
b Draw a diagram showing the various people in the role-set that influences your role as a student.
c Give an example of role conflict that you face in your role of student.

Questions and Suggested Projects

Review Questions

1 Explain what is meant by the 'nature–nurture' debate.
2 What are the major differences between humans and other species?
3 Explain the meaning and importance of the following:
    a culture   b role   c norm   d symbol   e socialisation.

Theme-linking Questions

1 Examine the extent to which the changes that take place as we age are due to social, rather than biological, factors.
2 How are we socialised into:
    a 'falling in love'   b wanting a 'good' job?
3 What are the traditional roles associated with males and females? Is there any evidence to suggest that they are beginning to change?
4 What part does schooling play in socialisation?
5 All occupational statuses are not considered equal.
    a Select ten occupations and rank them in order, from the highest to the lowest.
    b What basis did you use to rank the occupations? Why did you rank some higher than others?
    c Where do your beliefs about the different statuses of occupations originate from?

Stimulus–response Question

The importance of culture lies in the fact that it provides the knowledge and techniques that enable mankind to survive, both physically and socially, and to master and control, insofar as it is possible, the world around him. Man seems to possess few if any instinctive skills and no instinctive knowledge which might enable him to sustain himself, either singly or in groups . . . Man . . . survives only by virtue of what he learns.

Man is not, however, the only animal that learns to act instead of responding automatically to stimuli. Dogs can be taught a good deal and can learn from experience, as can horses and cats, monkeys and apes, and rats and white mice. But by virtue of his greater brain power and his capacity for language, man can learn more and therefore possesses greater flexibility of action than other animals. He can transmit a great deal of what he learns to others, including his young, and he can in part control the world around him – even to the point of transforming much of it. Man is the only animal to possess culture; indeed, this is one of the crucial distinctions between man and other animals.

Source: *Society*, Ely Chinoy, Random House, 1961, p21

a State one major advantage of man's greater brain power given in the above extract. (1)
b What two factors enable humans to learn more than other species? (2)
c What do sociologists mean by the term 'culture'? (2)
d Explain how we learn the culture of our society. (7)
e 'Norms and values vary dramatically from society to society.' Explain this statement, using examples to illustrate your answer. (8)

Essays

1 How do we learn the different roles we perform? Give examples to illustrate your answer.
2 a Explain, using examples, the differences between ascribed and achieved statuses.
  b Choose any two statuses and describe and explain the roles associated with them.
3 'Human beings are creatures of nurture, not nature.' What is the evidence for and against this view? Your answer could include:

> the nature–nurture debate
> isolated children
> the importance of culture
> the differences between humans and other species.

Suggested Projects

1 A library project on isolated children, perhaps concentrating on the validity of the evidence.
2 A study of how the guidance offered by child-care manuals has changed since World War Two.
3 A study of a particular role, e.g. student, and how different members of the role-set have different views of it.
4 A comparison of two cultures, concentrating on one particular area of social life.
5 A study of a deliberate attempt by a government to instil particular values into young people, e.g. Nazi Germany.

Answers to Activity 3

a, b and e are ethnocentric.
c is a statement of fact.
d is expressing a personal opinion, but is not saying classical music is better than pop music; it is, therefore, not ethnocentric.

2

Control and Order

Introduction

If people are to live in societies, which they must do, then they must generally conform to the rules of the society in which they live. Socialisation is the mechanism by which we come to accept the values and norms of society and the various groups we belong to, and this chapter will examine how the various agencies of socialisation help enforce rules, and what happens if those rules are broken. Many of the most important rules of society become laws, so special attention will be paid to the law and criminal behaviour.

Social Control

Some rules, of course, are more important than others, and so therefore are the consequences of breaking them.

Activity 1

What are the likely consequences of being caught doing the following:
a lighting a cigarette in your sociology class
b murdering your next-door neighbour
c wearing school uniform to a disco
d refusing to visit a sick relative in hospital?

KEY TERM

sanction a reward for keeping to a rule or a punishment for breaking a rule.

Sanctions for breaking rules vary from temporary ridicule from friends to death. A possible sanction in many small-scale pre-industrial societies is expulsion from society altogether; we cannot in Britain today compel offenders against the rules to emigrate, but we can exclude them from 'normal' society by locking them up in prison.

KEY TERM

social control the means society uses to ensure conformity to its rules.

KEY TERMS

conformity obedience to the rules of society or a group.
deviance the breaking of the rules of society or a group.

The rules of society, whether they are relatively minor ones like not shouting in church or major ones like not assaulting people we don't like, do not just appear from nowhere. Sociologists therefore are not just interested in what the rules are, but also in:

a who makes the rules
b how they are enforced
c how and why they change.

Conformity is much more likely to be achieved if people who conform are rewarded, and all societies and groups therefore develop a system of rewards or positive sanctions for those who obey the rules.

Activity 2

What positive sanctions would you receive if you did the following:
a visited a sick relative in hospital
b rescued a drowning child from a river
c swam for your school or college team
d worked hard for GCSE Sociology?

The rules of society or a group can be enforced through the threat of physical violence, but if people only obey the rules because they are frightened of the consequences of breaking them, one day they might conquer their fear and rebel. Such societies are therefore not as stable and secure as those where people obey the rules because they think those rules are just and fair.

Extract 1 The Warsaw Ghetto

Throughout history, social control has often been maintained through the threat, and the use of, physical violence. During 1941 and 1942 the Jewish people of Warsaw and the surrounding area were compelled by the Nazis, on pain of death, to move to the ghetto, a single, walled part of the town which they were forbidden to leave, and deprived of all outside contact.

By the early months of 1942 life in the ghetto had become a cruel and losing battle against hunger and disease. So short was fuel, that in a survey of 780 dwellings in the winter of 1941–42, it was found that as many as 718 had no heat at all.

Food was desperately short, the food allocation allowed by the Germans being only 194 calories per Jew per day. Outside the ghetto walls, the Poles of Warsaw were allowed 634 calories and the Germans 2,310 calories. With such precise calculations did the Nazis ensure that tens of thousands of Jews, without any means of earning a living, unable to keep themselves warm in winter, died of starvation. The adults and older children strug-gled as best they could to find food, to eke out their meagre rations, to subsist on 500 grams of sugar and 2 kilos of bread a month: even the bread was mixed with potato peel and sawdust. When there was no bread, there was no hope. Yet for the younger children, it seemed unreal. Avraham Kochavi recalled how his younger sister Adela would ask his mother repeatedly for some-thing to eat:

'She always said "Bread, bread, bread." And mother had nothing to give her. I somehow understood the situation and accepted it. But my sister was three years younger – she was eight years old. She didn't want to accept this because she didn't understand it. She always shouted "Bread, bread, bread – food." And there was none.'

Hunger and disease were the curse of the ghetto. Old men and children, too weak to move any further, would lie down in the streets and die. In October 1941, in order to ensure that food could not be smuggled in from outside, the Germans announced that anyone leaving the ghetto without permission would be shot. By the early months of 1941 more than one person in ten had died: a total of 40,000 people, each slowly and deliberately starved to death, trapped behind a wall in a city under Nazi rule, in a conquered land, in a Europe which could do nothing against the German will.

Source: *Final Journey*, Martin Gilbert, George Allen and Unwin, 1900, pp100–2

Part of the wall and fence which sealed the Jews inside the Warsaw ghetto.

(In 1942 over 300,000 Jews were deported from the Warsaw ghetto, most of them to the death camp at Treblinka. A year later, the Nazis levelled the ghetto to the ground, despite courageous resistance by the remaining Jews.)

a How did the Nazis attempt to maintain social control in the ghetto?
b Are there any societies in the world today where social control relies totally on physical force? If so, which?

How, then, do most of us usually come to accept that the rules of society are fair and just? Why, for example, do we believe that:
a teachers have the right to set homework
b democracy is preferable to dictatorship
c work is better than unemployment
d parents should be responsible for their children?

KEY TERM

social order the maintenance of generally accepted norms and roles in a relatively stable society.

The family, education, peer group, mass media, religion and the law are agencies of social control which help socialise us into accepting the rules of society. The more successful these agencies of control are the greater will be the degree of social order.

Note the words 'generally accepted' and 'relatively' in the definition of 'social order'. Norms and roles are never totally accepted by everyone and no society is ever completely unchanging. The questions the sociologist must ask therefore are:
  'To what extent is there agreement in society on desired norms and roles?' and 'How stable is a particular society and to what extent is it changing?'

The Family

'Look at it like this, Father – if they're going to rebel against their upbringing, why not bring them up the wrong way?'

'The good news is that I've decided to stop smacking you when you are naughty . . .'

Because children are dependent on adults for the first few years of their lives the family plays a key role in socialisation, and because most families are likely to socialise children into generally accepted values, norms and roles then the family is a key agent of social control. It is in the family that most children learn the basic moral, political and religious values of their society, and families have a wide range of sanctions available for children who do not conform.

In pre-industrial societies the family is likely to be the sole major socialising agency. In industrialised societies, on the other hand, there are several key socialising agencies. This raises the possibility that the different agencies may well attempt to transmit different values and norms. Differences of opinion on the desirable ways to behave may well arise between the family, the school, the media and the peer group. There is therefore never likely to be complete agreement on desirable values and norms, and, indeed, precisely what the values and norms are may be unclear and unknown to some people in some situations.

Activity 3

a Construct a brief questionnaire which asks people of your age where they obtained their values and norms from on the following areas of life:
   1 politics
   2 religion
   3 sex
   4 education.
Your questionnaire answers could be open-ended or allow your respondents a choice of a limited number of socialisation agencies (e.g. family, education, mass media, friends).
b Decide how many fellow-students you are going to interview, and how to draw up your sample. (See page 55 for information on the different types of sample.)
c Carry out your survey and present the data you obtain in the form of bar-charts, pie-charts, etc.
d What sociological conclusions can you draw from your survey about the sources of people's values and norms?

Education

The world of the school is very different from that of the family. For example, the organisation of the school is far more complex than that of the family; the head, teachers, caretakers and students all have different functions and responsibilities which cannot be easily changed or modified as they can within the

'Oh, by the way . . . according to my teacher I'm suffering from a lack of discipline in the home. See to it, will you . . .?'

family. Further, school rules are officially laid out, usually in writing, and are, in theory at least, applied equally to every student.

KEY TERM

formal organisation an organisation set up, with a definite structure and set of rules, for a specific purpose.

As a formal organisation, therefore, the school has particular purposes and aims; these are laid down by the Department of Education and Science, local education authorities, examination syllabuses and by the teachers themselves. These aims are to a great extent concerned with the types of values and norms schools wish to instil into their students.

Extract 2 Schools and Political Conformity

Schools therefore can play an important part in social control, by attempting to promote values which help maintain the existing social order. Political leaders have long recognised this and have frequently used schools in order to encourage conformity and discourage dissent.

The decision that the schools should have a definite part in promoting political consensus can be a conscious decision. The part the school plays in Russia is a good example. In our view much of the history taught in Russian schools is given a bias with the intention of making the children loyal to the Communist régime so that they will see the world in the way that the rulers of Russia wish them to do. However, it is possible that most countries do much the same thing unconsciously in their own schools. History textbooks provide many examples. For instance in describing the War of the Spanish Succession, British books tend to mention only British victories and omit French ones. French books tend to minimise or omit the part played by Marlborough. Both sides claim to have won the war. In the case of the Hundred Years War British texts make much of Crecy, Poitiers and Agincourt, so that British pupils are left wondering how we came to lose so many of our French possessions by 1453. Spanish textbooks have omitted any mention of the Armada.

It may be thought that it is easiest to build up loyalty to the country in such school subjects as history, geography and the teaching of the mother tongue, and that this process will be more powerful when the child is at the secondary stage. But this is not so. The textbooks of many countries could be quoted. A careful study of anthologies of verse for young children with their stress on national folk heroes would be relevant at this point. But here examples from German textbooks will be given. An elementary reading book dated 1906 will show how the ideal of militarism, then considered a political necessity by the rulers of Germany was inculcated into the young child.

"We want to play soldiers," said Albert. "Yes, soldiers," cried the others. He divided them into two armies, four boys in each. Charles led his army to a large sand heap. Albert had to storm this with his soldiers. Shouting "Hurrah! Hurrah!" they ran up the sand heap, came to grips with the enemy and took them prisoner. Thus Albert won the war with his soldiers."

Or, again under the Nazi elementary arithmetic was used to teach the young child the political aims of the new régime. The child became familiar with large numbers by reading how 13.25 millions were called up by Germany in the First World War and 11.25 millions by Germany's allies. These men carried on the 'heroic' fight, against the 47.5 millions of the league of Germany's enemies. Language can be used in an emotional way even in elementary arithmetic textbooks. Again, the child learnt how to multiply and divide using money from tables comparing the sums spent yearly on education and on lunatics; the intention was to show at the same time what an expensive liability the mentally handicapped were to the State. Similar problems were given using the number of Jews in Germany.

Source: *The Sociology of Education*, P. W. Musgrave, Methuen, 1965, pp143–45

GLOSSARY

consensus agreement

Source: *Granma: Proa a la Historia*, Havana, 1975, p42

The activities children are asked to do in such apparently non-political subjects as music and art can also indicate how the school can be used as an instrument of conformity. The picture on the left, for example, was painted by an eight-year-old Cuban girl and shows the revolutionaries, led by Fidel Castro, just disembarked from their boat Granma, and preparing to attack the armed forces of Batista, the Cuban dictator.

a If Castro had been defeated and Batista was still in power how do you think eight-year-old children would be painting the above event today?
b What values were the Nazis trying to instil into children at school in Germany in the 1930s?
c How can schools teach history and geography to encourage the values of patriotism and ethnocentrism?

Activity 4

Schools often try to produce different values in different types of children. Obtain a syllabus for:
1 a GCE A-level subject
2 a GCSE subject
3 a CPVE course
4 a Special Needs course.
(If you cannot obtain all of these, obtain others sufficient to cover the whole span of ability.)
a What are the differences and similarities in the aims of the syllabuses?
b What assumptions do the different syllabuses make about the type of student likely to be taking the course?
c What values are the aims trying to encourage?

Like all formal organisations, however, schools have relationships and values which are not officially laid down in rule-books and syllabuses. An important element of this informal aspect of the school is the values and norms which children pick up even though teachers are not consciously trying to teach them.

KEY TERM

hidden curriculum the values and norms transmitted by the school through its day-to-day processes.

The idea of the hidden curriculum suggests that students learn many things at school apart from what is officially laid down in syllabuses. The hidden curriculum varies from school to school, and teacher to teacher, but students are constantly picking up new values and new ways of behaviour. Students, of course, will not necessarily accept a teacher's view of 'decent' dress, what is 'good' literature or which jobs are most desirable. The hidden curriculum may be hidden from those who run the schools, but it is not so hidden from students, who are thus in a powerful position to reject it. The music teacher, for example, who constantly insults pop music is unlikely to have much success in persuading pupils to listen to Radio 3 rather than Radio 1.

Activity 5

Draw a diagram illustrating the different types of post filled by paid staff in your school or college. (If you are a student in a large school or college it might be more practical to draw a diagram containing the senior staff and one or two departments only.)

a Note down how many males and females fill each type of job.

b What image of males and females in society does the information contained in your diagram present to the students?

Peer Groups

Although peer groups are informal and we have a great deal of choice in deciding which ones to join, they are nevertheless important agencies of social control. The rewards for conformity to, and the punishments for deviance from, the norms of a peer group are likely to be powerful guides to our behaviour. Approval, ridicule, respect and ultimately exclusion from the peer group are sanctions often more powerful than those that parents and teachers can offer. Peer groups probably have most influence over young people, when the family is losing some of its control and work and a family of their own are yet to become important.

'Call yourself a magistrate! How can I ever show me face in the gang with a measly fine of £2?'

Extract 3 Skinheads and Conformity

Although youth groups like skinheads might be seen by many as deviant, within a skinhead group there is great emphasis placed on obedience to its values and norms. Read this study of a skinhead gang in East London.

Its most striking aspect was the conformity, only equalled by the council flats that they live in. The conformity of the uniform was a demonstration of the uniformity of the language, areas of discussion, interests, attitudes and actions. There is security in this sameness – individuality was a threat and could not be tolerated. Membership was based on the embracing of the conformity, termination of membership was achieved by non-conformity. This could be a difficult task if the member needed the approval of the other members, as the group pressures may be too strong to overcome. All the members of the gang were dependent on the gang, they were forced together due to their common experiences and common attitudes to the society at large. They gave each other the support that they did not receive from the community. The gang itself was often referred to as a community and even by some on odd occasions as their family. In this way the gang supplied a very real service to the members when they were in need of a sense of belonging. An identity and the knowledge that they were wanted by other people.

The gang had no authority structure, or defined leadership. There were no rules as such, everything was controlled by group pressure – by which we mean that every person tries to be and tries to get the others to be and behave the same. It was a kind of effort to lose themselves so that they couldn't be got at. If you can conform then no one can jump on you for being different. As everyone in the group behaved the same, the individual members were safe, even if all the members of the gang didn't conform with the dominant rules of society. John said, after a few incidents had been described, 'We just ran away from them all.' We see this as a sense of being detached, a kind of ignoring the people outside of the gang, and the physical and mental ability to escape from them all. The approval of activities within the gang overrides the disapproval from outside.

Source: *The Paint House*, Penguin, 1972, pp116–17

a How does the skinhead gang maintain conformity?
b What advantages does membership of the skinhead gang offer its members?
c In what ways do groups like skinheads frequently not 'conform with the dominant rules of society'?

The Mass Media

The mass media – television, radio, cinema, newspapers, magazines, advertising billboards – are different from other forms of social control in that we are unlikely to have direct and personal contact with them, as we do, for example, with parents, teachers and peer groups. This impersonal nature of the mass media means that the viewer, listener or reader has little, if any, influence over the form and nature of the communication, but also that the media cannot readily impose direct sanctions on us if we do not conform to their messages.

Activity 6

Construct a brief questionnaire in order to find out, in your class:
a how many hours, on average, your class-mates watch television each week
b which television programmes are most popular
c how often your class-mates go the cinema
d which newspapers are read
e which weekly and monthly magazines are taken. (See pages 56–57 for guidance on writing questions.)

Extract 4 *The Extent of Television Viewing*

Of all the forms of the mass media, it is television which has created most public concern and attracted most interest from sociologists. A major reason for this is the amount of time that we spend watching television, as the chart illustrates.

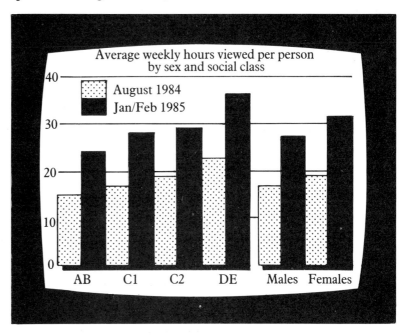

Source: Tony Garrett, *New Society*, 28 February 1986

a Which social class watches most television?
b Approximately how many hours a day does the average adult in Britain spend watching television?
c One reason is mentioned above for the great concern shown about the power of television. Can you think of any other reasons?

So what part do the media, especially television, play in social control? Although their effects on our behaviour and beliefs should not be exaggerated, they certainly do play a part in making us see the world in a particular way, and they are, of course, a key source of information about social, political and economic issues. Three important processes, gate-keeping, agenda-setting and norm-setting, within the media determine what information is presented to us and how.

KEY TERMS

gate-keeping the process whereby such people as newspaper and TV news editors have the power to decide which issues and news items are to be covered, and which are to face a 'closed gate' and are therefore not discussed.

agenda-setting the process whereby the media decide what issues should come before the public and how much importance should be given to each item.

norm-setting *how* items are presented to the public. The actual presentation of an item may well influence the audience's response.

Activity 7

Select two members of your class, one to watch a main news programme on BBC and one on ITV. They should note down, in order, the subject of the first ten news items. All other students in the class should avoid watching the news programmes in question. The two appointed students should produce a list, in random order, of the first ten items which appeared in the two programmes. (The two programmes are, of course, unlikely to be identical, so you may well have 12–15 items in your list.)

a In groups of three or four, imagine you are an editorial team for a half-hour television news programme. Decide what order you would put the news items on your list in, how many minutes you would devote to each item, and which items you would leave out.

b Compare the agenda you have set for your news programme with those of the other groups, and the actual agendas that appeared on BBC and ITV.

What do the similarities and differences between the agendas tell you about the nature of, and processes involved in, agenda-setting?

'I think we ought to turn it orf . . . it's frightening Mum and Dad . . .'

Extract 5   *The Social Production of News*

Newspapers, probably more than television, differ in the weighting they give to different items of news. Newspapers, unlike both BBC and ITV, do not have to give a 'balanced' view of the world, and they are targeted directly at particular types of readers who, the newspapers believe, want items presented in a particular way.

The media do not simply and transparently report events which are 'naturally' newsworthy *in themselves*. 'News' is the end-product of a complex process which begins with a systematic sorting and selecting of events and topics according to a socially constructed set of categories. As MacDougall puts it:

'At any given moment billions of simultaneous events occur throughout the world . . . All of these occurrences are potentially news. They do not become so until some purveyor of news gives an account of them. The news, in other words, is the account of the event, not something intrinsic in the event itself.'

One aspect of the structure of selection can be seen in the routine organisation of newspapers with respect to regular types or areas of news. Since newspapers are committed to the regular production of news, these organisational factors will, in turn, affect what is selected. For example, newspapers become pre-directed to certain types of event and topic in terms of the organisation of their own workforce (e.g. specialist correspondents and departments, the fostering of institutional contacts, etc.) and the structure of the papers themselves (e.g. home news, foreign, political, sport, etc.).

Given that the organisation and staffing of a paper regularly direct it to certain categories of items, there is still the problem of selecting, from the many contending items within any one category, those that are felt will be of interest to the reader. This is where the *professional ideology* of what constitutes 'good news' – the newsman's sense of *news values* – begins to structure the process. At the most general level this involves an orientation to items which are 'out of the ordinary', which in some way breach our 'normal' expectations about social life, the sudden earthquake or the moon-landing, for example. We might call this the *primary* or *cardinal news value*. Yet, clearly 'extraordinariness' does not exhaust the list, as a glance at any newspaper will reveal: events which concern elite persons or nations; events which are dramatic; events which can be personalised so as to point up the essentially human characteristics of humour, sadness, sentimentality, etc.; events which have negative consequences, and events which are part of, or can be made to appear part of, an existing newsworthy theme, are all possible news stories. Disasters, dramas, the everyday antics – funny and tragic – of ordinary folk, the lives of the rich and the powerful, and such perennial themes as football (in winter) and cricket (in summer), all find a regular place within the pages of a newspaper. Two things follow from this: the first is that journalists will tend to *play up* the extraordinary, dramatic, tragic, etc. elements in a story in order to enhance its newsworthiness; the second is that events which score high on a number of these news values will have greater news potential that ones that do not. And events which score high on *all* dimensions, such as the Kennedy assassinations (i.e. which are *unexpected* and *dramatic*, with *negative* consequences, as well as *human tragedies* involving *elite persons* who were heads of an extremely *powerful nation*, which possesses the status of a *recurrent theme* in the British press), will become *so* newsworthy that programmes will be interrupted – as in the radio or television newsflash – so that these items can be communicated immediately.

Source: *Policing the Crisis*, Stuart Hall et al., Macmillan, 1978, pp53–54

GLOSSARY

ideology set of ideas
elite most powerful groups of people

a Explain how the way a newspaper is organised influences the items it publishes.
b List the characteristics a news story should have if it is to be placed top of the agenda on television and in newspapers.
c Make up a news item which would be the lead story on page one of:
    1 both the *Sun* and *The Times*
    2 *The Times* but not the *Sun*
    3 the *Sun* but not *The Times*.

Activity 8

Find out answers to the following questions. The data you require should be easily available in your school or college or local public library. Don't hesitate to ask the librarian to guide you to the appropriate books and periodicals.

a Who owns the national daily and Sunday newspapers?
b Which political party, if any, does each paper support?
c Which television programmes are watched by most people?
d What are the most popular films currently being shown at the cinema?

Religion

While the mass media, especially television, have become more important, few people would dispute that the influence of religion as a means of social control in Britian has declined. Religion, however, has been one of the major sources of our laws, norms and values, and the behaviour of many people in Britain is still very heavily influenced by their religious beliefs. Further, there are many countries in the world where religious beliefs are a major determinant of social and political behaviour, and many countries, such as Northern Ireland, where religious differences play a major part in dividing the people and creating social conflict.

Religions vary so dramatically that any definition which tries to cover all of them is bound to be unsatisfactory, but it is probably safe to assume that all religions involve some sort of belief in some sort of supernatural power. But religion is not just a system of beliefs; it also includes a set of religious practices or rituals, and it is organised in a formal way, usually into churches with a specialised, paid clergy.

Activity 9

For each of the following religions, name a major ritual and state what function the ritual performs. You should be able to obtain the necessary information from reference books or encyclopaedias in your school or college library.

a Christianity
b Hinduism
c Islam
d Judaism.

Your answers to *Activity 9* have probably shown that religion is usually concerned with important events in life, such as birth, coming of age, marriage and death, and, in pre-industrial societies, often with the collecting and eating of food. Religion, therefore, is frequently used as a way of making sense of the world, especially sudden and tragic events that appear to have no logical explanation.

Extract 6 *Religion: An Explanation for Evil and Prosperity*

Using the example of Hinduism in India, the extract below illustrates the ways in which religion has often offered an explanation for the inequalities that exist in most societies.

An important relation between religion and 'the world' of everyday social life is brought about by religion providing society with a *theodicy*. The word literally means 'the justice of God' and refers to the problem, classically expressed in the Book of Job, of how to reconcile belief in an omnipotent and benevolent God with the presence of suffering and evil in the world.

Weber calls a theodicy any socially established interpretation of human suffering, injustice or inequality. He distinguishes between what he calls the theodicy of suffering and the theodicy of happiness. Those who suffer in the world, be it because of the actions of other men or because of 'acts of God', have a natural propensity to ask why they are thus afflicted, especially since other men are not. Religion has always provided answers to this question – though the answers are greatly different in different religious traditions. The theodicy of happiness, on the other hand, satisfies the need of those who are in a more favoured condition of life for the comforting reassurance that somehow this condition is what they deserve. Not all, but many, religious traditions have met this need as well. Weber maintained that the most rational and comprehensive theodicy to be found in history is that of classical Hinduism. Hindu theodicy was based on its belief in reincarnation and in *karma* (the doctrine that every human act has inevitable consequences for the actor, some of which extend beyond this present life). This means that every human being is precisely in the condition which he deserves. Those who suffer have no basis on which to complain, and those who are happy have no reason to feel guilty. It is this unique theodicy of Hinduism that explains the astonishing lack of rebellion against the Indian caste system, which, to modern eyes, imposed an intolerably harsh condition upon the lower castes. But since suffering is a universal human condition, even in the most privileged human strata, the need for theodicy is universal. Religion shows most clearly its function of providing ultimate meaning for human life in its ability to integrate the painful and terrifying experiences of life, and even death itself, into a comprehensive explanation of reality and of human destiny.

Source: *Sociology, A Biographical Approach*, Peter and Brigitte Berger, Penguin, 1976, pp382–3

GLOSSARY

omnipotent all-powerful
propensity tendency

a What questions asked by (**1**) the poor, and (**2**) the rich, does religion answer?

b According to the extract, why did the lower castes so rarely rebel against the inequalities of the caste system?

c Explain the last two sentences of the extract, using your own words and giving examples to illustrate your answer.

Extract 7   Karl Marx on Religion

Issues of religious truth and validity are the concern of theologians (people who study religion), not sociologists, who are concerned with the social, as opposed to spiritual, effects of religion. Karl Marx (1818–1883), however, denied the very validity and truth of religion, seeing it purely and simply as an instrument used by the powerful to keep the weak and poor in their places.

> 'Man makes religion, religion does not make man . . . Religion is the sigh of the oppressed creature, the heart of a heartless world, just as it is the spirit of a spiritless situation. It is the opium of the people.'

Source: 'Selected Writings', Karl Marx, in *Sociology and Social Philosophy*, eds. T. B. Bottomore and M. Rubel, Pelican, 1963, p41

a What does Marx mean by 'the opium of the people'?
b What might happen if the 'opium' was taken away?

It is not, however, inevitable that religion must operate as an agent of control and therefore support the established order. For nearly five centuries the Roman Catholic Church in Latin America did support the *status quo* (existing order), in particular persuading the poor that it was God's will that they endure squalor and poverty. But since the 1960s more and more Catholic priests have begun to take the side of the poor, arguing that true Christianity demands an end to the massive inequality of most countries in Latin America. Similarly, much of the opposition to apartheid in South Africa has been led by churchmen like Archbishop Tutu.

In Britain, although the Church of England is intimately linked to the state, it has become increasingly involved in political controversy in recent years, and can no longer be called, as it used to be, 'the Tory Party at prayer'.

Activity 10

In order to discover how significant religion is in the everyday life of Britain, study as many different daily newspapers as possible on one particular day, and two or three editions of your local newspaper. Record every time religion is mentioned. What do your findings tell you about the role of religion:
a in national issues of economic, political and social importance
b in the life of your local community?

A major debate among sociologists who study religion is about the extent to which religion is still important in Britain. Religion used to be at the very centre of life; is it today? An immediate problem is that it is almost impossible to discover how significant religion is in the lives of people. Non-religious people in previous centuries may have gone to church because of social pressures, while very religious people today may not go to church but may pray regularly at home. Church attendance figures therefore tell us very little about the extent of religious beliefs, but they do indicate very clearly that Britain is increasingly a multi-religious society. The number of people claiming to be members of Christian churches has been steadily declining over recent years, while the numbers of practising Muslims, Hindus, Sikhs and Buddhists have been increasing. There are, for example, now significantly more Muslims in Britain than Methodists and Baptists combined.

To the extent that Britain has become secular then obviously religion has declined in its importance as a means of social control. But even though a minority of Britain's population are members of any religious organisation, for many millions of people religion is a powerful source of values and beliefs. Religious thinking, practices and institutions are still important for the members of the various churches, but perhaps the most striking feature about religion in Britain today is its fragmentary nature. It is non-European religions such as Islam, and sects like the Mormons and Jehovah's Witnesses, which are growing in membership, not the established Christian churches. This fragmentation and this variety in beliefs and values suggests that, though religion is a central part of life for many people, it is playing a declining part in the maintenance of social order in societies such as Britain.

Crime and the Law

Law and social control

Of all the various agencies of social control, it is the law which possesses the most powerful negative sanctions; breaking norms which are considered so important that they have been made into laws can result in a fine, imprisonment or, in many societies, even death. The law is also unusual as an agent of social control in that there are people, such as the police and judges, specially employed to enforce it; teachers, parents and clergymen may play an important part in social control, but it is unlikely that they see this as their primary function.

'*Now* we'll find out why you were sent home early from school with 500 lines.'

Activity 11

Which laws have you broken which you do not mind admitting to your fellow students?

a Compare your list with that of your fellow-students.

b What do your lists tell you about the way different crimes are seen?

What is against the law does not, of course, remain static over time, and what is lawful varies widely from society to society. Drinking alcohol or selling Conservative Party literature, perfectly lawful activities in Britain, could get you into serious trouble in Saudi Arabia and Moscow respectively.

Activity 12

a State two acts which have been made crimes in Britain only since the Second World War.

b State three acts which used to be illegal in Britain but are now lawful. (Possible answers are at the end of the chapter.)

Sociologists, when studying law, are interested in two questions. First, who makes the law? In Britain it is Parliament which decides what acts should be lawful and which not, but important issues are how far MPs are influenced by public opinion, and whether particular groups of people outside Parliament are able to have a disproportionate influence on what becomes illegal.

Second, to what extent is there public support for the law? If people generally think the law is fair and just they are, of course, much more likely to obey it. A law which the majority, or even significant minority, think is wrong is unlikely to be successfully enforced, unless perhaps the punishment for breaking it is so severe that people obey purely out of fear of the consequences. In the United States between 1920 and 1933 the manufacture and sale of alcoholic drinks was prohibited; not surprisingly there was widespread evasion of the law by people who thought alcohol use neither immoral nor undesirable.

Activity 13

a Are there any laws in Britain today which do not enjoy support from either the public as a whole or particular ethnic or age groups?
b If so, what are the consequences of this lack of approval of the law?

'Walter's the leading light of our neighbourhood watch scheme!'

Crime and deviance

Deviance is the breaking of the norms of society or a group; it is therefore not necessarily the same as crime.

What is criminal in any particular society is usually not in doubt; laws are written down and formally sanctioned. One might not approve of a particular law, but one cannot easily disagree with what the law actually says. What is considered deviant, on the other hand, depends on one's point of view; homosexuality, for example, is regarded by some people as deviant, by others as normal.

Activity 14

a Give two examples in each case of acts you consider:
    1 deviant but not criminal
    2 criminal but not deviant
    3 both criminal and deviant.
b Compare your answers with those of your fellow-students.
c What do your answers tell you about the nature of crime and deviance?

Extract 8 Football Hooliganism

It is frequently claimed that crime and violence have increased over the years. It is, unfortunately, impossible to say whether this belief is true or not, because we do not possess reliable data with which to compare today with the past. It is true, however, that there have been violent and bloody periods in Britain's past, when it was much more dangerous to walk thc strccts than today. Football hooliganism, for example, is hardly new.

In recent years, politicians, media pundits and newspaper editors have all shown concern about the state of the contemporary game, the abuse of alcohol, the subsequent threat to property, the escalation of male violence, and the intrusion of politics into football (such as 'far right' organisations using football as a context for recruitment). All tend to posit the existence of a golden age of football, after which there has been a recent fall from grace.

Golden ages are always elusive, and finding one for football is extremely difficult: football has always reflected society. Returning to those days when opposing fans stood shoulder to shoulder, clapping the opposition, may be difficult because such a time hardly existed.

Taking a historical perspective, the traditional game of football was violent and a threat to property; was often lubricated by generous amounts of alcohol; attracted repressive legislation from the state; and often acted as a vehicle for political protest.

Modern football, about which there is so much concern, is a creation of the second half of the 19th century. Then football became a game with set rules, clear objectives and an agreed number of players. Before that time, its ill-defined predecessor had been banned from many urban centres of the industrial revolution because of its unruly nature. Undoubtedly, the old game survived in the unrecorded margins of early nineteenth century society, but it was suppressed because it created problems of social control in this new environment; the old game of football was a casualty of accelerating urbanisation.

Football in the pre-industrial period was subject to a high degree of regional variation. Pitches could be as much as three miles long with goals in separate villages. The numbers per side sometimes went into hundreds with the mass of people participating rather than observing, although smaller games were also more common and often took place in churchyards on Sundays.

The game's relationship with violence continued until the upheavals of industrial social change.

Shrove Tuesday was a popular time for big football matches, a time of release before embarking on the austerity of Lent. In the annual Derby between St Peter's Parish and All Saints, the pitch was a mile long and over a thousand people participated; such an event without alcohol and violence just wouldn't have been traditional. The annual match in Chester was abolished in 1539 because of the violence.

'Much harme was done, some in the great thronge falling into a trance, some having their bodies bruised and crushed; some their arms, heads or legs broken and some otherwise maimed.'

In 1583 the game was described as a 'devilish pastime' which gave birth to 'brawling, murder, homicide and a great effusion of blood'. In Wales, villages often had games on Christmas day; an account of one game in Cardiganshire in 1800 described how men and women participated in a spectacle which was nothing short of a serious, bloody fight. Football and violence were synonymous.

Source: 'Hooligans: the forgotten side', Norman Jones, *New Society*, 29 August 1986, pp16–17

GLOSSARY

pundit expert
synonymous the same

a Why do those concerned with football hooliganism today frequently suggest it is a new phenomenon?

b What problems of social control did football before the nineteenth century create?

c What image of football hooliganism is presented in newspapers and on television? (It would be useful to collect any newspaper articles which refer to football hooligans.) Look particularly carefully at the type of language used to describe hooligans.

'It says, "Why not get your window fixed in Bob-a-job Week?" '

Approaches to crime

Why do people commit crimes? In many ways this is a misleading question. People commit crimes for such a wide variety of reasons that any one simple explanation is bound to be wrong. Both drinking alcohol under age and murder are criminal offences, but a 17-year-old drinking a pint of beer in a pub is likely to be doing so for very different reasons from those which cause an armed robber to murder a post office clerk. Further, even the same act might be committed for very different reasons.

Activity 15

What different reasons or explanations can you give for someone:
a stealing a bar of chocolate from a supermarket
b committing murder?

However, the different ways in which crime has been approached are important. The reasons why we believe crime takes place will be a major factor in deciding how we behave towards criminals.

Biological approaches

Before the twentieth century it was widely believed that criminals inherited their criminality; they were born criminals, and any form of prevention or cure was therefore futile. Decent, law-abiding people had to be protected from these inherently evil and wicked criminals, who therefore had to be imprisoned or killed.

Few people today would accept that criminals are 'born, not made':
a There are few, if any, of us who have never broken the law; it is obviously not very helpful to argue that we are all inborn criminals.
b What is criminal varies from society to society.
c No one has ever proved that a particular gene results in a particular type of behaviour.
d It is impossible to isolate biological factors from a person's upbringing.

Psychological approaches

There are many different psychological approaches to crime, but most stress that some people develop, often through socialisation within the family, a type of personality which makes it more likely that they will commit crimes. Such factors as 'broken

'I've not been naughty, Daddy . . . I've just been manifesting the preliminary symptoms of a behavioural maladjustment syndrome.'

homes' and 'working mothers' have at times been believed to produce young people who are prone to delinquent behaviour, but studies which emphasise these sorts of factors rarely discuss precisely how difficult it is to define a 'broken home', and there is no substantial evidence to show that the majority of children from 'broken homes' or with 'working mothers' grow up to be any different from other children.

Sociological approaches

Both biological and psychological approaches assume that there is a major difference between criminals, especially those who commit serious crimes, and the rest of us. Sociologists, on the other hand, would suggest that the differences between criminals and 'normal' people are not quite so clear-cut. We may not imagine we could ever murder, for example, but have you ever read a newspaper story of a wife killing her drunken and violent husband, and thought you would have been tempted to do the same in similar circumstances?

Indeed, as important a question as why do people become criminals is why, most of the time, do most of us obey the law.

While both biologists and psychologists emphasise the personality of the individual criminal, sociologists look at the wider structure of society for an understanding of criminal behaviour. Different sociologists emphasise different aspects of society, but perhaps the two most important sociological approaches are those which have stressed the significance of, firstly, the strains caused by the clash between what people want and what they obtain, and, secondly, the ways in which people are labelled deviant.

Strain approaches

Approaches which stress the importance of strain often take as their starting point the finding from official statistics that criminal behaviour is more common among poorer people. Such people, it is argued, suffer a clash between values and means; they are socialised, through the media and education especially, into wanting a nice house, car, foreign holidays, fashionable clothes, meals out, etc., but are denied the opportunity, because of their poorly paid job or unemployment, of obtaining these desirable things. One possible response therefore is to try to obtain them by illegitimate means, i.e. by crime. Because many others are in the same position, criminal subcultures emerge which see much crime as acceptable. In other words, people in certain positions in society learn criminal behaviour as they learn all other behaviour.

Although   this   approach   has   the   advantage   of   relating

KEY TERM

subculture the norms, values and beliefs shared by a particular group in society.

criminal behaviour to the wider society, it does have several drawbacks:

a It assumes everyone wants the same material success, but not everyone who cannot afford foreign holidays, for example, feels deprived.

b It cannot explain crimes such as child abuse and rape.

c It implies that many poor people will turn to crime to obtain the desirable goods of society – the majority do not.

d It cannot explain why well-off people turn to crime. White-collar crimes such as fraud, tax evasion and expense account 'fiddling' are much more widespread than the official crime statistics suggest.

KEY TERM

labelling the processes by which individuals and groups classify and categorise social behaviour and other individuals.

'– on the other hand, David, from a Christian point of view, mugging people in the street is a criminal offence . . .'

Labelling Approaches

Sociologists have become increasingly interested in the ways certain individuals and groups are labelled, and in the implications these labels have for people's self-images and the ways in which they are treated by other people.

Activity 16

What do the following labels mean:
a mentally ill
b intelligent
c delinquent
d backward?

Your answers to *Activity 11* probably revealed that everyone has committed several crimes, yet few of us are seen, or see ourselves, as criminals. In one very important sense, therefore, we are not criminals until we have been so labelled. Whether someone is labelled a criminal will obviously depend on whether s/he is caught, but also to some extent on who s/he is and the circumstances in which s/he commits the act.

Important questions those sociologists who emphasise the importance of labelling ask include:
a Who does the labelling?
b Where do the ideas behind the label come from?
c Which people are most likely to be labelled?
d What are the effects of this label?

For example, only a small minority of people who steal are actually convicted of theft and therefore officially labelled a thief. It is this label which may affect how such people are treated by others, and it will probably have serious practical effects, such as restricting employment opportunities and the likelihood of obtaining credit. Further, the label may result in the person changing his or her self-image and, as legal opportunities may also now be limited, the individual may begin to act out the label.

> **Activity 17**
>
> Refer back to *Activity 16*. How would an individual given the following labels respond:
> a mentally ill
> b intelligent
> c delinquent
> d backward?

Your answers to *Activity 17* may have shown that not everyone labelled behaves in the same way; being once convicted of theft, for example, may not necessarily lead to deviance amplification, but may make the labelled individual determined never to steal again.

Labelling is not really an explanation of why crime takes place, but it does enable us to understand better what may happen when someone has committed a criminal act.

> **Activity 18**
>
> Elizabeth and Louise have, separately, been caught by a store detective stealing from a supermarket. Describe possible circumstances in which Louise would be labelled a thief, but Elizabeth would not.

A note of caution

Evidence for the breakdown of social order and the need for greater social control is often found in official crime statistics. Although such statistics are of great interest to sociologists and the general public alike, it is very dangerous to draw any conclusions from them as they do not accurately reflect the quantity and distribution of crime. (For more detail on the limitations of crime statistics see pages 48–49.)

Order and Control in Organisations

This chapter has looked at how order and control are maintained in society as a whole, and what means are available to persuade people to conform to the dominant values and norms of society. But all the organisations we belong to, such as schools, hospitals, clubs and sports teams, have their own values and norms and their own means of ensuring conformity. Most of the organisations we belong to, especially as we get older, we join voluntarily, and can therefore leave if we dislike the ways in which order is maintained. But in an institution we are compelled to join, social control can be maintained in a way we do not approve of but can do little to change.

Extract 9 *Women in Prison*

In the following extract, Pat Carlen describes the feelings of the women in Papa Block, Cornton Vale, Scotland's only women's prison.

The prisoners address the officers as 'Miss'. This in itself is a hated reminder of schooldays.

"We've got to say, 'Yes, Miss' and 'No, Miss', sort of 'three bags full, Miss,' this sort of thing." (Thelma Thompson)

"I work in Reception. If I want to go to the toilet, I have to say, 'Please, Miss, can I go to the toilet, Miss?'" (Ann Archer)

In their turn the officers monitor the women's deportment and personal cleanliness. At the age of fifty-nine Mandy MacDonald was resentful of being told by a young officer that she must keep her hands out of her pockets; Clare Carlton felt that she did not need a young officer to tell her how to keep her cell clean and tidy:

"We're all grown women in here. I'll be forty-seven on Saturday and when I get a young lassie of twenty-one telling me how to polish my floor, how to make my bed, it gets right up my nose." (Clare Carlton)

Women, like Clare, whose whole life has been steeped in the ethos of maternal responsibility, experience a very specific and painful loss of status when they themselves are treated as the children of a paternalistic regime which denies them their adulthood.

"I think most grown women know how to keep themselves and their room clean. Perhaps it's different with men . . . or with very young girls, but I think that most women who've had a home and reared a family don't need to be told." (Clare Carlton)

Thelma Thompson thought that it was *because* she was treated like a child in prison that she had deteriorated into a 'rambling' chatterbox!

"If they would treat us more like adults we would feel better. Sometimes it's hard to be an adult if you're getting treated like a child . . . You know . . . going in twos, 'Take your hands out of your pockets.' You talk like that to children, you don't talk like that to married women with children, or grandchildren." (Thelma Thompson)

Source: *Women's Imprisonment, A Study in Social Control*, Pat Carlen, Routledge and Kegan Paul, 1983, pp113–14

a How are the women prisoners labelled by the prison officers, and how did they think this had affected their behaviour?

b How is social control maintained in the prison?

c How do you think the officers would perceive relationships between themselves and the prisoners?

d No indication is given in the above extract of the offences committed by the women prisoners. Discuss whether and how your responses to the extract might vary if you were told firstly, the women were shoplifters and secondly, child-murderers.

Questions and Suggested Projects

Review Questions

1 What do sociologists mean by:
    a social order
    b social control
    c conformity
    d deviance?
2 What are the main agencies of social control in Britain today and what sanctions are available to them?
3 Briefly outline the key questions sociologists ask when studying crime?

Theme-linking Questions

1 How do politicians in democratic societies maintain their authority?
2 Examine the extent to which the changes in family structure in recent years may influence the socialisation children receive?
3 Children, young people and the elderly may all become members of peer groups.
    a Explain what advantages the different age groups would obtain from forming close friendships with people of their own age.
    b What sanctions do the three types of peer group possess?
4 Find out (for example from *Social Trends*) the different crime rates for males and females. What possible explanations can you offer for such differences?
5 Collect all the national daily papers for one day. Extract all articles which refer to:
    work and unemployment
    education
    crime
    sex
    males and females.
    a What differences exist between the various newspapers?
    b What are the dominant messages presented to the public on the above topics?

Stimulus–response Question

a

Source: Leeds Postcards

b

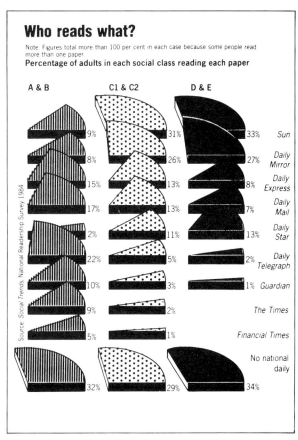

Source: Tony Garrett, *New Society*, 28 November 1986

a What proportion of people in social classes A and B read the *Guardian*? (1)

b According to the above figures, which paper has the best claim to be 'classless' in terms of its readers? (2)

c Extract **a** is based on the front page of the *Sun* on 4 May 1982. Give a brief sociological comment on it. (4)

d What do sociologists mean by:
1 agenda-setting
2 norm-setting? (4)

e 'The power of the mass media is much exaggerated.' What are the arguments for and against this view? (9)

Essays

1 'Deviance is in the eyes of the beholder.' Explain and discuss.
2 **a** What part does religion play in maintaining social order?
  b Examine the arguments for and against the view that Britain is now a secular society.

3 Examine the importance of schools as a source of values and norms. Your answer could include:

> the hidden curriculum
> sex-role socialisation
> political socialisation
> who controls the schools
> alternative sources of values and norms.

Suggested Projects

1 A study of how football hooliganism is portrayed in news papers.
2 A case study of social control in one institution, e.g. school or hospital.
3 A library study of a government's attempt at political indoctrination, e.g. Nazi Germany, the Soviet Union in the 1930s, the Khmer Rouge in Kampuchea.
4 A study of a local religious sect.
5 A 'victim study' to examine how likely people are to report different types of crime.

Possible Answers to Activity 12

a Drunken driving, insider dealing, incitement to racial hatred, secondary picketing.
b Homosexuality (males over 21), attempted suicide, abortion.

3

How Sociologists Find Things Out

Introduction

This chapter is concerned with the various methods sociologists use in order to find things out, and the types of data and information which can be used.

Each method and type of data has its advantages and disadvantages. Which method or type of data a sociologist chooses will depend partly on the nature of the issue being investigated, and partly on the available resources.

Both primary and secondary data can be sub-divided into two types: numerical and written.

I THINK WE'RE BEING BUGGED

Secondary Data

Official statistics

There are many topics in sociology which are largely dependent for information upon statistics issued by the government. Sociologists studying population, divorce, crime and educational achievement, for example, often base much of their work on such secondary quantitative data, but it must always be borne in mind that official statistics are rarely as accurate and valid as they at first sight appear.

Examples of the variety of official statistics appear throughout this book; they should all be handled with care. Some, like divorce statistics, do tell us exactly how many divorces take place in a particular year, but they tell us little about the meaning of marriage, perhaps reflecting above all the legal and financial ease of obtaining a divorce. Other statistics, like those on suicide, are likely to tell us more about how they are collected than anything else; in the case of suicide, more about how coroners categorise sudden deaths than the number of people who actually kill themselves.

Activity 1

Using your school or college library, find the statistics on the following. (You may need to ask the librarian for help.)
a The population at the last census of (1) Britain, (2) your town.
b The last general election result in your constituency.
c The number of crimes committed in your area.

Extract 1 *Crime Statistics*

As mentioned on page 42, crime statistics are widely quoted. The bar-chart and pie-chart below are examples of the types of crime statistics issued by the government, but increasingly such statistics are issued with important qualifications.

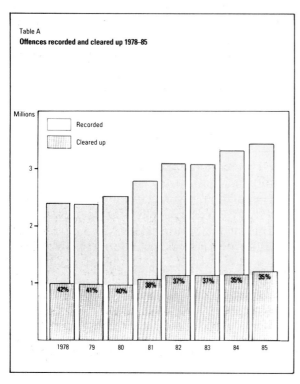

Table A
Offences recorded and cleared up 1978–85

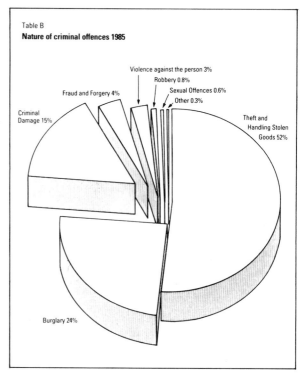

Table B
Nature of criminal offences 1985

Tables A and B show the number of offences recorded and cleared up in 1978–85 and the nature of the offences recorded in 1985 (the vast majority were offences against property). These statistics cannot however be taken at face value as a true indicator of the level of actual crime or, necessarily, of its true rate of increase. A number of reservations and qualifications have to be made:
(i) Research has shown that there is a deep pool of crimes which are never reported to or recorded by the police.
(ii) The ease with which people can report crimes or are under some obligation to do so affects the extent to which they act; thus greater police presence, improved police/public relations, the increase in the use of the telephone and the extension of insurance can all put up the level of recorded crime and so make the crime figures look more serious. Paradoxically, more police officers may result in more reported crime.
(iii) Police practice may play a part. Although every effort is made to ensure uniformity, it is up to the local forces to interpret instructions on recording offences and there are local variations. An upward shift in reporting or recording offences can quickly look like a 'crime wave'.
(iv) Rising affluence in society as a whole has led to a general increase in the opportunities for casual crime, as has the more general possession of cars and home equipment such as TVs, videos and home computers. Burglaries are common now in streets where thirty years ago there was little to steal.
(v) The growth of car ownership has been accompanied by a growth in vehicle-related crime. Streets which thirty years ago were almost empty are now full of parked cars, about one quarter of them left unlocked.

Source: *Criminal Justice*, Home Office, 1986, pp4–5

a According to the official statistics, did the proportion of crimes cleared up between 1978 and 1985 increase or decrease?
b What was the second biggest category of offence in 1985?
c Explain how police practice can appear to create a 'crime wave'.
d Give three possible reasons why people might not report a crime to the police.

Extract 2 *The Presentation of Statistics*

How statistics are interpreted will depend to a great extent on how they are presented.

Statistics can be presented in different ways. A burglary a minute all year throughout England and Wales sounds alarming; but the chances of the 'typical household' being burgled in a year are one in thirty-five, and the 'statistically average person' aged 16 or over can expect:
(i) A robbery once every 450 years.
(ii) An assault resulting in injury once every century.
(iii) The family car to be stolen or taken by joyriders once every 60 years.
(iv) A burglary in the home once every 35 years.
    The risks are very different in different places and for different types of people, so this approach obscures some much greater risks.
    Nevertheless, it indicates how small the overall risks are of experiencing these fairly serious crimes. They were compared by the first British Crime Survey with the chances of other misfortunes: the risk of burglary is slightly less than that of a fire in the home; the chance a family runs of car theft is slightly smaller than that of having one of its members injured in a traffic accident; the chances of being robbed are smaller than those of being admitted to hospital as a psychiatric patient.

Source: *Criminal Justice*, Home Office, 1986, p6

a Explain what is meant by the terms 'typical household' and 'the statistically average person'.
b Even though the actual risk is slight, many people are worried about the likelihood of experiencing a serious crime. Explain why this fear appears to be widespread.

Activity 2

a Obtain the latest figures on the proportions of the workforce who are working and unemployed. Present the statistics in a way which is, firstly favourable to the government, and secondly unfavourable.

b Obtain the examination pass rates of your school or college. Try to present them in a way which suggests the school or college is firstly successful, and secondly unsuccessful. (Depending on your school or college, one of these tasks might prove difficult!)

Secondary qualitative data

Useful as secondary statistical data is, it cannot tell us anything about people's feelings and motives, and what meanings they give to various areas of social life. Secondary qualitative data such as diaries, autobiographies, letters and television and newspaper reports can give the sociologist insight into and an understanding of how people see their world.

Extract 3 Loneliness

Loneliness is an issue which is rarely mentioned in sociology textbooks, perhaps because it is such a difficult topic to study. Jeremy Seabrook, in one of the few studies of the subject, first introduces each lonely person, and then lets him speak for himself.

Stephen is twenty-three. He is below average height, thin and self-effacing. He wears a plain grey suit with straight trousers, his hair in a pageboy cut. His gestures are nervous and his hands move a lot, as though they never know where to go next. He works in a department of the Co-op as salesman, and he lives alone with his divorced mother in a terraced house half a mile from the centre of a Midland town. I taught him for a year in a secondary modern school in 1964. Since then, I have seen him from time to time, always alone. When he was at school he was unobtrusive, diligent and eager to please; the kind of child on whose report teachers write 'It is a pleasure to teach him'. Now he is isolated and introspective.

I think I've always been shy, but as I've got older it's worse. I'm afraid of people. I don't quite know what I'm afraid of. Sometimes I think 'Well, what's the worst thing that could happen?' and then I realise, the worst thing they could do would be to hit me. But it still doesn't make any difference. When I'm at home, I feel I could talk to anybody. I can think of all sorts of things to say, but when I have to face people a kind of shutter comes down. I panic. I just want to run away from them. I just can't escape fast enough. And then sometimes I'll go home, and I could cry with feeling so miserable. I do sometimes. I sit in my room, and there's my mother downstairs with the television on, and she has it on loud because she's deaf. If I go in she looks at me and says 'Are you all right, dear?' And I smile and she goes back to Police Five or whatever it is . . . She's so placid. I hate her sometimes. She never gets upset, she never argues. I want to say to her, 'Why do you sit there like that, you know my life is all wrong, you know I have no friends, you know I can't get a girl-friend, why do you pretend everything's all right?'

Source: *Loneliness*, Jeremy Seabrook, Temple Smith, 1973, p34

a Why is Stephen lonely?
b What do such autobiographical accounts tell us about the extent of loneliness in society?
c If you were asked to do research on loneliness among people of your own age, how would you set about it? What problems would you face?

Secondary qualitative data must be interpreted particularly carefully. In *Extract 3*, for example, it is possible that Stephen is lying or exaggerating, or that a different researcher would have received a very different account. Further, Stephen's mother might have given a very different view of her son's loneliness. It is probably unwise to base a sociological explanation or theory on secondary qualitative data alone, but to use it to back up and/or illustrate other types of data or method.

Extract 4 The Photography of Poverty and Fashion

The two photographs below illustrate the ways in which photographs can be used by sociologists as a form of secondary qualitative data, and why they must be approached with care.

Wigan 1938, photographed by Kurt Hutton for *Picture Post*. It's now part of the iconography of unemployment in the thirties. Why? He is hurt and humiliated, isolated and inert. His pathos incites our pity. This still street life constructs our collective memory of defeat and despair. Yet it is opposed by another image of the Thirties, the Hunger Marches, when the poor took to the streets together.

1983. Gloria Chalmers. 'Who controls the past controls the future' George Orwell, *1984*.

Source: *Wigan Pier Revisited*, Beatrix Campbell, Virago, 1984

a If a photographer in the 1930s had wanted to show the anger and pride of the unemployed, rather than their pathos, what sort of photograph could s/he have taken?

b The second photograph is not a real fashion photograph at all, but an attempt by a photographer to comment on several things. What do you think she is trying to say about:

1 the 1980s
2 photography
3 fashion?

Does the photograph actually say anything about the 1930s?

c 'Who controls the past controls the future.' What did Orwell mean by this?

d Why must photographic evidence be especially carefully interpreted?

Primary Data

When a sociologist wishes to carry out first-hand research an immediate decision to be taken is which method of sociological enquiry to adopt. Simply, most sociological methods involve either asking questions or observing.

Activity 3

A central theme running through much of sociology is that the particular way a sociologist looks at the world will influence the picture or account that is presented at the end of the research. This can be illustrated by an analogy (a comparison of similarities) between sociology and photography.

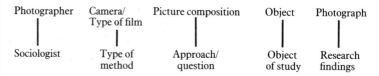

Photographer	Camera/ Type of film	Picture composition	Object	Photograph
Sociologist	Type of method	Approach/ question	Object of study	Research findings

a It is frequently claimed that the 'camera cannot lie', but how can a photographer create a particular desired image in a photograph?

b Using the information provided in the above diagram as a basis for your answer, briefly explain how what a sociologist finds out will depend on what is being looked for and the methods being used.

Experiments

Scientists such as chemists and physicists usually carry out their research by conducting experiments. Beginning with a hypothesis (an untested idea) the scientist carries out the experiment in carefully controlled conditions in such a way that the hypothesis can, in theory, be proved either right or wrong. For example, a scientist wishing to test the hypothesis that 'a high sugar intake increases the likelihood of rats getting cancer' would need two identical groups of rats, kept in an identical environment; the only difference between the two groups being that one, the experimental group, would be fed sugar, the other, the control group, would not. If the rats in the experimental group proved to have a higher incidence of cancer, the scientist could be fairly certain it was because of their sugar intake. Further, other scientists could carry out exactly the same experiment to check on the results.

'He's been falsifying research data for years!'

In practice, science is often not so perfect; scientific discoveries are often made through guesswork and luck rather than experiments, and 'identical' experiments do not always yield the same results.

Activity 4

a Why might scientific experiments go 'wrong'? Illustrate your answer from your study of chemistry, physics or biology.

b Although scientists frequently claim to be objective and unbiased, what is considered scientifically true changes over time. Give two examples to illustrate the changes in scientific 'truth'.

experiment a method of testing a hypothesis in a carefully controlled manner.

The problems involved in experiments in sociology are even greater than in the sciences. In particular, people are so complex and so different from one another that it is impossible to obtain two individuals or groups that are totally identical. A second problem, though one shared by participant observation, is that people are likely to behave differently when they are being observed.

Asking people questions

A social survey is likely to be carried out when a sociologist wishes to find out how a large number of people think or act; surveys involve either giving people a questionnaire to fill in themselves or actually interviewing them in person. Even if a sociologist is carrying out a small piece of research, perhaps by observation, asking people questions can provide an additional valuable source of data. There are, therefore, likely to be few pieces of sociological research which do not involve asking questions.

The first question a sociologist faces in carrying out a survey is, 'Which people do I question?' Occasionally, as in the ten-yearly census carried out for the government, it is possible to question everyone (or, at least, the head of every household), but usually considerations of time and expense mean that only a selected group of people can be questioned. A sample is therefore used by sociologists to ensure that the people they question or interview are an accurate representation of the population as a whole.

Extract 5 Sampling

There are various ways of obtaining a sample, which Gerry Rose illustrates by taking the example of a sociologist wishing to study the attitudes of the students at the University of X. Because of time and money considerations, a sample of 400 out of 8,000 students is to be questioned, but how does the sociologist select the 400? (The students can be sub-divided into different groups or strata i.e. male or female, and first, second, third, fourth and graduate years.)

'I'm a DON'T KNOW and my husband is a GET KNOTTED.'

Representative sampling plans

1. Simple random sample. A random sample of 400 (from the 8,000), for example by a lottery.

2. Quasi-random (or systematic) sample. Take every twentieth name from an alphabetic list (the starting point must be selected randomly).

3. Stratified random sample. First stratify by year and sex (there will be ten categories, first-year male to graduate female). Then either (3a) select one in twenty randomly from each group (proportionate stratified sample), or (3b) select forty randomly from each group (disproportionate stratified sample).

4. Cluster (or multi-stage) sample. Assume all students at the University of X are resident on campus. Select twenty starting addresses (rooms in colleges), and instruct interviewers to start here and work through adjacent addresses (along corridors, etc.) until twenty interviews have been completed from each starting-point. The result would be a cluster sample. In this case it is a two-stage sample: the first stage is the selection of starting addresses; the second stage is the procedure of sampling to complete twenty interviews.

Other sampling plans

The central question is how closely these approximate representativeness:

5. Accidental sample (or convenience sample). The first 400 students enrolled by the university registry.

6. Judgment sample. If experience has shown that sociology students are a good cross-section of students as a whole, select 400 sociology students.

7. Snowball sample. A small number of students, who are known by personal contact, are asked to nominate other students who would be prepared to be interviewed for the research; these, in turn, nominate others, and so on.

8. Quota sample. Assume there are ten interviewers on campus, and each is instructed to find four respondents from each of the ten age/sex stratification samples defined in (3). Thus we have a total of forty respondents per interviewer.

Source: *Deciphering Sociological Research*, Gerry Rose, Macmillan, 1983, pp50–51

KEY TERMS

sample a group selected for study, representative of the people the sociologist wishes to study.

sampling population the people the sociologist is interested in studying and who could therefore be included in the survey.

sampling frame the people the sample is actually taken from e.g. list of names. It is essential that the sampling frame accurately represents the overall population.

a Which four types of research can be seen as most representative of the 8,000 students as a whole?

b What are likely to be the disadvantages of (**1**) accidental, and (**2**) judgment samples?

c Opinion polls designed to discover voting intentions are usually based on quota sampling. What are the advantages and disadvantages of such a method?

Activity 5

Explain the advantages and disadvantages of using the following lists as sampling frames:

a telephone directory

b electoral register

c computer print-out of students at your school or college.

Having decided from whom to collect the necessary information the sociologist then has to decide what method to use for collecting it.

Extract 6   *The Problem of Setting Questions*

Whether the sociologist sends out questionnaires by post, or interviews the people in the sample personally, a major problem lies in the precise wording of the questions. The main pitfalls involved in asking questions are:

1 Questions which are not sufficiently specific. A question such as, 'Are you happy at school?' might produce a generalised 'Yes' or 'No' response; of course, 'happiness' may depend upon which aspect of school life is being considered.

2 Leading questions. 'Do you not think that smaller schools are better than larger ones?' prods the respondent towards an affirmative answer. Similarly, 'A lot of people now think sex before marriage is reasonable. What do you think?'

3 Presuming questions – where the respondent is assumed to do or to think something. For example, 'How long is it since you last had a cigarette?' presumes a 'Yes' answer to the unasked question, 'Do you smoke?'

4 Double questions. To the question, 'Do you think that Labour has made a mess of government during the past three years, and that the Conservatives should be given a chance?', the respondent might want to say 'Yes' to the first part, and 'No' to the second, or vice versa. A double question prohibits such a distinction.

5 Causal and coincidental links. An ambiguity or uncertainty, similar to 4 above, occurs when a causal relationship is attributed to something: for example, 'Do you think that educational standards have declined since the introduction of comprehensive schools?' It may be that a respondent would want to argue that educational standards have declined, but not necessarily since, or because, comprehensive schools were introduced. Standards might have declined coincidentally alongside the development of comprehensives. A straight 'Yes' might be made then, falsely implying acceptance of the causal relationship. Similarly, a 'No' response might be made so as to dispute the causal relationship even though the respondent feels that standards have declined. 'Yes' and 'No' answers therefore can mean either the same or different things to different people.

6 Terminology difficulties. Questions using vague words such as 'generally', 'sometimes' or 'seldom' will be interpreted differently by respondents and the resulting responses will not be strictly com-

parable. Questions using complex vocabularies may create different problems, as when the vocabulary is highly abstract and involves long words, or when it uses technical sociological language: for example, 'To what extent have you been socialised into internalising middle-class traits?'

7 Hypothetical questions. Answers to a question such as 'What would you do if you inherited half-a-million pounds?' might tell us something about escapist ideas, or desired expenditure, or greed. And which one would constitute the 'truth'?

The task of the researcher designing a questionnaire or an interview schedule must be to try to phrase questions in straightforward, every-day language, and to try to avoid ambiguities, leading questions, etc. Often, researchers will carefully try out early versions of questionnaires or schedules on some respondents so as to anticipate any problems in working or sequence.

Source: 'Finding Out', Ian Shelton, in *Perspectives on Society* ed. Roland Meighan, Ian Shelton and Tony Marks, Nelson, 1979, pp38–39

a What problems might the actual words used in a question create?

b Researchers often 'try out early versions of questionnaires'. What are the advantages of carrying out such pilot studies?

c Despite the obvious difficulties, asking questions is one of the major activities of sociologists. Why?

'Do I ever feel depressed? What kind of question is that? I'm a lemming.'

There are two main types of questions and answers:

a Open-ended questions allow the respondent to answer in a way s/he chooses. For example, the question 'What do you think of your sociology teacher?' allows an infinite number of possible answers.

b Pre-coded questions compel the respondent to give one of only a limited number of possible answers. For example, 'Do you think your sociology teacher is (i) excellent (ii) very good (iii) good (iv) average (v) poor (vi) very poor?'

Open-ended questions produce qualitative data, pre-coded questions produce quantitative data.

Activity 6

a Write one open-ended and one pre-coded question on each of the following:
   1 attitudes towards education
   2 religious beliefs
   3 political behaviour.
b What are the advantages and disadvantages of each of the six questions you have written?

Everyone answering a questionnaire answers the same questions in exactly the same order. Interviews can be structured in the same way as questionnaires, or they can be much more flexible.

The answers the sociologist receives will therefore depend on the wording of the questions, but in an interview they will also depend to some extent on the person who is asking the questions.

The age, sex, ethnic group, appearance and manner of the interviewer may all influence answers obtained in an interview. When asking questions therefore it is important to remain as neutral and detached as possible.

Observing people

In everyday life, we are constantly observing other people; indeed, much of what we learn comes from observation. Similarly, in sociology, there are many things about people we can learn only by watching them act in their everyday surroundings. Sociologists often distinguish between non-participant and participant observation, but in practice, complete non-participant observation is very difficult (unless, perhaps, one uses one-way mirrors or secret closed-circuit television). Just being present is in some ways participating and may well influence how people behave.

KEY TERMS

structured interview the exact wording of the questions and the order of asking is worked out beforehand and are the same for all respondents.

unstructured interview similar to a discussion, where the interviewer directs the discussion as appropriate and dependent on the respondent's previous answers.

KEY TERM

interview bias the effect the appearance, personality and behaviour of the interviewer has on a respondent's answers.

KEY TERM

participant observation a method of research in which the observer joins the group being studied and participates in their activities.

The participant observer seeks insight by taking part personally.

Activity 7

It is highly likely that at some time in your schooling one of your teachers has been observed by an inspector or adviser.

a Describe the extent to which the adviser or inspector participated in the class.

b Explain how and why the presence of the observer affected the behaviour of:
  1 the teacher
  2 the students.

c Explain how this change in behaviour made it difficult for the observer to obtain a 'true' picture of the class.

The major advantage of participant observation is that it allows the sociologist to gain insight into the feelings and meanings of those being studied. The researcher can usually get closer to an individual or group by observing over a period of time than by asking questions. If sociologists are to understand how and why people act as they do then they must get as close as possible to seeing the world from the point of view of those they are studying. But a male sociologist can never fully understand what being a woman means, just as a white sociologist can never see the world from a black person's point of view and vice versa.

Extract 7 *Black Like Me*

In some circumstances it may even be impossible for a researcher to become merely an observer. Such a problem faced John Griffin, a white man who wished to understand what it was like to be black in the Deep South of the United States in the 1950s.

How else except by becoming a Negro could a white man hope to learn the truth? Though we lived side by side throughout the South, communication between the two races had simply ceased to exist. Neither really knew what went on with those of the other race. The Southern Negro will not tell the white man the truth. He long ago learned that if he speaks a truth unpleasing to the white, the white will make life miserable for him.

If a white man became a Negro in the Deep South, what adjustments would he have to make? What is it like to experience discrimination based on skin colour, something over which one has no control?

[With the help of a doctor Griffin darkened his skin, and he shaved all his hair off.]

The transformation was total and shocking. I had expected to see myself disguised, but this was something else. I was imprisoned in the flesh of an utter stranger, an unsympathetic one with whom I felt no kinship. All traces of the John Griffin I had been were wiped from existence. Even the senses underwent a change so profound it filled me with distress. I looked into the mirror and saw reflected nothing of the white John Griffin's past. No, the reflections led back to Africa, back to the shanty and the ghetto, back to the fruitless struggles against the mark of blackness. Suddenly, almost with no mental preparation, no advance hint, it became clear and it permeated by whole being. My inclination was to fight against it. I had gone too far. I knew now that there is no such thing as a disguised white man, when the black won't rub off. The black man is wholly a Negro, regardless of what he once may have been. I was a newly created Negro who must go out that door and live in a world unfamiliar to me.

The completeness of this trans-formation appalled me. It was unlike anything I had imagined. I became two men, the observing one and the one who panicked, who felt Negroid even into the depths of his entrails.

I felt the beginnings of a great loneliness, not because I was a Negro but because the man I had been, the self I knew, was hidden in the flesh of another. If I returned home to my wife and children they would not know me. They would open the door and stare blankly at me. My children would want to know who is this large, bald Negro. If I walked up to friends, I knew I would see no flicker of recognition in their eyes.

[Griffin toured alone, as a black, through the Deep South, experiencing first-hand what it was like to be black in a prejudiced and brutal white-dominated society.]

Source: *Black Like Me*, John Howard Griffin, Panther, 1964, pp9, 19

a Why did Griffin think it necessary to take on the physical appearance of a black person?

b What does Griffin suggest is the importance of a person's colour?

c What other methods could Griffin have used to discover the extent of racial discrimination in the American South in the 1950s?

Activity 8

Either alone or with a friend carry out a brief participant observation study. Select an area of social life you have little knowledge or experience of. You could choose, for example, a religious service, sports club or leisure activity, theatre, classical music concert, or trade union meeting. After your observation answer the following questions:

a Could you, as an observer, fully understand what was happening? If not, why?

b Were the participants affected by your presence?

c What problems did you face in your role of participant observer?

d Did the people you were studying know they were being watched? What are the advantages and disadvantages of telling people they are being observed?

e What does your piece of research tell you about the advantages and disadvantages of participant observation?

'Frankly, Henshaw, if gates go on falling like this,
I can't see us ever finishing our paper on crowd hooliganism.'

The Setting for Research

The sociologist does not just have to decide which research method to use; a further question is where to carry out the research. This will depend partly on what the sociologist wishes to find out and partly on the time and financial resources available. Three research settings are especially important:

a Case studies – detailed studies of just one example, e.g. a factory, school class, family, teenage gang, etc.

b Longitudinal studies – studies of a group of people over a period of time. Perhaps the most famous longitudinal study in Britain is that directed by J. W. B. Douglas for the Medical Research Council. This study, based mainly on interviews for questionnaires, has followed the lives of 5,500 children born in the first week of March 1946, and has discovered a great deal which is of sociological, educational and medical value. It was, for example, the first study to link a mother's smoking to health problems in her children.

c Comparative studies – in this type of study the sociologist takes two or more examples of whole societies or particular institutions or groups and compares the differences and similarities between them.

Extract 8 Three Important Concepts

When carrying out any piece of research there are three key questions that sociologists must ask of the methods used: How reliable are they? How valid are they? and How representative are they?

Reliability
If a method of collecting evidence is reliable, it means that anybody else using this method, or the same person using it at another time, would come up with the same results. The research could be repeated, and the same results would be obtained.

Validity
Validity refers to the problem of whether the data collected is a true picture of what is being studied. Is it really evidence of what it claims to be evidence of? The problem arises particularly when the data collected seems to be a product of the research method used rather than of what is being studied.

Representativeness
This refers to the question of whether the group of people or the situation that we are studying are typical of others. If they are, then we can safely conclude that what is true of this group is also true of others.

Source: *Research Methods*, Patrick McNeill, Tavistock, 1985, pp12–13

a 'The problem arises particularly when the data collected seems to be a product of the research method.' Explain the meaning of this sentence.

b Why is it important that sociological methods are reliable?

c 'Participant observation is valid but not reliable; questionnaires are reliable but not valid.' Examine the arguments for this view.

Questions and Suggested Projects

Review Questions

1

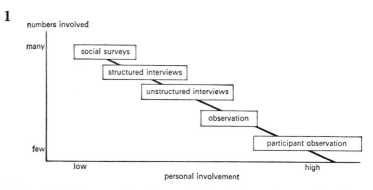

Relationship between number of respondents and degree of personal involvement of sociologist

Source: *Introducing Sociology*, ed. Peter Worsley, Penguin, second edition 1977, p89

Using the information contained in the above diagram explain briefly the key features of each sociological method.

2 Distinguish between
      a quantitative and qualitative data
      b primary and secondary methods
giving an example of each.

3 Explain why sociologists carrying out surveys usually take samples and why it is important that a sample is representative of the population as a whole.

Theme-linking questions

1 Explain the value and the limitations of secondary data on:
      a religious attendance
      b educational achievement
      c divorce.

2 Why is it particularly difficult to do research on:
      a political decision-making   **c** the Royal Family
      b child abuse   **d** professional criminals?

3 What would be the most appropriate methods or sources of data to use if you wished to carry out research on the following? Give brief reasons for your answers.
      a migration patterns in Britain
      b attitudes towards work among supermarket employees
      c how children learn sex roles
      d the extent of racial discrimination in your community.

4 Study your GCSE sociology syllabus to see if you can find any important social issues in Britain that are omitted. Select two such issues and explain how you would go about finding data on them.

Stimulus–response Question

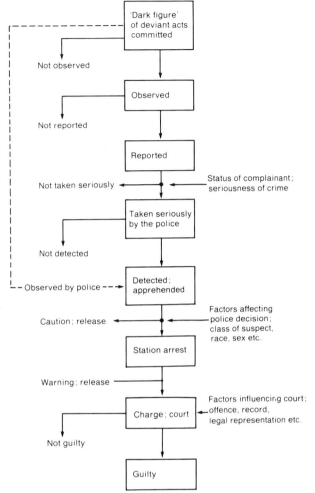

The social construction of official statistics (adapted from *Deviance, Reality and Society*, S. Box, 1981)

Source: *Methods in Sociology*, Murray Morison, Longman, 1986, p79

a According to the above diagram which two factors determine whether a reported deviant act is taken seriously by the police?
(2)

b What are the two possible outcomes of a deviant act being observed? (2)

c Explain the meaning of the terms:
  1 dark figure   **2** status of complainant. (4)

d Give one example of a crime the police are likely to take seriously and one they are not. (2)

e Explain carefully the difference between deviance and crime. (4)

f What are the implications of the above diagram for the validity of official crime statistics? (6)

Essays

1 'The method of research a sociologist uses depends above all on the topic being studied.' Explain, giving examples to illustrate your answer.

2 **a** What are the main types of secondary data available to the sociologist?

   b Explain, using examples, the value and limitations of secondary data on education or employment or family life or religion.

3 A friend has been asked to carry out a survey at her place of work on the attitudes of her colleagues towards the introduction of flexitime. Explain to her what factors she needs to take into account in asking her questions. Your answer could include:

   sampling

   open-ended or pre-coded questions

   written questionnaire or an oral interview

   structured or unstructured interviews

   the wording of questions.

Suggested Projects

All sociology projects will, of course, use research methods or secondary data. It is unlikely that many projects will be based on the study of methods alone, but there are some possibilities:

1 A study of how people in a particular social setting behave differently when they are being observed.

2 A study of how honest people are in answering questionnaires. (A project not without its obvious problems!)

3 A library study of the use sociologists have made of a particular method or type of data, e.g. longitudinal study.

4 A study of how crime statistics are presented in the media.

5 A study of participant observation using two observers of a particular social activity and comparing their accounts.

4

Social Stratification

Introduction

Chapters 4–8 examine the key differences that exist between people. This chapter looks at the ways in which some groups of people come to have more wealth, status and power than others, concentrating on the nature of social class in Britain today.

Social Differentiation

Activity 1

a Write a list of the things you immediately notice about someone you meet for the first time.
b Compare your list with those of your fellow students. What does this comparison tell you about the ways in which we look at other people?

Having quickly noticed certain things about someone, we then often try to find out what job, if any, s/he has, and where s/he lives. Sociologists are interested in the differences between groups of people because these differences are important; it *does* matter whether one is male or female, old or young, rich or poor, ugly or beautiful. Note that sociologists are not saying that it *should* matter, but that it does matter in the sense that the social groups we belong to have a profound influence on every area of life.

'Do you think the directors ever pretend to be us?'

KEY TERM

social differentiation the process whereby individuals and groups are placed in a variety of categories, e.g. classes, ethnic groups, age groups.

What elements of social differentiation are represented in the above cartoon?

With the exception of sex, where most of us are fairly definitely male or female, it is not, of course, possible to draw sharp and distinct boundaries between groups. There is not a sudden point at which we become old, and we cannot rigidly divide the population into two or three separate classes. But this does not necessarily imply that the categories we use to differentiate people are meaningless. Indeed, we must use categories and labels if we are to make sense of the world around us. One cannot, for example, neatly divide people into three height categories: tall, average and short. In reality people are ranged on a continuum of heights, rather than being in one of three distinct groups. Nevertheless, it is on many occasions useful to talk of tall or short people, and the particular problems each may face, while at the same time recognising that the categories we use reflect our way of looking at the world rather than the world itself. For example, a man of five foot would be defined as short in Britain, but as tall in Pygmy society.

Activity 2

a What are the main categories used in society to distinguish people of different:
   1 classes
   2 physical appearances
   3 intellectual abilities
   4 weights?
b Explain the advantages and disadvantages of using these categories in sociology.

Some differences between people are obviously more important for the structure of society than others. Hair colour and height may matter to the individual, but they are not usually major means of differentiating people, and they do not normally have a major effect on someone's position in society. Four types of difference are perhaps of key importance in industrial societies: class, gender, ethnicity and age.

The Nature of Social Stratification

Social stratification necessarily involves social inequality.

Members of different groups or strata usually perform different occupational tasks, and this serves to justify or legitimate the system through the belief that certain occupations are more important for society than others, and should therefore carry more pay and status.

If the members of the lower strata believe that the system of social stratification is unfair and ought to be changed, then instability and potential conflict are created. The more powerful strata therefore usually attempt to develop in the minds of the lower strata the belief that the benefits of the rich are just and deserved. Wealth and power may, for example, be seen as the results of God's will or the legitimate rewards of hard work.

A key distinguishing feature between the different systems of stratification is the degree of openness. In an open society movement between strata is possible and a person's position depends primarily on achievement; in a closed system movement is not possible and ascription determines a person's position (see p16 for an explanation of ascription and achievement).

In no society are all roles totally achieved or ascribed. Each system combines both ascription and achievement, but the relative emphasis given to each varies widely. It is useful to distinguish on this basis four types of stratification system; slavery, estate, caste and social class.

Slavery

Slavery draws a sharp and rigid dividing line between two groups of people. One person owns another and can treat him or her as a piece of property. Slaves have few, if any, legal rights, and their children will, in turn, usually become the legal property of the slave owner. Not surprisingly, societies based on slavery are marked by extreme inequality. Examples of systems of stratification based on slavery are ancient Greece and Rome, and eighteenth- and nineteenth-century southern United States. Slavery is easier to justify (at least to the slave owners) if the slaves belong to a different ethnic group from the slave owners, and both in the ancient world and America slaves were usually originally captured and taken forcibly to the slave owner. Some 20 million Africans were transported to North America, a very high proportion of them dying on the journey.

Extract 1   *Slavery on a Cuban Sugar Plantation*

Esteban Montejo talking, at the age of 104 in 1963, of his early life on Cuban sugar plantations, reveals well the type of life a slave led.

'Like all children born into slavery, I was born in an infirmary where they took the pregnant Negresses to give birth . . . Negroes were sold like pigs, and they sold me at once.

I do remember running away from "the plantation" once; I decided I'd had enough of that bloody place, and I was off! But they caught me without a struggle, clapped a pair of shackles on me, screwed them up tight and sent me back to work wearing them.

I saw many horrors in the way of punishment under slavery. That was why I didn't like the life. The stocks . . . were the cruellest. Some were for standing and others for lying down. They were made of thick planks with holes for the head, hands and feet. They would keep slaves fastened up like this for two or three months for some trivial offence. They whipped the pregnant women too, but lying face down with a hollow in the ground for their

bellies. They whipped them hard, but they took good care not to damage the babies because they wanted as many of those as possible. The most common punishment was flogging; this was given by the over-seer with a rawhide lash which made weals on the skin . . . Life was hard and bodies wore out.'

Source: *The Autobiography of a Runaway Slave*, Esteban Montejo, Penguin, 1970, pp15, 32

a State three punishments given to slaves by the plantation overseers.

b Why were the slave owners concerned not to damage unborn babies?

c Who benefited, and why, from the system of slavery on the plantations?

Activity 3

Using the history section of your library as a resource, write a paragraph on the system of stratification in one of the following:

a ancient Greece or Rome

b the Southern States in the eighteenth and nineteenth centuries

c the labour camps of Hitler's Germany or Stalin's Russia.

Estate

In feudal societies, such as England in the Middle Ages, there are several strata, or estates, the distinctions between which are supported by the law. The main estates of feudal England – the nobility, the clergy and the serfs – had very different legal rights and responsibilities. The estates system was based on the owner-ship of land, and each estate had its own occupational functions. Although the system was a largely closed one, intermarriage and individual social mobility were possible. In particular, the Catholic Church, with its insistence on priestly celibacy, provided op-

portunities for occupational mobility both for the younger sons
of the nobility and the sons of the better-off commoners.

Extract 2 The Serf in Feudal Society

The great majority of the population of feudal England were
serfs. No doubt the living conditions of serfs varied, but generally
they had few opportunities to obtain wealth or power. The serf:

had no land or rights, but he did have security in that he could not be thrown out of employment, and when he became too old to work he had to be taken care of by his feudal master, who at times intervened even to the point of deciding who the serf's children should marry. If a serf could learn a trade he stood a small chance of making money, for on every manor there were craftsmen who mended the carts and ploughs, shoed the horses, made the furniture, wove and dyed the cloth and wove baskets, for which they received wages. But few serfs rose to become freemen or craftsmen; the feudal system discouraged competition so there was little incentive and most stayed on the land.

It is easy enough to describe the structures of the feudal system but more difficult to imagine how people thought. Was there a lot of muttering at the size of the meals eaten in the manor house compared with those lower down the scale? Did the servants envy their masters their stone houses with tapestries on the walls and stone floors while their own families lived in wattle and daub dwellings with earth floors. Did the poor ever begrudge having to go to bed as soon as darkness fell instead of being able to light an expensive candle?

Source: 'Life in the Middle Ages', Diana Villar, *The Lady,* 12 June 1986, pp1143, 1148

a What were the advantages and disadvantages of the estates
system for the serf?
b What opportunities were there for social mobility in feudal
society?
c Why do we know so little about what the serfs thought? What
are the implications of this lack of knowledge for our study of
history?

Caste

The caste system of India has its origins over 2,000 years ago. It
is a very closed system and is closely linked to occupation. In
theory, there are four main castes in India:

Brahmins – priestly aristocracy
Kshatriyas – warriors
Vaisya – traders
Sudra – peasants

These four large groupings are known as *varna* and are in many
ways like feudal estates. Of more importance in the day-to-day
life of the average Indian is the *jati* or sub-caste. Jati usually have
their own occupation, and marriage must usually take place to
someone of the same jati.

Outside the caste system are the Untouchables or Outcastes;
these are regarded as so inferior by caste Indians that even to
touch an Outcaste is polluting. Traditionally the Untouchables

performed the lowest jobs – sweeping streets, skinning carcasses and scavenging – though today most are agricultural labourers.

Two Hindu beliefs are particularly important in supporting the caste system:

a The idea of *karma* tells Hindus they were born into particular sub-castes because of their actions in previous lives or incarnations, i.e. one's caste position is deserved.

b The idea of *dharma* or duty to the caste system and its rules; behaviour according to dharma will be rewarded in the next life while the breaking of caste rules will result in birth into a low caste.

Discrimination on the grounds of caste has been illegal since the early days of independent India (1947) and the Untouchables are given equal rights in law. But to enforce the laws, especially in rural areas, has proved almost impossible, and caste is still a key element of Indian life.

The apartheid system of South Africa bears many similarities to a caste society, though it has been maintained primarily through the use of force.

> **KEY TERM**
>
> **caste** a traditional system of social stratification, based almost entirely on ascription and legitimated by the Hindu religion.

Activity 4

a Explain how systems of stratification based on slavery, estate and caste are legitimated (made acceptable).

b Using diagrams, illustrate the key differences between the three systems of stratification.

> **KEY TERM**
>
> **social class** a system of stratification typical of industrial societies. Classes consist of people in a similar economic position, but the boundaries are not clearly drawn, and social mobility, upwards or downwards, is higher than in other systems of stratification.

Social Class

In stratification systems based on slavery, estate or caste, people know their place in society; there can rarely be any doubt about which group an individual belongs to. Class is not so simple.

Bloody snob! Conkers out of season!

> **Activity 5**
>
> **a** Construct a questionnaire to give to a small number of fellow students, friends or relatives, to find out:
>   1 If they think there are social classes in Britain today.
>   2 If so, what social classes there are, and what the differences are between them.
>   3 Which social class do they think the following belong to: primary school teachers, pop stars, computer programmers, professional tennis players.
> **b** Collect and summarise your findings.
> **c** What conclusions can you draw from your findings about the nature of social class in Britain today?

As might be expected, there are many different views of how social class should be defined. Systems of stratification based on class do however place a higher emphasis on achievement than ascription, and therefore have higher rates of social mobility than other systems of stratification.

Extract 3   *Class and Status*

Although social class is based primarily on economic factors such as wealth, income and occupation, we judge and rank people in a wide variety of ways.

Class labels tell us about one over-arching aspect of people's social relationships and about one sort of social interaction . . . In 1982 Ralf Dahrendorf described class as a kind of 'layer cake in which clear distinctions can be drawn between the bottom of the cake, the jam in the middle, and the chocolate on top'. However, as he was very well aware, in contemporary Britain there are a myriad status differences – to do with lifestyle, spending habits, leisure interests, religious or voluntary group activities, manners, accent, place of residence, and so on – which cut across the broad division into social-class groups. These are impossible to rank in order or even to assess objectively, since they depend on subjectively perceived differences along dimensions of taste and personal preference. For many families . . . these may be more important than class definitions in deciding their pattern of relationships outside the home – for example, visiting, entertaining and shared leisure activities. However, as Brian Jackson suggests, status differences often operate in essentially marginal areas of experience.

'Almost everyone shops some-times at Marks and Spencer . . . almost everybody might have the same washing powder in their kitchen . . . but if the crucial element in social difference is income and working conditions it is hard to see how using the same mass products as people more prosperous and powerful than yourself breaks the class barriers . . . the merest glance at half-a-dozen of the major London stores – Harrods, Heals, Liberty's, Selfridges, John Lewis, C & A – tells you that they reflect, serve and perhaps reinforce quite different social groups'. (It is worth noting that Jackson does not say the different shops *create* different groups.)

Source: *Modern English Society*, Judith Ryder and Harold Silver, Methuen, third edition 1985, pp212–213

GLOSSARY

myriad great number
objectively in an unbiased manner
subjectively dependent on one's own views

a According to Dahrendorf, who is the 'jam', and who the 'chocolate'?

b Explain, in your own words, the meaning of:
 1 'status differences operate in essentially marginal areas of experience'
 2 'they reflect, serve and perhaps reinforce quite different social groups'.

c Summarise the arguments that appear in the extract for and against the view that social class is of key importance in Britain today.

Activity 6

a List the main food and shoe shops in your town, or if you live in a large city, one particular shopping area.
b Which types of people does each shop try to attract?
c Explain how you would carry out research to discover the relationships between each shop and type of customer.

Karl Marx (1818–83)

Extract 4 Marx on Class

Marx's theory may be stated briefly in the following propositions:
1) in every society beyond the most primitive, two categories of people may be distinguished: (a) a ruling class, and (b) one or more subject classes.
2) the dominant position of the ruling class is to be explained by its possession of the major instruments of economic production, but its political dominance is consolidated by the hold which it establishes over military force and over the production of ideas.
3) there is perpetual conflict between the ruling class and the subject class or classes; and the nature and course of such conflict is influenced primarily by the development of productive forces, i.e. by changes in technology.
4) the lines of class conflict are most sharply drawn in the modern capitalist societies, because in such societies the divergence of economic interests appears most clearly, unobscured by any personal bonds such as those of feudal society, and because the development of capitalism brings about a more radical polarisation of classes than has existed in any other type of society, by its unrivalled concentration of wealth at one extreme of society and of poverty at the other, and by its gradual elimination of the intermediate and transitional social strata.
5) the class struggle within capitalist society will end with the victory of the working class, and this victory will be followed by the construction of a classless society.

Source: *Elites and Society*, T. B. Bottomore, Penguin, 1966, pp24–25

KEY TERMS

capitalism an economic system where the means of production are privately owned.

communism a classless economic system where the means of production are collectively owned.

means of production property (e.g. slaves, land or capital) used to create more wealth.

bourgeoisie those in capitalist societies who own the means of production.

proletariat workers in capitalist societies who receive wages for their labour.

In capitalist societies there are two classes, the bourgeoisie and the proletariat. The bourgeoisie or capitalists own the means of production (e.g. factories, wealth); the proletariat have nothing but their labour which they must sell to the bourgeoisie. There is a fundamental clash of interests because higher wages for the proletariat mean lower profits for the bourgeoisie. Although the bourgeoisie control society in their own interests, Marx believed that the industrial proletariat would eventually overthrow the bourgeoisie, and that a classless communist society would be established in which the means of production would be owned by all the workers.

a Why is there conflict between the bourgeoisie and the proletariat?

b What does Marx mean by:
   1 'major instruments of economic production'
   2 'production of ideas'
   3 'polarisation of classes'?

Marx's ideas have not gone unchallenged; among the many criticisms made of his theory are:

a It is unrealistic in Britain today to talk of a small owning class. Insurance companies and pension funds, in which many of us have an interest, are now major shareholders in private companies, and the privatisation in recent years of previously publicly-owned industries has widened share ownership beyond the traditional bourgeoisie.

b The classes have not polarised, as Marx predicted, and indeed there is a large professional middle class between the bourgeoisie and the proletariat. Further, there are such wide differences *within* the working class that it is difficult to see it developing sufficient awareness or consciousness of its interests to take collective action against the bourgeoisie.

c No developed capitalist society has had a proletarian revolution; Marx underestimated the extent to which capitalist societies could change by gradual reform.

Activity 7

a About one in three of the world's population live in societies officially labelled 'Marxist'.
  1 List as many of these countries as possible.
  2 Find out all you can about the distribution of wealth and power in one 'Marxist' society. What conclusions can you draw from your findings?
b Virtually everyone has heard of Marx, whether interested in politics or not. Construct a brief questionnaire to discover how much your friends and relatives really know about his life and ideas.

Max Weber (1864–1920)

Where Marx saw class as being based on relationships in the economic structure, Max Weber saw systems of stratification, especially in industrialised societies, as being rather more complex. He identified three 'orders' or dimensions of stratification:
stratification:
a the economic order – the distribution of wealth
b the status order – the distribution of prestige or status
c the political order – the distribution of power.

According to Weber, status and power are largely determined by economic position, but they can be obtained independently by, for example, belonging to a religious or political group. Further, some occupations are high in economic position, but low in status, and vice-versa.

Weber accurately predicted the rise of the 'new middle class' – bureaucrats, managers, teachers, social workers, etc. – who do not own the means of production, but who rarely see themselves as members of the working class.

The value of Weber's approach lies in its emphasis on the complexity of systems of stratification in industrialised societies.

'I have an executive brief-case, toy, car, house – and I still haven't been made one.'

> **Activity 8**
>
> **a** Draw a diagram to illustrate Weber's three orders of stratification.
> **b** Identify and locate on your diagram:
>   1 an occupation which is high in the economic order, but low in status and power
>   2 a poorly paid occupation which is high in status and power.

Class and Occupation

In practice, most sociologists, like most people in everyday life, use occupation as an index of social class. This has several advantages; a person's occupation has a profound influence on other areas of life; it is relatively easy to discover and quantify; and there is a wide measure of agreement on the ranking of occupations.

There are many different ways of categorising occupations, but a crucial distinction is usually made between non-manual and manual occupations. This is a distinction we often make in everyday life, and indeed the term non-manual is often taken to be the same as middle class, and manual the same as working class. But note the crudeness and artificiality of the distinction: the brain surgeon, classed as non-manual, has to perform manual operations, while the bricklayer, classed as manual, has to be trained and carefully plan the work to be done.

Official government research, including the census, is usually based on the classification adopted by the Office of Population Censuses and Surveys whose head is the Registrar General. The Registrar General's classification distinguishes five groupings, one of which is further sub-divided:

I   Professional and higher administrative, e.g. doctors, barristers
II   Intermediate professionals and administrators, e.g. teachers, social workers
III Skilled
    a Non-manual, e.g. typists, shop assistants, clerks
    b Manual, e.g. electricians, joiners
IV Semi-skilled, e.g. machine operatives, bus conductors
V   Unskilled, e.g. labourers, road sweepers.

Britain's Changing Class Structure

The extent to which the class structure of Britain has changed in recent years has been an issue of major concern to sociologists, but, partly because of the difficulty of defining social class, there are a variety of different interpretations of these changes. Chapter 8 examines the extent of inequality in Britain today, but sociologists have also been interested in whether classes as a whole have declined or increased in importance. Whether one thinks class important in Britain today will depend partly on how class is defined and partly on one's political values, but in assessing the existence and the differences between social classes the following types of evidence should be taken into account:

a income
b wealth
c working conditions
d housing tenure
e leisure activities
f educational achievement
g voting behaviour.

You will be in a better position to judge the importance of class after studying these topics. A useful question to ask throughout your study of sociology is 'How significant are class differences in this topic?'

Those who argue that class is declining in importance have usually pointed to changes in the working class as causing this change.

Arguments that suggest that *in some ways* some working-class people have adopted middle-class styles of life include:

a the increased affluence of most manual workers, since the 1950s especially
b the increase in home ownership among manual workers, encouraged by the sale of council houses
c the significant number of working-class people who vote Conservative.
d wider share ownership.

But clearly there are still significant differences between the middle and working classes as whole groupings. An alternative view is that the better-off members of the working class and the lower levels of the middle class have in some ways come together.

> **KEY TERM**
>
> **embourgeoisement** the process whereby the working class become bourgeois or middle class.

> **KEY TERM**
>
> **convergence** the process whereby the upper working class and the lower middle class develop certain common characteristics.

Extract 5 *The Different Working Class Images of Society*

Many writers have suggested it is misleading to talk about the working class as a whole. David Lockwood, for example, identifies three very different types of working-class environment which result in very different views of society.

Proletarian traditionalism is typical of working-class groups living in homogeneous communities which are socially and occupationally isolated and characterised by large-scale industrial enterprise. These are typically communities with heavy industries and predominantly working-class populations with low rates of social and geographical mobility . . . Thus, communities centred on mining, ship-building and dock work, employing large numbers of workers in similar jobs of a single-class character, exemplify most clearly Lockwood's proletarian traditionalism. The sense of community is reinforced by the mutual dependence the worker feels for his colleagues (given the often hazardous nature of such jobs) and by the sense of identity felt at 'doing a man's job', and is reflected in the amount of leisure time which is spent with workmates.

These community experiences, according to Lockwood, . . . give rise to a view of the world in which two classes stand opposed in an arena of conflict between 'us' and 'them'.

Deferential traditionalism characterises working-class groups living and working in more heterogeneous environments, in effect relatively more isolated from other members of the working class. Their work situations involve them in personal . . . relationships with middle-class employers . . . Agricultural workers in rural areas and workers in small-scale industries (e.g. family-run businesses) and in small towns are the obvious example of this working-class type.

These workers subscribe to a model of society as a legitimate hierarchy, with deference and trust accorded to social superiors by virtue of their possession of intrinsic skills for elite positions.

Lockwood's third group of manual workers are free of the traditionalist perspectives which distinguish their proletarian and deferential counterparts. The **privatised** manual worker lives in the community milieu of the housing estate and is involved in specialised but routine occupations which are well rewarded but lack autonomy and offer little intrinsic satisfaction . . . Work is a means to the end of money with little inherent reward: . . . low job involvement and instrumental attitude to work produce no strong attachment to workmates but manifest themselves in a privatised home-centred existence focusing on a preoccupation with their families and homes. Enduring fairly boring employment is the price they are prepared to pay for the financial rewards they desire for their families.

Privatised workers, although seeing themselves as working class, give greater salience to social divisions based on income and material resources with status judged by personal possessions and conspicuous consumption.

Source: *Introductory Sociology*, Tony Bilton et al, Macmillan, 1981, pp226–228

GLOSSARY

homogeneous of the same kind
deferential exaggerated respect for those one sees as betters.
heterogeneous of varying kinds
milieu surroundings
autonomy personal freedom
salience importance

a Identify the three types of working-class environment discussed above, and give an example of an occupation likely to belong to each.
b What is meant by:
    1 'privatised manual worker'?
    2 'instrumental attitude to work'?
c Which of the three types of working class would you expect to be increasing currently? Give reasons for your answer.

Writing in the mid-nineteenth century, Marx had referred to the *lumpen proletariat*, those members of the working class either in very badly paid, temporary employment or unemployed. Some writers have claimed that in Britain today there is such an *under-class* – the long-term unemployed, those in part-time and/or temporary work, some people dependent on state benefits and certain members of ethnic minorities. The members of this under-class have perhaps become increasingly separated from the majority of the working class in recent years, especially in terms of their standard of living, and it is these people, of course, who are most likely to live in poverty (see Chapter 8).

Activity 9

a Using a map of your town or community, identify areas of housing according to the social class of the people who live there. Produce as detailed a class breakdown as possible.
b Explain any differences you identify between the social class composition of each area.
c What are the consequences of such differences?

Extract 6 Changes in the Middle Class

If it is misleading to talk of the working class as a whole, then arguably the middle class is even more diversified and fragmentary.

The growth of middle-level occupations, such as clerks and technicians, has fuelled the controversy as to whether the class balance of Britain is shifting towards the middle class and away from the working class. The proportion of people in non-manual occupations has grown at the expense of manual occupations and there has been an increase in the number and importance of jobs requiring formal educational qualifications. Is Britain (and indeed most industrialised western countries) then becoming an overwhelmingly middle-class nation. Does this explain the recent electoral successes of the Conservative Party?

Some have doubted this and argued that many of these so-called middle-level positions are really rather lowly involving routine, repetitive tasks which should be correctly classified as working-class. This debate has raged, in particular, around clerical work. Typing and form filling in large offices under close supervision for relatively poor rates of pay was hardly the stuff of a responsible middle-class job. But is this typical of these new positions? Don't some of them require years of training, and carry considerable responsibility for the organisation of the work of others? Managers and professionals could be considered to fall into this category. Some sociologists have tried to solve this debate by dividing middle-level occupations into two. One is called the service class, in view of the way in which this group of workers serves the functions of capital, the other is seen to be part of the working class (involving the routine clerical workers).

Other sociologists have commented that clerks do not stay clerks all their lives, so it is inappropriate to put the occupants of these positions in one class on the basis of their temporary occupational status. These writers go on to challenge the concept of class as a set of occupational slots, and argue instead that the focus should be on groups of people with similar job histories.

How have sociologists researched these questions? Some have engaged in detailed empirical studies of particular occupations. One of the classic early studies was that in which Lockwood investigated the position of the 'black coated worker', as he called clerks. This involved a close examination of the work and market situation of the clerk and to some extent their beliefs, looking for similarities and dissimilarities with typical working-class and middle-class occupations. He decided that while the market situation of the clerk in terms of earnings and benefits was not much better than that of a skilled manual worker, their position in the enterprise distinguished them from the manual workers in terms of work situation.

Source: 'Social Inequality: sociology's central issue', Sylvia Walby, in *Exploring Society*, ed. Robert C. Burgess, Longman, 1986, pp49–50

a Why is it often claimed that clerks are not truly middle class?
b Explain the meaning of:
  1 market situation
  2 work situation.
c How is the clerk's work situation different from that of the manual worker?
d Why has the proportion of the workforce in non-manual occupations grown in recent years?

Social Mobility

A key feature of systems of stratification based on class is that they allow social mobility – the movement from one layer of society to another, either up or down. However, the study of social mobility is fraught with difficulties:

a How is it measured? Most research bases it on occupational movement, but not everyone in society sees social mobility in this single sense, and not everyone ranks occupations in the same way.
b People do not necessarily stay in the same occupation all their life; a 'snapshot' study therefore may present a very misleading picture.
c Most studies are based on fathers and sons alone. Apart from the fact that they therefore omit half the population, family members are not necessarily socially mobile in the same direction. For example, a woman may be promoted at work at the same time as her husband is made redundant.

KEY TERMS

intergenerational mobility between generations; when a child has a better or worse job than his or her parents.
intragenerational mobility within one generation; a person obtains a better or worse job him or herself.

It is usual to distinguish two main types of social mobility: intergenerational mobility and intragenerational mobility.

'Solicitors can make a lot of money. Yes, if I were you I'd mug a solicitor.'

Extract 7 The Oxford Mobility Study

The most recent major study of social mobility was carried out by a group of sociologists at the University of Oxford.

The study was based on a representative sample of 10,000 men in England and Wales, who were interviewed in 1972. For present purposes, we may emphasise two of the general conclusions which emerged. First, the data indicate that during the last fifty years or so British society has been characterised by a relatively high level of social mobility. Thus, for example, more than 7 per cent of the sons of manual workers had obtained 'class I' (higher professional and managerial) occupations. Due to the size of the 'manual' categories, this meant that by 1972 well over a quarter of all men in class I jobs had come from working-class homes. The extent of such mobility, Goldthorpe argues, suggests that the higher levels of the occupational structure have been much more open to new recruits than has commonly been supposed. However, when we turn from the absolute volume of mobility to the relative chances of men from different classes, a somewhat different picture emerges: sons of men in the top two occupational classes were nearly four times as likely to attain such occupations themselves as were the sons of manual workers. So, judging in terms of *relative* chances of social mobility, it cannot be concluded that British society has become any more 'open' during the period in question. On the contrary, the data suggest that this pattern of unequal opportunity has remained remarkably stable.

The second general conclusion is that the mobility patterns which have been observed are mainly a result of changes in the occupational structure. After all, the expansion of higher-level managerial, administrative and technical jobs, and the contraction of manual ones, has made a considerable volume of 'upward' mobility inevitable: 14.3 per cent of the fathers were in class I or II occupations, but 26.5 per cent of their sons.

Source: '*Social Stratification*', Pete Martin, in *Applied Sociological Perspectives*, ed. R.J. Anderson and W.W. Sharrock, George Allen and Unwin, 1984, pp28–29

a What proportion of men in class I jobs in 1972 came from working-class homes?
b What has been the main reason for the patterns of mobility?
c Why has 'this pattern of unequal opportunity . . . remained remarkably stable'?
d Would you expect rates of female social mobility to be higher or lower today than before the Second World War? Explain the reasons for your answer.

Questions and Suggested Projects

Review Questions

1 What are the main forms of social stratification? What are the key differences between them?
2 Using no more than 100 words for each, outline the approaches to social class of:
    a Karl Marx **b** Max Weber **c** the Registrar General.
3 List the different ways in which a person may obtain status in Britain today.

Theme-linking Questions

1 Explain how changes in the nature of work and the occupational structure have affected the different social classes in Britain.
2 Outline the relationships between social class and:
    a leisure activities **b** family life
    c political behaviour **d** educational achievement.
3 Examine the varying ways in which members of the different social classes define and experience age and ageing.
4 What sociological methods would you use to carry out a study on attitudes to social class? What problems would you face?

Stimulus–response Question

Most people who live in class societies are aware that they do, though their ideas about class may not coincide with the sociologist's model of the class-system nor with his evaluation of their particular class position. A person's class position may also be differently evaluated by others besides sociologists; by neighbours, workmates, relatives, etc. A further difficulty is that we are dealing with rapidly changing societies, in which social class changes rapidly also, and in which people realise that such changes are taking place. So it becomes difficult to draw hard-and-fast borderlines between classes when hundreds of thousands of people move into occupations different from those of their parents, or marry people of different class backgrounds, or feel perhaps that class is not as important or as rigid as it was in Dickens's day.

Source: *Introducing Sociology*, ed. Peter Worsley, Penguin, second edition 1977, pp420–421

1 Name the five types of people mentioned in the passage who may evalute a person's class position. (2)
2 State the three reasons mentioned for the difficulty of drawing 'hard-and-fast borderlines between classes'. (3)
3 What boundaries are drawn between classes by:
    a Karl Marx
    b the Registrar General? (2)
4 Identify three reasons why most people have different jobs from those of their parents. (3)
5 Even though X's neighbours, relatives and friends see X as working class, X might well see him or herself as middle class. What consequences is this difference likely to have for X's attitudes and behaviour? (5)
6 Explain why sociologists are so interested in social class. (5)

Essays

1 Explain how and why Britain's class structure has changed in recent years.
2 **a** Outline Marx's theory of social class.
   b What are the advantages and disadvantages of basing a person's social class on occupation?
3 Compare and contrast the caste and class systems of stratification. Your answer could include
       an outline of each system
       closed and open systems
       ascription and achievement
       social mobility
       role of religion in legitimating caste
       the difficulty of defining class
       the importance of occupation
       changes in both systems.

Suggested Projects

1 A study using secondary sources of slavery in the world today.
2 A study of the importance of caste among local Hindus.
3 A study, based on surveys, of how people in your community define social class.
4 A study of the class structure of a village community.
5 A study of how and why different types of people rank occupations.

5

Gender

Introduction

This chapter is concerned with the social differences between men and women, and how we learn particular ways of behaviour depending on whether we are born a boy or a girl. Gender differences obviously occur in many areas of sociology, and differences in education are discussed on pages 228–231, and those in the family on pages 201–203. It is the world of work, however, which perhaps provides the most important illustration of the differences between men and women, and this will be examined in this chapter.

Sex and Gender

'One of the most dominant themes which runs through much of sociology is the question of how far our behaviour is determined by our biology and how far it is influenced by the society in which we live.' (see page 1). In no topic is this question of more importance than in gender. Put simply, do men and women have different personalities and behaviour patterns because they are born different or because society makes them different? There are obvious biological differences beween males and females, but in view of the wide variations in how women and men act, both within and between societies, most sociologists argue that our behaviour as men or women is learned, not inborn. We must always be careful to distinguish between the biological and the social differences between men and women.

Our sex is determined even before we are born, and can be changed only through medical operations, and even then not totally. Our gender behaviour, on the other hand, depends on how we are brought up and how we ourselves choose to act. The terms male and female refer to the differences between the sexes; masculine and feminine to the differences between the genders. What is considered appropriate masculine and feminine behaviour varies greatly between societies and over time, and even from group to group within a particular society.

'Oh! That explains the difference in our pay'

KEY TERMS

sex the biological or physiological differences between men and women.
gender the social and cultural (i.e. learned) differences between men and women.

Extract 1 Gender Roles: Nature or Nurture?

A key sociological question is why are the roles of males and females different?

One answer often put forward is that this is the way nature wanted it to be. Men and women are, after all, differently put together. Women can bear children, men cannot. The difference in roles, according to this view, merely reflects the difference in biology.

It is also often said that men and women are born not just with biological differences, but with psychological ones too. Men are said to be naturally dominant, aggressive, and independent. Women are said to be naturally passive, meek, and dependent. Therefore, this view goes, men are naturally best fitted to deal with the harsh conditions outside the cosy domestic scene, while women are best fitted to stay within the domestic ambit. If women do take paid work, then it is best for them to stick to tasks such as teaching, nursing, cleaning, and so on, as these most closely reflect their biological role. This is what nature intended. Any other system would be unnatural.

The curious thing is, nature seems to have worked rather differently in other societies. Probably the most famous demonstration of this was made by the American anthropologist Margaret Mead. In her book *Sex and Temperament in Three Primitive Tribes* (1935) she describes three tribes in New Guinea. They each considered 'natural' a system of sex-roles quite different, not only from our own, but also from the others.

In one tribe, the Arapesh, both sexes acted in a way our society thinks of as typically feminine. Both men and women were gentle and passive, and they shared equally the tasks of bringing up children.

In another tribe, the Mundugumor, both sexes acted in a way our society would consider typically masculine. Women as well as men were aggressive and independent, and both sexes detested the business of childbirth and child-rearing.

In the third tribe the situation was more like our own, in that men and women played different roles: but the roles tended to be the reverse of those our society considers 'natural'. In this tribe, the Tchambuli, it was the women who were the practical, managing ones, and the men the ones who spent their time in gossip, shopping, and making themselves look attractive.

Source: *New Society*, 23 November 1978, p.i

GLOSSARY

anthropology study of societies, usually non-industrial.

a Summarise in two or three sentences the argument that states that men and women are born with different personalities.

b Draw a chart or diagram which summarises the findings of Margaret Mead in the three New Guinea tribes.

c Mead's research methods and findings have, in recent years, been severely criticised. In particular, it has been argued that she was so keen to prove that gender roles are culturally determined that she found what she was looking for. How do you think this may have happened, and what are the main difficulties of carrying out participant observation and interviews in societies one knows little about beforehand.

Activity 1

a Describe the type of person each of the following suggests to you:

    1 a feminine female   3 a feminine male
    2 a masculine female 4 a masculine male.

b List any complimentary or abusive names that can be attached to each of the above.

c Which of the four is most commonly looked down upon? Why do you think this is?

Gender Role Socialisation

Like all our roles, we are socialised into our gender roles. (See pages 13–10 for a general discussion of socialisation.) While studying gender role socialisation, however, two important points must always be borne in mind:

a Not everyone agrees on what is appropriate gender behaviour for boys and girls, men and women, and this disagreement has increased in recent years.

b Children are not passive recipients of socialisation. We can, if we wish, choose to reject the norms and values imparted by parents, teachers and friends.

Almost from the day we are born, the socialisation processes of most of us are saturated with gender-specific norms and values.

Extract 2 Nursery Rhymes and Gender

Children's literature is a fascinating source for the sociological study of socialisation. The two nursery rhymes below, for example, convey particular images of males and females.

Miss Muffet	Peter
Little Miss Muffet	Peter, Peter pumpkin eater
Sat on a tuffet	Had a wife and couldn't keep her
Eating her curds and whey	He put her in a pumpkin shell
There came a big spider	And there he kept her very well.
Who sat down beside her	
And frightened Miss Muffet away.	

Source: *The Oxford Nursery Rhyme Book*, ed. by Iona and Peter Opie, Oxford University Press, 1955, pp39, 81

a What messages about male and female behaviour can be found in these two nursery rhymes?

b What are the advantages and disadvantages of using such secondary qualitative data as nursery rhymes in the sociological analysis of gender?

Look at this, a sex stereotype's joined the playgroup.

Activity 2

a Using young children you know as your sample, examine the extent to which boys and girls today:
   1 play different games
   2 have different toys
   3 read different books and comics.
b Interview the parents of the children in your sample about their own childhood in order to find out if games, toys, books and comics have become less gender-specific.

Extract 3 Ways of Learning Gender Conformity

Gender socialisation, like all socialisation, operates in a variety of ways:

1 Positive reinforcement – children not necessarily punished for gender-inappropriate behaviour, but subtly rewarded for being 'just like a girl' or 'a big strong boy'.

2 Parental expectation – parents' preconceived ideas about male or female behaviour bring about a self-fulfilling prophecy.

3 Identification and imitation – the behaviour of significant adults and children's heroes and heroines prompt children to take on that behaviour themselves.

4 Peer group pressure – the desire to conform, to be accepted as 'normal' begins early and may increase around adolescence.

Source: *Gender*, Pat Mayes, Longman, 1986, p11

a What is meant by 'gender-inappropriate behaviour'?
b Give an example to illustrate each of the four ways of learning gender conformity.

Heroes and heroines, as *Extract 3* points out, provide important role models for children, but there are also role models we come across in our everyday lives. Part of the hidden curriculum of the school, for example, is that different types of post in the school tend to be filled by the different sexes (see page 27 Activity 5); we thus learn that caretakers are usually male, cleaners usually female.

Activity 3

As a group, carry out research in order to discover the extent to which TV programmes and commercials present different role models and images of males and females. You will have to devote considerable care and time to planning your study.

a Outline the different ways, if any, in which TV programmes and commercials present gender-appropriate behaviour for males and females.

b It is often argued that TV presents stereotypes of males and females. Does your study suggest this is the case? If so, what are the main characteristics of the two stereotypes?

c Explain the difficulties you faced carrying out this study.

Extract 4 A Sexist Advertisement and Reply

What does the above advertisement tell you about social attitudes towards men and women? It may help you answer this question if you try to think of a male equivalent to the advertisement.

Sexuality

The different views of appropriate behaviour for males and females can perhaps be seen at their clearest in attitudes to sexuality.

Extract 5   How Boys Slag Off Girls

It is among young people, who are both discovering their sexuality and are most subject to peer group pressure, that these different attitudes are most obvious. Sue Lees' research is based on interviews with over a hundred 15-year-old girls in three London comprehensive schools.

Boys and girls talk about sexuality in quite different ways. Though both are concerned with reputation, the basis on which it rests is very distinct. For boys, sexual reputation is enhanced by varied experience: bragging to other boys about how many girls they have 'made'. For a girl, reputation is something to be guarded. It is under threat not merely if she is known to have sex with anyone other than her steady boyfriend, but also if she goes out with several different boys, or is merely seen with different boys, or dresses in a certain way.

For a boy, reputation does not appear to be predominantly determined by his sexual status or conquests. More important is his status among his mates, where sporting prowess may count most. For a girl, the defence of her sexual reputation is crucial to her standing both with boys and girls – certainly around the age of 15 or so.

This emphasis on the importance of a girl's reputation is shown up in a whole battery of insults which are in use by both girls and boys in their day-to-day life.

The commonest insult, used by both sexes, is *slag*. But *all* the insults we came across seemed to relate to a girl's sexual reputation. It is crucial to note that the insults might bear *no* relation at all to a girl's actual sexual behaviour. (It is sometimes just sour grapes.) It is a question of perception and of codes of language. But this did not make things any easier for the girls. An unjustified tag can stick as easily as a justified one.

Some girls laughed the insults off; others felt threatened, afraid and upset. But even if the accusation was unjustified, few girls felt able simply to ignore the insult, or to give as good as they got.

One problem for girls – if the abuse came from boys – is that there aren't equivalent terms that they can use against boys. There are no words that amount to an attack on their whole personality or social identity. The only really derogatory word for a boy is *queer* or *pouff*. Because this refers to abnormal sexuality, there are limits to the occasions it can be used. As one girl told me:

'One thing I noticed is that there are not many names that you can call a boy. But if you call a girl a name, there's a load of them. You might as well make a dictionary of names you can call a girl.'

Source: 'How Boys Slag Off Girls', Sue Lees, *New Society*, 13 October 1983, p51

a What appears to be the main determinant of a boy's reputation?
b Why do you think 'there are not many names that you can call a boy', and so many for girls?
c What does this difference tell you about social attitudes to male and female sexuality?

Gender and Occupation

Before Britain became an industrial society, both men and women participated fully in economic life, as they do in most agricultural societies today. In the early days of industrialisation, in the late 18th and early 19th centuries, men, women and children worked in the new factories and mines (for child labour, see page 111–112), but gradually women and children were excluded. Other employment opportunities for women, in the professions for example, were restricted. In the late 19th century women were largely restricted to those jobs, such as domestic service, considered suitable for females. Within marriage, both sexes worked, but the work of the husband was paid and outside the home, the domestic work of the wife unpaid, although a large proportion of working-class women also did paid work such as cleaning for the better off and taking in laundry.

In Britain today, however, a majority of women under the age of 60, both married and unmarried, work outside the home. This 'return to paid employment' of married women began during World War One (1914–1918), and the trend has continued since then.

Extract 6 *Women's Return to Paid Employment*

There are many reasons why more women now have paid employment:

1 Two world wars made it necessary to employ women to replace men away in the forces. Also the 'war economy' of the defence industries employed women.

2 Changes in industry, most notably the expansion of the service sector, led to the employment of women as telephonists, typists, clerks and so on.

3 Improved contraception released women from child-rearing for greater periods of their life.

4 The family wage has proved inadequate for many families' needs.

5 Increased expectations about material circumstances often necessitates a second wage.

6 Improved educational standards heighten women's aspirations; many women work because they want to.

Source: *Gender*, Pat Mayes, Longman, 1986, p53

a Explain what is meant by 'increased expectations about material circumstances'.
b Why has the expansion of the service sector led to greater employment for women?
c What changes in the family and in the home have made it easier for married women to take paid employment?

But if most women are now in paid employment, this does not mean that they are paid as much as men (see page 127), or that they are in the same kinds of jobs as men.

Extract 7 *The Occupations of Full- and Part-time Working Women and Working Men*

Occupational order	Full-time	Part-time	All working women	Working men (1980 GHS)★
	(percentages)			
Managerial general	–	–	–	1
Professionals supporting management	2	0	1	6
Professionals in health, education and welfare	16	10	13	5
Literary, artistic and sports	1	1	1	1
Professionals in engineering and science	1	0	1	5
Other managerial	5	1	4	12
Clerical	41	22	33	6
Selling	6	13	9	4
Security	0	0	0	2
Catering, cleaning and hairdressing	10	41	23	3
Farming and fishing	1	2	1	2
Material processing (excluding metal)	1	1	1	3
Making and repairing (excluding metal)	6	4	5	6
Metal processing, making, repairing	3	1	2	20
Painting, assembling, packing	6	3	5	5
Construction and mining	0	–	0	6
Transport	1	1	1	11
Miscellaneous	0	0	0	1
	100	100	100	100
Base	1877	1477	3354	8024

★1980 GHS General Household Survey

Source: *Women in Employment: a lifetime perspective*, Office of Population Census and Surveys, 1984 (quoted in *Gender*, Pat Mayes, Longman, 1986, p95)

a In which two occupational orders do most women work?
b State three occupational orders which are heavily male dominated.
c From the information in the above table, what appear to be the relationships between gender and occupational status?
d How might sociologists explain the relationships between gender and type of occupation?

Activity 4

How many women are currently:
a Cabinet Ministers
b Members of Parliament
c University Vice chancellors
d Polytechnic Directors
e Bishops?

Extract 8 Hairdressing: an Example of 'Women's Work'

Many occupations have a male or female image. Most of us take for granted that secretaries and florists will be female, and that bricklayers and train drivers male. Girls are not naturally better secretaries than boys, but, once established, such gender-related assumptions tend to be self-perpetuating. Attwood and Hutton's research is based on interviews with first- and second-year hairdressing apprentices.

Many of the female apprentices, especially those who had not done well at school, saw their future selves primarily as working wives and mothers . . . They recognised the need to work after marriage and expected to stay at home when children are very small. However, they said that they intended to return to work when their children were old enough. Most stopped short, however, of wanting to do anything involving the commitment they saw as characteristic of a full-time career. Many clearly had given thought to combining work with motherhood and saw working from home as a solution . . .

Some explained that, whilst they saw themselves as working, they nonetheless subscribed to the traditional family role division and saw their work as primarily a way of supplementing family income and contributing a 'second wage'. Some saw their work as secondary to their husbands' careers and saw hairdressing as 'women's work'. This was confirmed by their view of male hairdressers as homosexual and in this way 'lesser men'.

Source: '"Getting On". Gender Differences in Career Development: A Case Study in the Hairdressing Industry', Margaret Attwood and Frances Hatton, in *Gender, Class and Work*, ed. Eva Gamarnikow, David Morgan, June Purvis and Daphne Taylorson, Heinemann, 1983, pp123–124

a What is meant by 'the traditional family role division'?
b Why is hairdressing seen as 'women's work'?
c How do many of the female apprentices link their future roles as wives and mothers to their roles as workers?

KEY TERM

patriarchy the structure of male power and control over women.

Patriarchy

The key dimensions of differentiation in society – class, gender, ethnicity, and age – are usually structured in such a way that some groups of people have power over others. Slave owners have power over slaves, the middle-aged usually have power over the young, and it is common for some ethnic groups to be in a superior position to others. Similarly, it is usual for men to be more powerful than women.

Activity 5

There is wide disagreement over the extent to which Britain is a patriarchal society. Outline the arguments for and against the view that men have power and control over women in the following areas of social life:

a marriage and the family
b sexual activity
c politics
d work
e education.

Questions and Suggested Projects

Review Questions

1 Explain the difference between the terms 'sex' and 'gender'.
2 List the main ways in which children are socialised into gender roles.
3 Outline the occupational differences that exist between men and women in Britain today.

Theme-linking Questions

1

> . . . of 465 judges, only one is black . . . and just 17 are women; their average age is 66.7. Nine of every ten judges went to public school and eight in ten to Oxford or Cambridge.

Source: *New Society*, 16 January 1987, p3

How might sociologists explain the above figures?
2 How have changes in the law in recent years attempted to improve the position of women? How successful have they been?
3 The lives of female members of certain ethnic minorities are frequently very different from those of other women. Examine the lives of women in one such ethnic minority.
4 Examine the relationships between gender and affluence and poverty.

Stimulus–response Question

Feminist sociologists have pointed out the significant impact of gender upon a whole host of social experiences and institutional areas. Just as social class can be shown to have an important influence upon such diverse matters as educational opportunity and health care, gender also, it is argued, affects almost every aspect of our daily lives and the social institutions in which they are lived. Moreover, as anthropological and comparative material makes clear, what constitutes the appropriate masculine and feminine behaviour, roles and attitudes in our society are not natural, inevitable and unchangeable but social constructions elaborated in distinctive ways in different historical periods.

Feminists argue that gender is as important a dimension of inequality as social class. Class divisions are the form of inequality created in a capitalist society where the capitalist class retains the wealth and the power. Gender divisions are the form of inequality created in a *patriarchal* society where men have advantages and power not afforded to women.

Source: 'Introducing Feminist Sociology', Mary Maynard, *Social Science Teacher*, Vol 12, 3, pp89–90

1 Which two dimensions of inequality are discussed above ? (2)
2 What is meant by the term 'patriarchal society'? (2)
3 Explain what anthropological and comparative material tell us about gender roles. (3)
4 How do children learn their gender roles? (6)
5 'Gender differences are becoming less important; women now have the same opportunities as men.' Examine the evidence for and against this view. (7)

Essays

1 Examine how peer groups and the mass media can influence young people to behave in a way considered appropriate to their sex.

2 **a** Explain how sociologists distinguish between the terms 'sex' and 'gender'.

  b Examine the extent to which our gender roles are determined by nurture as opposed to nature.

3 Explain why the proportion of women who work has increased during the twentieth century. Your answer could include:
the effects of two world wars
changes in the economic and occupational structures
changes in the family and marriage
changing beliefs and attitudes among women
full- and part-time work.

Suggested Projects

1 A case-study of a local factory or office to examine how occupation, pay, and promotion prospects are still gender-related.

2 An observation study of young children to see if language, games and toys vary according to sex.

3 A study, based on interviews, of three generations of women in a small number of families to examine the extent to which female roles have changed.

4 A study of 'masculinity'. What does it mean, and how important is it to men that they are seen as masculine.

5 A comparative study of gender roles in two different societies.

6

Race and Ethnicity

Introduction

Of all the various dimensions of social differentiation, none is potentially more important in terms of its effects on individuals than race or ethnicity. Countless millions of people have been killed throughout history for no reason other than that they belonged to the 'wrong' racial or ethnic group. (See, for example, Chapter 2 *Extract 1* pages 21–23.)

This chapter looks at
a the nature of race and ethnicity
b racism and racialism
c racial differences in Britain today, especially in employment. (For race and education, see pages 231–233.)

The Nature of Race and Ethnicity

All human beings share a common origin and belong to a common species. However, the biological differences that exist between groups of people have often been seen as a reason for social differentiation.

KEY TERM

race a biological view: a group of people with certain inherited physical features in common, e.g. skin colour, type of hair, nose and eye structure.

A common classification is to divide people into three races – Caucasoid, Mongoloid and Negroid – but this division is a crude oversimplification; firstly, it does not include many groups such as the Red Indians of North America, and, secondly, it ignores the fact that in many countries of the world a large proportion of the people have ancestors of different racial groups. In other words, it is difficult, if not impossible, to locate many people in one of these three groupings. In any event, there are major differences *within* each race; compare, for example, the 'typical' Swede with the 'typical' Italian.

However, some biological differences *are* more important than others; when applying for a job, for example, the colour of one's skin *is* likely to matter more than the colour of one's eyes or hair.

KEY TERM

race a sociological view: a label commonly attached to a group of people who are seen as having certain physical characteristics in common.

KEY TERM

ethnic group a group of people who share a common culture and who see themselves as being united through a common origin and many shared activities.

Source: adapted from *Social Trends 1987*, HMSO, 1987, Table 1.7

It is this second, sociological, view of race which will be used in this chapter.

Activity 1

a As a sociology class exercise, write down the countries of birth of every student's grandparents.
b Produce a table listing all the countries referred to by your group, in order of the number of mentions.
c What does your table tell you about the people of Britain?

Because the term 'race' emphasises physical differences between groups of people, sociologists use the term 'ethnic group' to refer to those people who share a common culture.

Many ethnic groups which encourage or insist upon intermarriage do have certain physical characteristics in common, but this is not necessarily the case.

Extract 1 Britain's Ethnic Mix 1985

Ethnic origin	Thousands	Percentage UK-born
White	51,222	96
West Indian or Guyanese	547	53
Indian	689	35
Pakistani	406	44
Bangladeshi	99	28
Chinese	122	24
African	102	32
Arab	61	12
Mixed	232	76
Other	117	26
Not stated	637	69

a What proportion of Britain's population in 1985 was white?
b What proportion of people of West Indian or Guyanese origin was born in the UK? Would you expect this proportion to increase or decrease in the future? Give reasons for your answer.
c 'White' is classed as being an 'ethnic origin' in the above table. To what extent is this a valid classification?

Members of different ethnic groups not only have different cultures but also may well be treated in very different ways; some ethnic groups, for example, are likely to face much less discrimination than others. Britain is now a multi-racial society, and it is essential to always remember that there are members of many *different* ethnic groups living here.

Activity 2

List the main ethnic minority groups in Britain today, and identify the norms and values, and shared activities, which give each group its own cultural identity.

Racism and Racialism

There is no inevitable reason why skin colour should be of any more social significance than hair colour, but only rarely have all races and ethnic groups been seen as equals.

KEY TERM

racism a set of beliefs which state that a particular racial or ethnic group is in some way inferior.

This set of beliefs can operate at two different levels:

a at the individual: people who believe members of other racial or ethnic groups are inferior are said to be *racially prejudiced.*

b at the societal: this exists when the society, especially its economic and political institutions, is organised in such a way that members of certain ethnic groups are placed in a disadvantaged and inferior position. The apartheid system of South Africa provides the most extreme example of this *institutional racism.*

Extract 2 How People Learn to be Racist

Sociologists would argue that we learn our beliefs about the different racial and ethnic groups in the same way that we learn our other beliefs, i.e. through socialisation. The following song, heavy with irony, supports this view.

You've Got to be Carefully Taught
You've got to be taught
to hate and fear,
you've got to be taught
from year to year.
It's got to be drummed
in your dear little ear,
you've got to be carefully taught.

You've got to be taught
to be afraid
of people whose eyes
are oddly made,
and people whose skin
is a different shade
you've got to be carefully taught.

You've got to be taught
before it's too late,
before you are six
or seven or eight
to hate all the people
your relatives hate
you've got to be carefully taught!
you've got to be carefully taught!

Source: 'South Pacific', Richard Rodgers and Oscar Hammerstein II

a According to the above song, who have children got to be taught to be afraid of?

b The song says 'you've got to be taught . . . before you are six or seven or eight.' What are the sociological arguments for and against this view?

c How are children taught 'to hate and fear'?

Racist beliefs may well deflect criticism from the real causes of people's problems. Jews, for example, were blamed by the Nazis for Germany's massive economic and social problems of the 1920s and 1930s. Unemployment in Britain today may be blamed by racially prejudiced people on black immigrants taking all the jobs of the whites. This process is known as scapegoating.

KEY TERM

scapegoating wrongly blaming a person or group for a social problem when the real blame or fault lies elsewhere.

While they are blaming members of other ethnic and racial groups for their problems, racially prejudiced people are not, of course, blaming those people or institutions really responsible.

Activity 3

a Which groups of people benefit from using ethnic and racial minorities as scapegoats? Give examples to illustrate your answer.
b Apart from ethnic or racial minorities, which other groups of people are used as scapegoats?

By no means everyone, of course, holds racist views, and the 1984 British Social Attitude Survey suggests that young people are much less racially prejudiced than their elders.

Activity 4

Imagine you have been commissioned to investigate the degree of racial prejudice in your area.
a How would you set about your research?
b What problems and difficulties would you face?

There were these thick paddies . . .

Extract 3 *The New Empire within Britain*

In the article from which the extract below is taken Salman Rushdie accuses Britain of being a fundamentally racist society.

If you want to understand British racism – and, without understanding, no improvement is possible – it is impossible even to begin to grasp the nature of the beast unless you accept its historical roots; unless you see that 400 years of conquest and looting, centuries of being told that you are superior to the fuzzy-wuzzies and the wogs, leave their stain on you all; that such a stain seeps into every part of your culture, your language and your daily life; and that nothing much has been done to wash it out.

Think . . . about the ease with which the English language allows the terms of racial abuse to be coined:

wog, frog, kraut, dago, spic, yid, coon, nigger, Argie. Can there be another language with so wide-ranging a vocabulary of racist denigration?

What is it like, this country to which the immigrants came, in which their children are growing up? This is not the England of fair play, tolerance, decency and equality – maybe that place never existed anyway, except in fairy tales. In the streets of the new empire, black women are abused and black children are beaten up on their way home from school. In the rundown housing estates of the new empire, black families have their windows broken, they are afraid

to go out after dark, and human and animal excrement arrives through their letter boxes. The police offer threats instead of protection, and the courts offer small hope of redress.

Britain is now two entirely different worlds, and the one you inherit is determined by the colour of your skin.

What has been created is a gulf in reality. White and black perceptions of everyday life have moved so far apart as to be incompatible. And the rift is not narrowing; it is getting wider. We stand on opposite sides of an abyss, yelling at each other and sometimes hurling stones, while the ground crumbles beneath our feet.

Source: 'The New Empire within Britain', Salman Rushdie, *New Society*, 9 December 1982, pp417–418

a According to Rushdie, how can we best understand racism in Britain?

b What are Britain's 'two entirely different worlds'?

c For which groups of people, other than racial minorities, has a vocabulary of abuse developed?

d Is Rushdie correct in arguing so powerfully that Britain is a racist society?

Activity 5

Delegate at least one member of your sociology class to watch each episode of every British 'soap' on TV during one week. The delegated student should record every appearance of a member of an ethnic minority group and the part they played in the programme.

a At the end of the week produce a complete list of all appearances.

b What does your list tell you about the portrayal of members of ethnic minority groups on TV?

Racism refers to a set of beliefs, but sociologists are just as interested in people's actual behaviour towards members of other racial and ethnic groups.

A racialist society, therefore, is one where acts of racial discrimination are widespread. In Britain, research in the 1960s and 1970s consistently showed that black people were discriminated against, especially in employment and housing.

Evidence on the extent of racial discrimination led to the Race Relations Acts of 1965 and 1968, and the strengthening of the law which took place with the 1976 Race Relations Act. This Act (which is, in many ways, similar to the 1975 Sex Discrimination Act) makes it unlawful to discriminate on grounds of colour, race, nationality or ethnic or national origin. The Act distinguishes two types of discrimination:

a direct: straightforward, deliberate discrimination, e.g. an employer who states in an advertisement 'whites only need apply'.

b indirect: applying unjustified conditions which act in the interest of some racial groups as opposed to others, e.g. an employer stating that applicants for a job must have been educated in Britain (thus precluding adult immigrants) when a British education is not necessary for the job.

The Commission for Racial Equality was established by the 1976 Act to monitor and advise on issues of racial discrimination.

There are exceptions to the Race Relations Act of 1976 which allow racial discrimination in certain circumstances, and it is often very difficult to prove that discrimination has taken place, even when it is strongly suspected.

Activity 6

a Why do you think it is difficult to prove cases of racial discrimination?

b Re-read the section on law (pages 35–37). Do you think that racism and racialism are likely to be reduced because Parliament has stated that racial discrimination is unlawful? Give reasons for your answer.

Race and Employment

Members of ethnic and racial minorities are likely to face discrimination, however subtle, in many walks of life, but it is probably discrimination in employment which has the most far-reaching consequences, for it is a person's job, or lack of one, which is the most important determinant of his or her standard and quality of living.

There is not, of course, total racial discrimination in employment; some ethnic or racial minorities might face little or no discrimination, and some members of even the most discriminated against groups go through their entire working lives facing no personal instance of discrimination. There is, however, considerable evidence that many members of ethnic minorities, especially perhaps those of West Indian and Asian origin, do face discrimination at work. Such discrimination can operate in a variety of ways:

a offering jobs to members of some ethnic groups rather than others

b restricting some ethnic groups to certain types of jobs

c offering better training and promotion prospects to some ethnic groups.

Extract 4 *Ethnic Origin and Unemployment*

As the chart below clearly illustrates, one's chances of being unemployed depend, to a very great extent, upon one's ethnic origin.

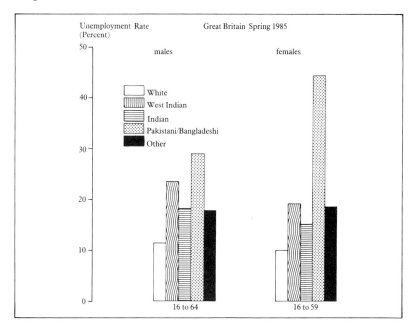

Source: *Employment Gazette*, January 1987, p26, HMSO

a Which ethnic minority group has the highest unemployment rate?

b Complete the following sentence: a person of West Indian origin is . . . as likely as a white person to be unemployed.

c What are the social and political consequences of high unemployment among young members of racial and ethnic minorities?

Extract 5 *The Occupational Distribution of Ethnic Groups*

Males and females have different patterns of employment, and so, to some extent, do the different ethnic groups, as the 1985 Labour Force Survey carried out for the Department of Employment shows.

The overall occupational distribution for both ethnic minority and white men was broadly similar, with the largest occupational groups in both cases in processing (about one-quarter) and managerial (about one-eighth) occupations. There were, however, some significant differences (mirroring the industrial structure) with smaller proportions of ethnic minority men than whites employed in construction and mining, and farming and fishing and larger proportions in catering jobs and in metal and electrical processing occupations.

Among both ethnic minority and white women, over 60 per cent were in three occupational groups; clerical and related occupations, catering and cleaning jobs, and professional and related occupations in health, education and welfare. White women were especially concentrated in clerical and related occupations (30 per cent compared with 23 per cent of ethnic minority women), whereas ethnic minority women were relatively numerous in processing and assembling occupations.

Source: *Employment Gazette*, January 1987, pp22–5

a Which types of jobs are small proportions of ethnic minority men employed in?
b Explain why catering has a larger proportion of ethnic minority men?
c Explain why a higher proportion of white women work in clerical and related occupations.
d What further information would you need in order to be able to assess whether members of ethnic minorities have equal opportunities at work?

Activity 7

Find out how many people of West Indian and Asian origin are currently:
a members of the Cabinet
b Members of Parliament
c leading trade union officials
d Football League club managers
e national TV news readers.
What do your findings tell you about the position of people of West Indian and Asian origin in Britain today?

Extract 6 *Discrimination: an Example*

The extent of racial discrimination is almost impossible to assess. People might wrongly think they are being discriminated against, but also might not realise they are. The extract below illustrates one of the best methods of finding out if discrimination is taking place.

At half past twelve, Friday lunchtime, on 28 May, Errol Davidson walked up to a pub called the Corner Pin – just across the road from Wimbledon greyhound stadium in south London. He didn't want a drink – he wanted a job, and that morning the Corner Pin had placed an ad in the local paper; they needed bar staff. Errol knew the job was still open because a friend had rung less than hour before to check it out.

So into the lounge bar he walked, and told the manager's wife he'd seen the ad. It was to be a brief exchange:

'Yes . . . no – it was seen to last night.'

'It was seen to?'

'Yeah, so he's took somebody on, yes.'

'So someone's on?'

'Yes, yes.'

Out walked Errol, and then, one hour later, in walked Andy. Andy was the same age as Errol, had the same experience and was similarly dressed. By this time the pub was noisily coping with the lunchtime trade: the manager couldn't see Andy just now – could he come back tomorrow at eleven? So the job's still open? Yes.

The crashingly obvious punchline, of course, is that Errol is black and Andy is white. For Errol, the quite casual act of discrimination is almost banal: for most blacks it is an unremarkable fact of everyday life. But, this time, the discriminator has been caught in the act, because Errol and Andy are part of a team of jobless young people working on a week-long series of spot-checks run by the Commission for Racial Equality.

Source: *Racial Equality at Work*, David Henshaw, *The Listener*, 1 July 1982

a Explain the meaning of 'the quite casual act of discrimination is almost banal'.

b Which method of research was used by Errol and Andy?

c Describe how you could carry out a similar piece of research to investigate discrimination in renting furnished accommodation.

Questions and Suggested Projects

Review Questions

1 Explain the difficulties involved in defining the term 'race'.
2 Why is it difficult to investigate suspected cases of racial discrimination?
3 How have governments attempted to reduce racial discrimination?
4 What is meant by:
    a ethnic group
    b racism
    c racialism
    d scapegoating?

Theme-linking Questions

1 How do newspapers present the different ethnic groups? Collect examples to illustrate your answer.
2 Religion plays an important part in the lives of many members of ethnic minority groups. Explain the functions religion can perform for these people.
3 Examine the extent to which ethnic minorities in Britain form part of an under-class.
4 What are the relationships between housing patterns and ethnicity?

Stimulus–response Question

Overseas doctors now make up almost a third of hospital doctors in England and Wales. Most of them are here to stay . . . Racial disadvantage and discrimination are a daily reality for many members of ethnic minorities. Doctors in the National Health Service are no exception. Overseas doctors (with broadly similar qualifications) wait longer for promotion to higher grades and have to make more applications for posts than their white British colleagues. They also change their career options more frequently in order to improve their chances of progress. Generally the low status of overseas doctors in the NHS has been accompanied by poor training opportunities, thus forcing them into careers in the less attractive specialties.

Specialty   Proportion of overseas-born doctors in hospital specialties in England and Wales; consultant posts, as at 30 September 1983

	%
General medicine	9
General surgery	9
Other surgery	17
Obstetrics and gynaecology	10
Anaesthetics	17
Geriatric medicine	46
Accident and emergency	35
Psychiatry	26
All specialties	17

Source: adapted from *Overseas Doctors*, Muhammed Anwar and Ameer Ali, Commission for Racial Equality, 1987, (Foreward by Peter Newsam, p7; Table 18, p35)

a What three factors mentioned in the passage suggest doctors from overseas are disadvantaged in the National Health Service?   (3)

b Which three specialties have the highest proportion of overseas consultants?   (1)

c What proportion of
      1 all hospital doctors
      2 all consultants
are from overseas?   (2)

d Explain why the highest proportion of overseas consultants work in geriatrics.   (3)

e Explain the difference between racial prejudice and racial discrimination and give an example of each.   (4)

f Imagine you have been appointed Community Relations Officer in your area with responsibility for persuading local employers to introduce an equal opportunities policy for all racial and ethnic groups. Explain how you would set about your job and identify the main problems you would face.   (7)

Essays

1 Explain how and why some people learn to be racially prejudiced.

2 a Examine the relationships between race and employment.

  b What attempts have governments made to reduce racial discrimination in employment? How successful have they been?

3 'Black people in Britain today have fewer opportunities than white.' Discuss. Your answer could include:
racism and racialism
racial prejudice and discrimination
the different ethnic groups in Britain
race and education
race and employment
race and housing
the 1976 Race Relations Act.

Suggested Projects

1 An interview-based study of attitudes to ethnic minorities among different age groups.

2 A study of how different ethnic groups are portrayed in children's literature.

3 A participant observation study of the various groups working in the field of race relations in your area.

4 A library study of race relations in two contrasting countries.

5 A study of one aspect of the culture of one ethnic minority, e.g. family life, religion.

7 Age

Introduction

Between birth and death we all age at exactly the same chrono-logical rate. If age was just this simple it would be of little interest to sociologists; we would certainly need to look at the effects of physical changes on our social activities, but generally the topic would be left to biologists to study.

However, age has a social as well as a biological dimension. It is a major means of distinguishing and differentiating between people – note, for example, the way newspapers usually give the age of people they name, even when it is of no relevance to the story. The importance of age and ageing can hardly be overestimated. It influences most of our relationships and activities, and many of us go to considerable trouble and expense to give the impression of being older or, more usually, younger than we really are.

Activity 1

State two occasions in each case when people may:
(1) underestimate; and (2) overestimate their age.

LUCY........BY DAVE FOLLOWS.

As a means of differentiating people, though, there are two major differences between age, on the one hand, and sex, ethnicity and class on the other.

Firstly, it can be argued that there are very few, if any, inevitable differences between males and females and that even the very existence of social class is not inevitable. But simple biology does place important limits on what people of different ages can do; a ninety-year-old, cannot be reasonably expected to run as fast as a twenty-year-old, for example.

Secondly, again unlike sex, ethnic group and class, we all move from one age group to another, from childhood through youth and adulthood to old age (unless, of course, we die early). This means that permanent and total conflict between the generations is unlikely; if it did exist we would have to keep changing sides as we got older.

This chapter will concentrate on three age periods which sociologists are particularly interested in: childhood, youth and old age. It may initially seem odd to omit adulthood from this discussion, but to a great extent the rest of sociology, and this book, is about adulthood, and the status of being an adult does not dominate one's life to the extent that being a child, a youth or old does.

The Social Meaning of Age

> 'He's old for his age.'
> 'She's young at heart.'
> 'You're as young/old as you feel.'

These three popular sayings illustrate the relative aspect of age, that while there can be no doubt about a person's chronological age the social meaning of that age varies widely from context to context, and society to society. A politician aged fifty, for example, may be regarded as young and inexperienced while a teacher of the same age may well be seen as old and worn out.

Extract 1 Old Age among the Aborigines

In industrial societies old people tend to suffer a decline in power and status, and often standard of living too. In other societies growing old may have very different implications, for example, in Australia:

all aborigines . . . move through the age-grade system; a man becomes successively a hunter and a warrior and eventually reaches the heights of elderhood. His social development is identical with that of his age-mates, and is determined by the physical fact of ageing. So although a society like this is highly stratified and constitutes a 'gerontocracy', in which the older men hold the decisive authority, every man in his time becomes an elder. He is not fixed for life in a lowly position.
(Note that it is the elder *men* who hold the decisive authority.)

Source: *Introducing Sociology*, Peter Worsley, Penguin, 1977, p397

GLOSSARY

gerontocracy government by the old.

a Explain what is meant by 'his social development is identical with that of his age-mates'.
b What are the advantages and disadvantages of the Aborigine age-grade system?

In many non-industrial societies age is so important that various rituals mark entry into the different age-grades, of which entry into adulthood is often the most significant and is accompanied by puberty rites.

Activity 2

a Using the reference section of your library (the *Penguin Guide to the Law* is a useful resource) find out the minimum ages at which you can:
  1 be tattoed
  2 buy a pet
  3 drive a bus
  4 own a shot gun
  5 be convicted of a crime
  6 consent to a homosexual act in private
  7 marry, with parental consent.
b What do the variety of answers to the above question tell you about when adulthood begins in Britain?

It is perhaps not surprising that the teenage years in industrial societies are marked by so much uncertainty; a seventeen-year-old may one minute be treated like an adult (e.g. 'Act your age', 'You're old enough to know better'), the next like a child ('No, you can't stay out till . . .', 'You're not old enough to . . .'). What happens, of course, is that complex bargaining and negotiating take place over precisely what the latter are allowed to do; that the outcome varies from family to family can lead to considerable conflict between adults and young people.

Childhood, youth and old age therefore have no clear-cut starting and finishing points (apart, obviously, from the biological ones of birth and death), but they are all important labels that we attach to certain categories of people. This label affects not just a person's legal rights, but also virtually all his or her relationships with other members of society. Important as age is, however, it is not the only means of differentiating people; class, sex, ethnic group, state of health and dis/ability may, for example, be as, if not more, important. The fact that two people are of the same age does not necessarily mean they have anything else in common.

LUCY........BY DAVE FOLLOWS.

Extract 2 *The Double Standard of Ageing*

The extract below discusses the way that the social meaning of age varies according to gender. The key point of Sontag's argument is that it is the social, not the biological process, of ageing which progressively destroys women.

Old age is a genuine ordeal, one that men and women undergo in a similar way. Growing older is mainly an ordeal of the imagination – intrinsic to which is the fact that it afflicts women much more than men. It is particularly women who experience growing older (everything that comes *before* one is actually old) with such distaste and even shame.

The prestige of youth afflicts everyone in this society to some degree. Men, too, are prone to periodic bouts of depression about aging – for instance, when feeling insecure or unfulfilled or insufficiently rewarded in their jobs. But men rarely panic about aging in the way women often do. Getting older is less profoundly wounding for a man, for in addition to the propaganda for youth that puts both men and women on the defensive as they age, there is a double standard about aging that denounces women with special severity. Society is much more permissive about aging in men, as it is more tolerant of the sexual infidelities of husbands. Men are 'allowed' to age, without penalty, in several ways that women are not.

This society offers even fewer rewards for aging to women than it does to men. Being physically attractive counts much more in a woman's life than in a man's, but beauty, identified, as it is for women, with youthfulness, does not stand up well to age.

Women become sexually ineligible much earlier than men do. A man, even an ugly man, can remain eligible well into old age. He is an acceptable mate for a young, attractive woman. Women, even good-looking women, become ineligible (except as partners of very old men) at a much younger age.

Thus, for most women, aging means a humiliating process of gradual sexual disqualification. Since women are considered maximally eligible in early youth, after which their sexual value drops steadily, even young women feel themselves in a desperate race against the calendar. They are old as soon as they are no longer very young. In late adolescense some girls are already worrying about getting married. Boys and young men have little reason to anticipate trouble because

of aging. What makes men desirable to women is by no means tied to youth. On the contrary, getting older tends (for several decades) to operate in men's favor, since their value as lovers and husbands is set more by what they do than how they look. Many men have more success romantically at forty than they did at twenty or twenty-five; fame, money, and, above all, power are sexually enhancing.

The prejudices that mount against women as they grow older are an important arm of male privilege. It is the present unequal distribution of adult roles between the two sexes that gives men a freedom to age denied to women. Men actively administer the double standard about aging because the 'masculine' role awards them the initiative in courtship. Men choose; women are chosen. So men choose younger women. But although this system of inequality is operated by men, it could not work if women themselves did not acquiesce in it. Women reinforce it powerfully with their complacency, with their anguish, with their lies.

Source: 'The Double Standard of Ageing', Susan Sontag, *Saturday Review*, 23 September 1972

a What does Sontag mean by the 'double standard of ageing'?

b The above article was written in 1972. Do you think the same double standard still applies, or have women become less worried, or men more worried, about ageing?

c Which means and agencies of socialisation help to reinforce this double standard of ageing?

Childhood

For the first few years of its life a child is totally dependent on adults for its survival. This period of dependency in humans lasts much longer than that of any other species, but it takes many forms and its length varies widely both between and within societies. In Britain today, for example, parents are legally responsible for their children until the late teens and education is compulsory until the age of sixteen. But more important than children's special legal position is their social and economic position in society.

'He's quite remarkably average for his age.'

It is frequently argued that childhood has changed dramatically over the last few centuries, and, more particularly, that childhood is a relatively recent invention. Philippe Aries, in an influential study, 'Centuries of Childhood' (1962), has argued that childhood is a product of the modern, industrial world. Childhood, he argues, is now markedly different from adulthood, whereas children used to be seen as miniature adults. In law, for example, the special rights and privileges, as well as the disadvantages, of childhood are mainly as recent as the nineteenth century; until then children as young as seven were held to be as responsible for their actions as adults and could therefore receive the same punishment for breaking the law.

The relationship between adulthood and childhood can perhaps best be seen by taking the example of dress; until the nineteenth century children wore the same type of clothes as their parents. As childhood came to be seen as a special and unique period, Aries argues, so a special and unique type of clothing for children was developed.

Activity 3

a In order to discover how childhood has changed during this century, interview relatives, friends or neighbours of different generations. If possible, include old people who were children before the First World War. Your questions could ask, for example, about:
   1 how children were treated by adults
   2 dress
   3 schooling
   4 play and games.
b Write a summary of the ways in which childhood appears to have changed.
c What are the advantages and disadvantages of using interviews to discover how childhood has changed?

Although Aries is certainly correct in arguing that childhood has changed dramatically, it would be a dangerous oversimplification to claim that it is simply a recent Western invention. We really know very little of how children were treated by their parents and how they lived their lives until recently, but young children at least do usually appear to have been seen as different from, and not just miniature, adults. It seems reasonable to assume that there was in the past enormous variety in the lives of children, dependent above all on the social class of their parents, just as there is today.

In Britain, differences in attitudes and behaviour towards children were probably at their most acute in the nineteenth century. The sons of the aristocracy and bourgeoisie did not usually begin working until their late teens or early twenties, and their sisters would probably achieve adulthood (though very much a second-class variety) through marriage at roughly the same age. The children of the working class could hardly have led more different lives.

Extract 3 Working-class Children in Nineteenth-century England

In Britain today there are strict laws about the employment of children, but in the early years of the nineteenth century young children worked in appalling conditions in mines and factories. If the factory and mine owners were indifferent to the misery endured by their child employees it should not be assumed that parents were similarly unconcerned about the lives of their children. Many child workers were orphans, and even for those with parents the alternative to work was probably starvation.

Concerning child-labour in the factories, one writer said:

In stench, in heated rooms, amid the constant whirling of a thousand wheels, little fingers and little feet were kept in ceaseless action, forced into unnatural activity by blows from the heavy hands and feet of the merciless over-looker, and the infliction of bodily pain by instruments of punishment invented by the sharpened ingenuity of insatiable selfishness.

Gibbins, the author of a popular educational text late in the nineteenth century, wrote that children:

. . . were fed upon the coarsest and cheapest food, often with the same as that served out to the pigs of their master. They slept by turns and in relays, in filthy beds which were never cool; for one set of children were sent to sleep in them as soon as the others had gone off to their daily or nightly toil. There was often no discrimination of sexes; and disease, misery, and vice grew as in a hot-bed of contagion. Some of these miserable beings tried to run away. To prevent their doing so, those suspected of this tendency had irons riveted on their ankles with long links reaching up to their hips, and were compelled to work and sleep in these chains, young women and girls as well as boys suffering this brutal treatment. Many died and were buried secretly at night in some desolate spot, lest people should notice the number of the graves; and many committed suicide.

Source: *The Family and Marriage in Britain*, Ronald Fletcher, Penguin, 1966, p101

a What effect do you think these working conditions would have on the personalities of the child labourers?
b Imagine you are a seven-year-old factory worker in the early nineteenth century. Describe a typical day.

If children today are of little productive importance, they have taken on a new role as consumers. Between a fifth and a quarter of Britain's population is under sixteen, and manufacturers and retailers have not been slow to realise the enormous children's market. Children have in recent years become a large and powerful market in themselves; sweets, comics, toys and, as they grow older, records, magazines, 'young teenage' cosmetics and clothes are obvious examples of commodities that are targeted directly at children. Further, children may also influence adults to buy particular goods or brands; TV commercials for such products as breakfast cereals, fish fingers and 'junk food' are aimed at children, not because children will themselves buy them, but because they will put pressure on their parents to do so.

Activity 4

Carry out research in your local shopping centre to discover:
a how many and which types of shops are aimed specifically at or for children
b how department stores and supermarkets are set out in order to appeal to children.

The growing popularity of special activity holidays for children in part reflects the view that children have different needs and interests from adults, while at the same time helping to reinforce that view.

Although in some ways, then, children are encouraged to see themselves as a special category of people, there may well, at the same time, be pressures encouraging children to see themselves as young adults. At a biological level, the age of puberty has fallen dramatically since the middle of the nineteenth century, on average by four months every decade.

But, as Neil Postman argues in 'The Disappearance of Childhood' (1983), social factors are mainly responsible for what he sees as the crumbling barriers between childhood and adulthood. It is, Postman argues, television which is largely responsible for the disappearance of childhood; the world of the adult is revealed to the child every night, and the special world of childhood is eroded. Aries uses the example of fashion to illustrate the invention of childhood; Postman does likewise to illustrate its disappearance. Girls of eight and nine wear make-up, eleven-year olds copy adult fashions, and males and females of both five and sixty-five wear jeans.

The reality, as always, is more complex; childhood is in some ways different from adulthood, in other ways similar. The precise balance of differences and similarities varies from society to society, from century to century and between families in the same society. It is adults, however, and not children, who decide where that balance shall lie.

Extract 4 The San of the Kalahari

The San (or Bushmen) of the Kalahari Desert in Southern Africa bring their children up so that they can become useful members of the hunting and gathering society.

Bringing up the children is a group activity, and particular delight is taken in helping the infant to learn to walk. As a result, San children do not go through a period of crawling, and are able to walk properly by the age of six or eight months. Mother's milk forms the basis of the child's food until he or she is nearly four. Children between three and six stay behind during the day while their parents go out hunting and gathering. They play a great deal: the boys invent imaginary hunting exploits, the girls play at fruit-gathering. But an elderly member of the band, who has not joined the hunters or gatherers, will have stayed behind to keep an eye on the children and to talk to them. After the children have tired of playing, they will gather round the elderly person to hear tales of the past and stories; but, most importantly, they are told about hunting, weapons, fire, and so on. At about the age of five or six, a girl will join the women on gathering expeditions, and spend about two years learning about the plant-life of the area and the role of women in the society: boys spend longer playing, but gradually are taught to make bows and arrows and spend their time practising and developing their marksmanship. There is a puberty ceremony for boys, which is carried out between the ages of twelve and fifteen, which involves tattooing, and, as an indication of prowess and bravery, the tracking of an animal alone in the night.

Source: *The San of the Kalahari*, David Stephen, Minority Rights Group, Report No. 56, 1982, p8

a What part do the elderly San play in the upbringing of children?

b What gender differences appear to exist among San children?

c What are the key similarities and differences between the life of a British and a San child?

Extract 5 *Children of a Slave Generation*

In both the affluent societies of the West and societies such as the San, childhood is for most children a time to be protected and looked after by older people. In many other countries, however, child labour is still common.

In most countries, legislation exists against the use of child labour and against the sexual exploitation of children. However, the gap between the law and what actually happens is often tragically wide.

All too often these children are exploited through low wages and atrocious conditions which adults, who can protest, would not tolerate. This type of exploitation is particularly prevalent in small backstreet sweatshops which are much harder to regulate than larger industrial enterprises.

Both Unicef and the Anti-Slavery Society have documented instances of inhumane conditions in such sweatshops in India, South East Asia, Hong Kong, South Korea, Africa, Turkey, Italy, Spain, Latin America and the Caribbean. Case studies tell of long working hours, of cramped conditions, of children having to sleep on the floor of their workplace, of beatings, of employers feeding their juvenile workforce at subsistence level, of injuries and death from fire, molten metals or unguarded machinery, of health ruined by exposure to toxic chemicals or by the inhalation of coal dust, graphite dust, glue fumes or particles from textiles and carpets.

The largest sector of child employment in the world is agriculture. Possibly the myths generated by Western urban society about the simple, good, healthy, rural life have made us slow to recognise the harsh reality of children being put to work in fields as soon as they can walk, and of being made to perform heavy physical tasks for long hours.

Unfortunately, legislation prohibiting child labour can result in children being put to informal, uncontrolled, less visible work which is even more exploitative, such as work sub-contracted into the home.

Children may work 10 or 11 hours a day in their ill-lit hovels at such tasks as sewing sequins onto dresses, folding cardboard boxes or pasting labels onto a variety of products. Even children of three or four can be put to work for eight hours a day or more sorting beads or unravelling piles of human hair.

The informal and marginal part of the Third World urban economy – the flower sellers, shoe-shine boys, car minders, windscreen cleaners, street vendors, garbage pickers – is also difficult to regulate, as are those most marginal of all, whose activities are frowned upon or illegal – beggars, petty thieves, prostitutes.

Many of these are street children. Some live permanently on the streets, having been abandoned or having severed all ties with their homes, and are alone in their struggle for survival. These children are open to exploitation by adult criminals who enlist their services, by pimps and drug-pushers, by gangs of older boys and corrupt police who operate 'protection' rackets.

Source: *The Guardian*, Robin Lloyd-Jones, 19 December 1986

a In which form of employment are most children found?

b Who are the street children of the Third World?

c Why are so many children employed in the conditions described in the above extract?

Youth

In pre-industrial societies there is often no period of youth between childhood and adulthood; the transfer from childhood to adulthood will probably be marked by puberty rites and ceremonies which tell everyone in society that the child has become an adult and should be treated accordingly. In industrial societies, however, there is an important period between childhood and adulthood which has attracted a great deal of interest from sociologists, as well as public concern.

In particular, sociologists are interested in the extent to which young people possess their own values and norms which are different to those of older people. It is sometimes argued that the difficulties of being young today are so great that young people develop their own culture or subculture. These two terms, 'culture' and 'subculture', are often used interchangeably in discussions of youth, and different writers use the terms in different ways, but it is probably best to see culture as referring to the way of life of a particular society, and subculture as referring to the different values, beliefs and norms of a particular group within that society.

This is not to say, of course, that all, or even most, people in Britain share the same culture in every respect, but that there may be certain dominant values, beliefs and norms which are widely accepted.

The question sociologists ask therefore is; do young people have their own subculture, or are they really very similar to older people? In answering this question, sociologists have concentrated on young people, but there is a wide variety of adult values, beliefs and norms in a country like Britain which clearly makes any comparison with 'adult culture' very difficult.

Young people do face peculiar problems and difficulties in society, but, like adults, they are divided by class, sex and ethnicity and therefore have widely different life-styles. Generally, however, young people lack status and are at the receiving end of other peoples' decisions; at school they are pupils, at college students, at work apprentices, juniors or trainees, and in the family they are probably still children.

KEY TERM

youth subculture a distinctive set of values, beliefs and norms sometimes claimed to exist among young people.

'I can't wait to be grown-up and do exactly as I please.'

For many young people the school-leaving age is when the realities of the social and economic world outside the school gate come face-to-face with the dreams and aspirations which have been fostered by parents, teachers and the media. Young people with few or no qualifications quickly discover that even if they do find employment, their job is likely to be badly paid, boring and have no prospects. Unemployment is likely to be an even more demoralising experience.

There is often an uncertainty about how young people should behave which can result in arguments about clothing, choice of friends and staying out late, for example. It is perhaps not so much that young people do not know how they should behave, more that adults do not know how they think young people should behave.

Extract 6 *The Ambiguous Position of Youth*

Peter and Brigitte Berger in this extract clearly outline why youth can be such a confusing and difficult time. They are writing of the United States, but most of what they say applies equally to all advanced industrial societies.

Society's Ambiguous Demands: 'Act your Age'?

It is not easy to be young: the comforts of childhood are in the process of disappearing, and the rewards of adulthood are slow in making themselves available. It is unclear when youth begins and when it ends. And it is far from clear what it means while it is apparently going on. No clear dividing lines separate the different stages of biography. Modern society has few, if any, of those 'rites of passage' which, in many other human societies, mark the thresholds between clearly defined stages in the individual's progress through life. Young people in modern society are nevertheless frequently exhorted to 'act their age', while, at the same time, society is very ambiguous as to what this actually means. The young individual in this society is subjected to a highly bureaucratic educational establishment and to fierce competitive pressures to succeed within it. And he is supposed to take all of this with great seriousness. At the same time, his capacity to participate in important decisions affecting his life is seriously doubted by adults. Young men are expected to serve in the military but (at least until very recently) they were not permitted to vote. Young women are subjected to completely contradictory expectations, one set of expectations in terms of a traditional value system that emphasizes the virtues of being 'feminine', the other set vigorously affirming the equality of the sexes and both the right and the necessity for a woman to have an independent career. Young men and young women alike are presented with a bewildering choice not only of careers and occupations but of lifestyles and belief systems. What is more, the adult world is not only fairly unhelpful in the face of the situation of youth but seems to react to it with hysterical inconsistency: one day youth is hailed as some sort of messianic hope for the society, the next day it is denounced as a sinister, subversive conspiracy.

Source: *Sociology: A Biographical Approach*, Peter and Brigitte Berger, Penguin, 1976, pp236–237

a The above extract is titled 'Society's Ambiguous Demands'. What exactly do the authors mean by this?
b Why do the authors suggest the period of youth is particularly difficult for girls?
c Rewrite the last sentence of the extract, using your own words.

Activity 5

a Carry out an observational study of the different ways in which youth and older people dress.

b List the main leisure facilities in your area and indicate whether they attract a particular age group. If so, state which.

c Construct a brief questionnaire in order to find out if young people have similar or different political and religious views from their parents.

d Examine the extent to which your findings suggest there are important differences between the generations.

'It **is** the school uniform.'

Your answers to *Activity 5* have probably shown that most young people respond to their ambiguous and uncertain position by being remarkably like their parents' generation. Disagreements with parents over clothes, hair and staying out late may seem important at the time, but they hardly suggest a fundamental clash of values. On moral, political and religious issues, there appear to be few significant differences between the generations. However, some young people do respond to their position in society by banding together and developing their own values and norms, and it is these groups, such as the teddy boys, mods, rockers, skinheads and punks, which attract attention from the media. The distinctiveness of these groups should not be exaggerated; many young people drift in and out of membership, some young people might be only partial followers of a particular group, and few remain members for long.

If all young people share some experiences, their positions in society, their life-styles and, perhaps above all, their futures, depend on their social class. Each youth group or sub-culture can only be understood by locating it in the context of the social class of its members and their common experiences. For example, the chauvinism and emphasis on masculinity often found in traditional working-class culture is reflected and exaggerated in working-class groups like the skinheads.

Extract 7 *Working-class Youth Cultures*

John Clarke and Tony Jefferson here explain how the values and norms of skinheads originate and develop. These values and norms do not just arise by chance, but reflect the position of working-class young males in society. The authors suggest how certain elements in traditional working class life – the emphasis on community, the pub and sexism – are exaggerated and distorted by the skinheads.

The Skinheads

The connection between the skinheads and football is not, as some would suggest, fortuitous – that they could have gone anywhere but just happened to pick on football grounds. Rather, this traditional working class activity is crucial because it allows some of the skinheads' crucial concerns to be symbolically articulated. Most importantly, the support of a particular team provided a focus for the assertion of territorial loyalties, involving both a unified collective identity ('We are the Holte Enders', etc.), and an assertion of territorial rights – not those of property ownership, but of community identification.

The other major skinhead location also has strong cultural roots in the working class – the pub, which also acted as a territorial base and landmark. Here, supported not by pot or pills, but by a rather more traditional drug, beer, was the place where exploits could be discussed, plans laid, and time killed.

However, the violence associated with the skinheads was much more closely articulated around football. Fighting both expressed involvement in the game, and was a source of excitement both directly, in the physical activity of the fight, and indirectly, in its providing a topic of conversation to dispel the continual threat of boredom in the periods between fights and other group exploits.

The violence, both actual and discussed, acted as an expression of toughness, of a specific working class self-conception of masculinity, and of particular symbolic importance here is the activity of 'queer bashing'. The skinhead definition of 'queer' extended to all those males who looked 'odd', that is to all those who were not overtly masculine looking, as this statement indicates:

Usually it'd be just a bunch of us who'd find someone they thought looked odd – like this one night we were up by Warley Woods and we saw this bloke who looked odd – he'd got long hair and frills on his trousers.

This emphasis on overt masculinity was visible in the most obvious areas of skinhead symbolism, most importantly, the clothes and the 'prison crop' hair style from which their name derived. The clothes, heavy denims, plain or striped button-down shirts, braces and heavy boots, created an image which was clean-cut, smart and functional – a youthful version of working clothes. The haircuts completed the severe and puritanical self-image, a formalized and very 'hard' masculinity. (It is also important to note that both the mods and the hippies had gone some way to undermining traditional stereotypes of masculine and feminine appearance and behaviour.)

Thus we would argue that by reading the skinheads' style in terms of its creators' structural and cultural context, it offers a reassertion of some elements of traditional working class culture. Certainly, it is displaced into a symbolic leisure style, but it arises in a period when the norms of that culture and its social base had been threatened by erosion and disappearance, and when social conflicts were becoming increasingly visible and demanding forms of articulation.

Source: 'Working Class Youth Cultures', John Clarke and Tony Jefferson, in *Working Class Youth Culture*, G. Mungham & G. Pearson (eds), Routledge & Kegan Paul, 1976, pp154–156

a Rewrite the last paragraph in your own words.
b If one accepts Clarke and Jefferson's arguments, how could football hooliganism be best reduced?
c Using the approach adopted by Clarke and Jefferson, attempt to locate the style of other youth subcultures (including middle-class ones) in the social position of their members.

Working class young people who are black face additional difficulties caused by racial discrimination, and are thus likely to develop their own subcultural styles. The beliefs, dress and life-style of Rastafarians, for example, can only be understood by placing them in the context of the particular problems faced by young British blacks.

Youth sub-cultures, then, in so far as they do exist, are for most young people temporary; they rarely dominate a young person's whole life, and equally rarely reject the dominant values of adult society. Members of youth subcultures might inconvenience and annoy older members of society, but ultimately they pose no real threat to the established order.

Old Age

It is common for sociologists and politicians, and many of the public, to assume that old age begins with retirement. But many retired people themselves, especially those in their sixties, do not consider themselves old, and they face none of the problems we all too readily assume old people suffer from. Old age, perhaps even more than childhood and youth, is a relative concept: in other words, what old age actually means varies widely both over time and between societies and, crucially, between individual people.

About a fifth of Britain's population is over retirement age, but more significant is that the number and proportion of *very* old people is increasing more rapidly than the retired as a whole. It is frequently claimed that this will increase the 'burden of dependency' – a rather derogatory term used to refer to the way the declining proportion of the population which works has to support, through taxation, the rising proportion of those who do not work. It is, of course, the very elderly who are most likely to need medical and social services.

Sociologists usually concentrate on the 'problems' of old age, but, when asked, most old people do not appear to be as unhappy and dissatisfied as younger people often think they are.

Many of the problems we associate with old age, such as poor housing and the risk of hypothermia, are probably more to do with poverty than old age. In the same way that the position and life-style of children and young people can only be understood in the context of their social class, the positions and life-styles of old people also depend above all on their class and occupation when they were younger. It is, therefore, dangerous to talk of 'old people' as if they were a group with everything in common.

There are, of course, some problems that old people, especially the very old, of every class are more likely to face than younger people. Ill-health, disability and lack of mobility are not problems peculiar to old people, but they are more common among them for simple biological reasons we can do little about. Isolation and loneliness too are probably more common among old people, but the causes are social rather than biological. The declining birth rate this century (which means today's old people have fewer children and many have none), increased rates of geographical mobility and, paradoxically, greater life expectancy (which means that many old people will long survive their spouses, siblings and friends) are all contributory factors in the isolation of some old people. There is no evidence that the old are treated in a worse manner than in previous centuries, and most elderly parents maintain very close and regular contact with their children. But there are more old people either without children at all or without children living nearby. It is perhaps these two groups who are most likely to be isolated in very old age.

Activity 6

Arrange a visit to a local branch of a voluntary organisation concerned with the welfare of the old. Find out:
a what the main difficulties are for the old in your area;
b what statutory and voluntary services are provided for them.

At the same time as people are living longer, the age of retirement has in practice been reduced for many people. Although in Britian women do not receive an old age pension until sixty and men not until sixty-five, it has become more and more common for people to take early retirement. Governments have encouraged this trend as a mechanism for reducing unemployment and providing jobs for younger people.

In pre-industrial societies there is unlikely to be a sudden and abrupt termination to productive economic activity. Old people, both men and women, may well gradually reduce their productive work as they become less strong and healthy, but it is likely to be such a slow reduction that it causes no problems of adjustment or feelings of worthlessness, and few old people are unlikely to be able to contribute anything to the economic well-being of an agricultural society.

In societies where most people work away from home for an employer, retirement is sudden and total. Most employees still receive little preparation in how to cope with leaving work, even though in many ways it is as big a step as beginning work.

The problems and difficulties of retirement should not be exaggerated; most people adjust relatively easily, especially if they enjoy the financial resources and good health necessary to develop their interests. But some people do find it difficult; their relationships might have been work-centred, or they might find it difficult to establish a new and different relationship with their spouse. Perhaps most importantly, work provides for some people routine, structure, meaning and purpose in life. Suddenly take away that work and life can appear unsatisfying and unfulfilling.

Activity 7

a Interview a small number of retired people to find out
    1 if they 'prepared' for retirement
    2 the advantages and disadvantages of being retired.
   Try to include different types of workers, men and women, and both married and unmarried people in your interviews.
b On the basis of the information you obtain from your interviews, write a sociological account of retirement.
c How could workers be better prepared for retirement?

Extract 8 *Approaches to Old Age*

As we have seen, different societies have different attitudes towards old age. Equally, different people in a particular society have varying attitudes towards old age, and the extract below summarises the different approaches adopted by sociologists. Note especially how the experts on old age disagree and how the adoption of one particular theory leads to a particular view of how the old should be treated by the young.

With the large increase in the elderly population since the war, sociologists have become increasingly interested in old age as an area for study. This is particularly so in the United States, where the elderly are a powerful lobby. Several main theories have been put forward to account for the social processes of getting old:

Disengagement Theory: This has been one of the most widely held theories of ageing . . . It maintains that people entering old age must be phased out of important roles for society to function. By phasing out the old in this way, their deaths are not disruptive to the functioning of society. Disengagement theorists say that happiness in old age consists of individuals' recognising that they are no longer young, and that there are more competent people to take their places.

Activity Theory is the opposite of disengagement theory. It claims that to be happy in old age, people need to keep active. Happiness is achieved by denying the onset of old age and by maintaining a middle aged way of life, values and beliefs for as long as possible. Activity theorists take the view that if existing roles or relationships are lost, it is important to replace them, or there will be a drop in the level of life satisfaction. One of the main criticisms of this theory is that people need a high morale to keep up an active lifestyle, and that it takes little account of people who are ill or demoralised.

Subculture Theory: The American gerontologist, Arnold Rose, has suggested that old people form a subculture which shapes and forms their behaviour.

Supporters of this theory believe that old people are a legitimate sub-culture because (a) they form a very large group in society, (b) they are separated from the rest of society by retirement, emphasis on youth and so on, and (c) because old people have an 'age consciousness' – they recognise that they are 'different' from the rest of society.

Personality Theory maintains that activity and disengagement theories are wrong in focusing on the amount of *activity* people get involved in. It is personality types that are important in determining life satisfaction. The American gerontologist, R. J. Havighurst, defines two main types of old people – the 'reorganisers', who are happy keeping their middle aged lifestyle, and the 'disengaged,' who are equally happy with the rocking chair approach to life.

Labelling Theory: This is based partly on the ideas of Erving Goffman, and suggests that, through the process of labelling, people are forced into acting out specific roles. Once somebody has been labelled 'senile', for instance, this label has a major impact on the way they will be perceived and treated by others. It is difficult then for that person to change the label, because all subsequent behaviour will be interpreted in the light of the new identity. Someone who has been labelled old, senile, dependent or sick will experience a marked reduction in the number, types and options of roles available.

Source: 'Society Today', *New Society*, 19 November 1981, pp.ii

GLOSSARY

gerontology the study of old people.

a Which theory or approach do you think best explains the position of old people in Britain today?
b Outline the arguments for and against the view that old people today form a sub-culture.
c 'Once somebody has been labelled senile . . . this label has a major impact on the way they will be perceived and treated by others.' Explain this sentence in your own words, and give examples to illustrate the process of labelling.

Questions and Suggested Projects

Review Questions

1 Explain, in your own words, and in not more than two sentences each, the meaning of the following:
   a 'Age has a social as well as a biological dimension.'
   b 'Childhood, youth and old age are all important labels we attach to certain categories of people.'
   c 'Youth culture'.
   d A 'youth culture can only be understood by locating it in the context of the social class of its members'.
2 What are the arguments for and against the following:
   a Childhood is a recent invention.
   b Young people today have their own culture.
   c Old age is a time of problems and difficulties?

Theme-linking Questions

1 What evidence is there to suggest that children possess a culture of their own? You could examine, for example:
   a the language of children
   b stories, games and jokes
   c TV programmes.
2 Which age group usually possesses the most power in industrial societies? Why?
3 Give two examples each of:
   a actions which would be considered deviant in a sixteen-year-old but conformist in a 75-year-old
   b actions which would be considered deviant in a forty-year-old but conformist in a sixteen-year-old
   c actions which would be considered conformist in a forty-year-old but deviant in a 75-year-old.
   What do these examples tell you about the nature of age in Britain today?
4 It is frequently argued that work plays a major part in giving people an identity and a purpose in life. What implications does this have for retirement?
5 Describe the main ways in which social class influences the way of life of a:
   a five-year-old girl
   b fifteen-year-old boy
   c 45-year-old woman
   d 75-year-old-man.

Stimulus-response Question

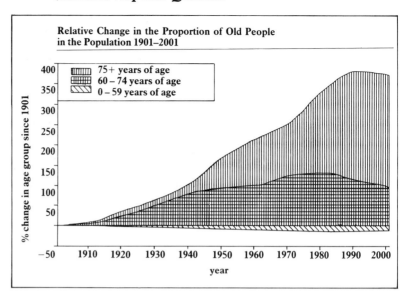

Relative Change in the Proportion of Old People in the Population 1901–2001

(legend)
75+ years of age
60 – 74 years of age
0 – 59 years of age

y-axis: % change in age group since 1901
x-axis: year

Source: 'Old People', Stuart Lowe and Ross Day in *Social Policy Today*, Longman, 1986, p1

a By how much will the 75+ age group increase between 1901 and 2001? (1)

b What will happen to the proportion of 60–74-year-olds in the population between now and 2001? (1)

c What is meant by the term 'burden of dependency'? (2)

d Explain why the number and proportion of the 75+ age group has increased since 1901. (7)

e Explain the consequences of this increase in the number and proportion of the over-75s on levels of taxation, and health, housing and social security services and benefits. (9)

Essays

1 Compare childhood in Britain today with either childhood in Britain in the nineteenth century or childhood in another society.

2 a What are the main problems facing young people in Britain today?

 b Outline the main differences and similarities between the social and economic position of young people today and that of their parents' generation.

3 What are the main consequences of the fact that Britain has an ageing population? Your answer could include:

the burden of dependency
the high rate of increase of the very old
ill-health and disability
housing
isolation
effects on the family.

Suggested Projects

1 A study of how people have different perceptions of age in men and women.
2 A comparison of how old people are treated in a private nursing home and a geriatric ward.
3 A survey comparing the attitudes of people of two different age groups on a particular topic (e.g. politics, education).
4 A participant observation study of the 'secret world' of childhood.
5 A study of disabled young people, concentrating on discovering whether their youth or their disability is more important in determining friendships and activities.

8 Inequality: Affluence and Poverty

Introduction

Chapters 4–7 have examined the key elements of social differentiation in Britain; class, gender, ethnicity and age. This chapter looks at the extent of inequality in Britain today, concentrating on income and wealth differences and those groups of people most likely to be in poverty.

Most writers on inequality base their work on family units, as does the social security system. It is thus difficult to examine poverty as an issue which affects individuals in a family in different ways. It is, however, quite possible that, in a family with an average income, some members may well be affluent and others poor. A working teenager may be able to afford a foreign holiday, for example, while her parents cannot.

This chapter will therefore examine economic and social inequality between social classes. The life chances of the different ethnic groups will depend above all on the social classes their members belong to, although working-class members of disadvantaged ethnic groups may well suffer a double disadvantage.

Economic Inequality

Activity 1

a Carry out a brief survey in your sociology group or among friends and relatives to ask how much they think is earned (weekly, gross, and including overtime) by:
   1 doctors (GPs)   2 ambulance drivers
   3 secondary school teachers   4 farm workers
   5 the Prime Minister.
b Construct a table showing the mean figure and the range of incomes for each occupation.
c What does your table tell you about people's knowledge about what other people earn?
   (You should be able to find out what the above people actually earn from your library.)

Even though few of us are very knowledgeable about what other groups of workers earn, it is not usually very difficult to find out; finding out how wealthy particular individuals or groups are is, however, very difficult. Not everyone would willingly disclose how much their various possessions and investments are worth, and indeed the calculation is not easy to make anyway. With the rise in house prices and the spread of home ownership in recent years, an increasing number of people do now possess at least one very valuable asset. Further, many millions of people in the future will inherit, when their parents die, a house which can be sold for a considerable sum.

KEY TERMS

income earnings from work, investments, property etc.
wealth assets or property, e.g. land, stocks and shares, houses, consumer durables.

This distinction between wealth and income is not, however, totally clear-cut, for wealth does, if invested, provide an income, and any income not spent contributes to a person's wealth.

Extract 1 *The Different Forms of Wealth*

The wealth owned by the rich takes a different form from that of the rest of the population, as the diagram below, with figures for 1986, shows.

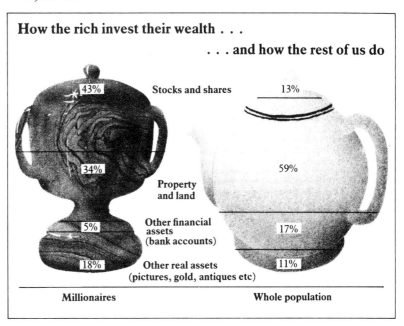

How the rich invest their wealth . . .

. . . and how the rest of us do

43%	Stocks and shares	13%
34%	Property and land	59%
5%	Other financial assets (bank accounts)	17%
18%	Other real assets (pictures, gold, antiques etc)	11%
Millionaires		**Whole population**

Source: Tony Garrett, 'The Rich in Britain', *New Society*, with LWT, 22 August 1986, piv

a What proportion of the wealth of millionaires is in the form of property and land?
b What form of wealth shows the greatest difference between millionaires and the rest of us?
c Explain the implications and consequences of the statistics in the above diagram.

Extract 2 *The Distribution of Wealth*

Two issues of major importance are:
a how is wealth in Britain today distributed
b is that distribution changing?
(Table 1 refers to 1986)

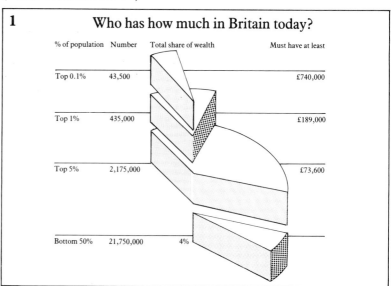

1   Who has how much in Britain today?

% of population	Number	Total share of wealth	Must have at least
Top 0.1%	43,500		£740,000
Top 1%	435,000		£189,000
Top 5%	2,175,000		£73,600
Bottom 50%	21,750,000	4%	

Source: Tony Garrett, from estimates by Professor Sharocks, Essex University, for 1986

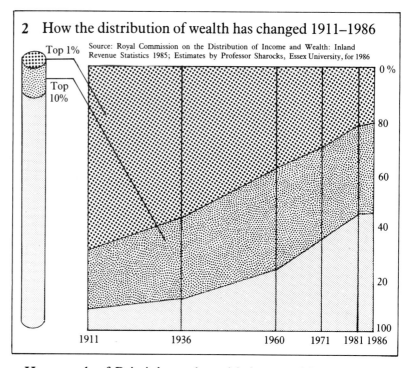

2   How the distribution of wealth has changed 1911–1986

Source: Royal Commission on the Distribution of Income and Wealth: Inland Revenue Statistics 1985; Estimates by Professor Sharocks, Essex University, for 1986

Top 1%
Top 10%

1911   1936   1960   1971   1981 1986

Source: Tony Garrett, 'The Rich in Britain', *New Society*, with LWT, 22 August 1986, ppv, vii

a How much of Britain's total wealth is owned by the bottom 50% of the population?

b How much wealth do you need to be among Britain's richest 1%?

c What share of Britain's wealth is owned by the more affluent half of Britain's population?

d What share of Britain's wealth did the most affluent 10% of the population own in:
    1 1911 **2** 1986?

e What is the general trend indicated by the above figures?

Income from employment is not as unequal as the distribution of wealth, but there are still massive differences between the incomes of the highest and lowest paid. The well paid, in addition, are much more likely to receive fringe benefits such as company cars and private medical insurance.

Activity 2

a Collect as much information as you can on the salaries and wages of different jobs currently being advertised. For information, look at your local paper, the 'quality' daily and Sunday papers, and the cards in your local Jobcentre.

b Rank the occupations in order of income. (If fringe benefits are offered cost them out and include in the income.)

c What explanations can you offer for the different wages and salaries you have discovered?

Extract 3 Weekly Earnings in Some Occupations, 1986

How much do they earn? (weekly averages)

Women in jobs

Hairdressers	£78.1
Barmaids	£89.3
Checkout operators	£90.3
Cleaners	£98.2
Repetitive assemblers	£113.4
Record clerks	£118.1
Telephonists	£123.3
Secretaries	£141.2
Nurses	£143.7
Engineers etc	£165.3
Office managers	£196.3
Primary school teachers	£198.1
Secondary school teachers	£201.7
Policewomen	£218.6
Academics	£229.8

Men in jobs

Farm workers	£121.0
Barmen	£123.5
Roadsweepers	£135.9
Dustmen	£147.0
Nurses	£164.1
Salesmen	£186.3
Primary school teachers	£227.1
Secondary school teachers	£227.3
Miners (pit face)	£233.0
Civil engineers etc	£264.3
Journalists	£304.6
University academics	£321.0
Police inspectors, fire officers	£352.4
Finance/tax specialists	£403.2
Doctors	£425.3

Source: New Earnings Survey, 1986

Source: Tony Garrett, 'Database', *New Society*, 23 January 1987

a Which is the lowest paid job in the above charts?

b How much more than a farm worker did a doctor earn in 1986?

c Explain why some groups of workers earn more than others.

Two Examples of Social Inequality: Health and Housing

Two of the clearest and most obvious examples of social inequality are provided by health and housing.

Although health standards and life expectancy have increased for all social classes and in all regions, there are still significant differences between different social groups.

Extract 4 The Heartbeat Wales Survey

The Heartbeat Wales Survey, published in 1987, shows how the life-styles of the different social classes affect health.

New evidence of a widening health gap between those in work and the unemployed is revealed in a survey . . . covering 22,000 people, the largest of its kind in Britain.

A team from Heartbeat Wales, a Government-backed health education pilot project to fight heart disease, has spent two years analysing a survey of Welsh families which asked people aged between 12 and 64 detailed questions on their attitudes to health, their medical history and use of health services.

The unskilled and unemployed were much more likely to follow unhealthy lifestyles with increased risk of strokes and heart attacks. But people in long-term unemployed households were found to have the greatest incidence of high blood pressure, smoking, obesity and alcohol problems. While heart disease death rates in men have improved slightly over the last decade, non-manual groups and professional workers have done markedly better in improving health.

According to the survey, the unemployed tend to smoke and drink more, but take less exercise. More than 60 per cent of the long term unemployed smoke, compared with 40 per cent of all Welsh men. Two to three times as many people in manual groups suffered from angina and respiratory problems.

Low income families ate more unhealthy foods like processed meat and fried meals, buying much fewer fresh vegetables and fibre-rich foods.

Those out of work for more than a year may develop unhealthy lifestyles because of being unemployed. A significant widening of income levels between manual and non-manual workers in the last 10 years could also be a factor, the report adds.

Professor John Catford, director of Heartbeat Wales, said: 'Our evidence suggests the health gaps are getting worse. There is no reason why these results for Wales cannot be generalised to the rest of the UK.'

Source: *The Independent*, 20 February 1987

a Which types of people are most likely to be obese?

b Explain why low income families eat more unhealthy foods.

c What are the main features of a 'healthy life style'?

d It is often argued that the middle class benefit more from health-care services than the working class. Explain what advantages middle-class people might have in using health services.

Extract 5 Infant Mortality

Although infant mortality rates have declined for all social classes, the chances of a baby surviving still depend partly on its social class.

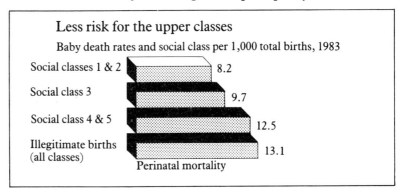

Less risk for the upper classes

Baby death rates and social class per 1,000 total births, 1983

Social classes 1 & 2 — 8.2
Social class 3 — 9.7
Social class 4 & 5 — 12.5
Illegitimate births (all classes) — 13.1

Perinatal mortality

Source: Tony Garrett, 'Database', *New Society*, 1 August 1986

GLOSSARY

perinatal mortality still births and deaths in the first week of life.

a How much more likely is a baby born into classes 1 and 2 to live past its first week than a baby born into classes 4 and 5?
b Explain why babies born into classes 4 and 5, and those born illegitimate, are less likely to survive.
(See Chapter 10 for changes in infant and adult mortality rates.)

Extract 6 Housing Standards by Tenure

Health depends on a complex variety of factors such as income, values and norms, the medical services available, diet, smoking, exercise and luck. Housing depends above all on a person's financial resources.

Housing Standards: by tenure, 1971 and 1984

Great Britain   Percentages and numbers

	Percentage of households[1]						Sample size (= 100%) (numbers)	
	Lacking sole use of				With central heating			
	Fixed bath/shower		WC inside building					
	1971	1984	1971	1984	1971	1984	1971	1984
Owned outright	12	3	13	3	39	66	2,654	2,312
Owned with mortgate or loan	4	–	5	–	57	82	3,206	3,357
All owner-occupiers	7	1	9	1	49	75	5,860	5,669
Rented from local authority/new town	3	1	5	1	24	58	3,691	2,805
Rented privately unfurnished[2]	33	9	37	7	15	47	2,043	947
Rented privately furnished	58	29	57	29	17	36	320	217
All tenures	12	3	13	2	34	66	11,914	9,638

[1]Excludes those living in caravans or houseboats.   [2]Includes those renting from a housing association, and those renting with a job or business.

Source: General Household Survey, 1971 and 1984

Source: *Social Trends 1986*, HMSO, 1986, Table 8.6

a What percentage of **1** owner-occupiers, **2** those renting privately furnished accommodation did not have an indoor toilet in 1984?

b Which type of housing generally seems to have the best facilities?

c What are the main overall trends revealed in the table in *Extract 6*?

d What are the financial advantages and disadvantages of buying one's own house?

Activity 3

a Find out how much the following cost:
  1 a three-bedroomed semi in the North or Midlands
  2 a country estate in the South-east
  3 a flat in the centre of London
  4 a terraced house in an area of high unemployment.

You can obtain information from newspapers, estate agents or relatives and friends in other parts of the country.

b What social and economic problems are caused by the high price of houses in London and the South-east?

Poverty and the Poor

Activity 4

a Complete the following sentence, 'Poverty is not having . . .'

b Compare your answer with your fellow students; produce a list of items that are produced by everyone and a list of items mentioned only by some people.

c What conclusions can you draw from your two lists?

Your answers to Activity 4 have probably shown you that, as so often in sociology, defining the terms we use is highly complex. The word 'poverty' means different things to different people, but it is usual in sociology to distinguish two major types: absolute poverty and relative poverty.

KEY TERMS

absolute poverty having insufficient resources to obtain the basic necessities of life, e.g. food, clothing, shelter, heating.

relative poverty having insufficient resources to maintain a standard and style of living considered appropriate in the community.

Sociologists writing about poverty in modern Britain have generally based their work on a relative definition of poverty. Few people live in absolute poverty in the sense that death caused by an absence of the basic necessities of life is uncommon, though not unknown. A relative definition means that poverty can only be understood in the context of time and place, and will therefore change over time and vary from place to place. Poverty in Britain in the late twentieth century might well therefore have been seen as affluence in the nineteenth, as it would be in much of Africa and Asia today.

Extract 7 A Definition of Poverty

Peter Townsend, in his major study of poverty in Britain, adopts a relative view of poverty.

> Individuals, families and groups in the population can be said to be in poverty when they lack the resources to obtain the types of diet, participate in the activities and have the living conditions and amenities which are customary, or are at least widely encouraged or approved, in the societies to which / they belong. Their resources are so seriously below those commanded by the average individual or family that they are, in effect, excluded from ordinary living patterns, customs and activities.

Source: *Poverty in the United Kingdom*, Peter Townsend, Penguin, 1979, p31

a Explain the meaning of 'ordinary living patterns, customs and activities'.
b Using Townsend's definition of poverty, explain how a family in Britain today might be considered to be in poverty in the following contexts:
    1 leisure activities
    2 birthdays and Christmas
    3 clothing
    4 diet.
c What criticisms can be made of the type of definition adopted by Townsend?

Extract 8 *The Extent of Poverty in Britain*

In 1983 London Weekend Television commissioned an opinion poll to discover what people in Britain regarded as essential and what they themselves lacked.

24 items ranked by percentage of survey sample describing them as essential, and percentage of sample lacking items because they cannot afford them

	Described essential by %	Lacked by %		Described as essential by %	Lacked by %
Heating to warm living areas of the home if it is cold	97	6	New, not second-hand, clothes	64	8
			Hobby or leisure activity	64	9
Indoor toilet (not shared with another household)	96	1	2 hot meals a day (for adults)	64	4
Damp-free home	96	8	Meat or fish every other day	63	9
Bath (not shared with another household)	94	2	Presents for friends or family once a year	63	5
Public transport for one's needs	88	3	Holiday away from home for 1 week a year, not with relatives	63	23
Warm waterproof coat	87	7			
3 meals a day for children	82	4			
			Leisure equipment for children, eg sports equipment or bicycle*	57	13
Self-contained accommodation	79	3			
2 pairs of all-weather shoes	78	11	Television	51	†
Enough bedrooms for every child over 10 of different sex to have own bedroom	77	10			
Refrigerator	77	1			
Toys for children*	70	2			
Carpets in living rooms and bedrooms	70	2			
Celebrations on special occasions like Christmas	69	4			
Roast joint or equivalent once a week	67	7			
Washing machine	67	5			

*For families with children only   †Less than 0.5%

This is what the survey showed when applied to the population as a whole:

* approximately 3 million people in Britain today cannot afford to heat the living areas of their homes
* around 6 million go without some essential aspect of clothing – such as a warm waterproof coat – because of lack of money
* some 1½ million children go without toys or, for older children, leisure and sports equipment

because their parents don't have enough money
* nearly 3½ million people don't have consumer durables such as carpets, a washing machine or a fridge because of lack of money
* around 3 million people can't afford celebrations at Christmas or presents for the family once a year

The results show that a few of the people who cannot afford one or two of these necessities are not on low incomes. But those who cannot afford three or more necessities are heavily concentrated among those on the lowest incomes. **On this basis 7½ million people in Britain today – one in seven of the population – are poor.** Five and a half million – one in ten – cannot afford five or more necessities, a level of deprivation that affects their whole way of life. And among the poor, many live in intense poverty. Three-quarters of a million people cannot afford most of the necessities for living in Britain today.

Source: London Weekend Television Ltd and Market and Opinion Research International (MORI), 'Breadline Britain', 1983, pp 8, 10

a Which two 'essential' items are lacked by most people?
b Which two 'essential' items are fewest people without?
c What does the table in *Extract 8* tell you about the view of diet commonly held in Britain today?
d Imagine you are a typical African child reading the above extracts. How would you respond?

Extract 9 *Who are the Poor?*

Who then are those lacking three or more of these items? **Breadline Britain** found that the poor fell into five groups: *the unemployed; single parents; the sick and disabled; pensioners* and *low-paid workers*.

Among these, the two groups most at risk are *the unemployed* and *single parents*. Among single parents, those with younger children are especially at risk, and among the unemployed deprivation rises with the length of unemployment.

The next most vulnerable group is the *sick and disabled*. As a group, *pensioners* are less at risk, though this may be due to lower expectations. Many did not think of themselves as having a particularly low standard of living. Among them, single pensioners are poorer than couples and living standards decline with age as resources dwindle.

Least at risk are families with a head of household in full-time work, and in families with two wage-earners there is little chance of ending up poor. But there are large numbers of families in which the wife does not work and the husband's wages are too low to met the costs of bringing up children.

Risk tells us what proportion of a particular group are likely to be deprived. But also important is what proportion these groups constitute of all the poor. This depends on the overall size of the group in the population. For example, even though single parents have a high risk of being poor, they only constitute a small proportion of all those in poverty, because they account for a relatively small proportion of the population.

The survey found that three groups – the unemployed, the sick and disabled, and those households with a head in full-time work – accounted for most of those lacking necessities. In contrast, single parents and pensioners accounted for fewer of the poor. These groups also overlap to some degree. Some people, for example, will be disabled *and* unemployed, some single parents *and* unemployed.

Source: London Weekend Television Ltd and Market and Opinion Research International (MORI), 'Breadline Britain', 1983, pp 10–11

a Which two types of people are most likely to be in poverty?
b Explain why single parents have a high risk of being poor, but only make up a small proportion of the total poor.
c Explain which types of old people are most likely to live in poverty.

Activity 5

a Identify how the different types of people most likely to be in poverty are portrayed on television and in the press. Collect as many newspaper cuttings as possible.
b What are the implications of your findings for the likely popularity of any government attempts to reduce the poverty of the different groups?

Approaches to Poverty

The causes of, and thus the responses to, poverty are a source of major disagreement to the general public and politicians alike. Indeed, it is perhaps one of the major issues which distinguishes people of different political views. Any single theory of poverty is unlikely to be able to explain the existence of many different types of poor people, but sociological approaches are likely to stress that poverty can only be understood in the context of the wider society.

Poverty as an individual issue

This approach argues that if people are poor then it is their own fault. Laziness or lack of motivation, for example, are the causes of poverty. The weaknesses of this approach can perhaps best be seen if you look again at the groups of people most likely to be in poverty; to argue that it is the fault of the old and the disabled that they are poor hardly seems satisfactory.

Poverty as a cultural issue

This approach argues that the poor have a culture of their own, the *culture of poverty*. This idea is usually associated with Oscar Lewis, an American who carried out research among the poor of Mexico and Puerto Rico. According to Lewis, the culture of poverty is characterised by acceptance, apathy, fatalism and despair, and the poor do not organise with each other to try to improve their conditions. Their involvement in the life of the community is therefore minimal; it is the family which is the critical institution for such people. The material, as well as the cultural, life of the poor, is also a major barrier to escape; poor housing and diets, unemployment and unskilled work, combine with the attitudes of the poor to produce a cycle of deprivation whereby poverty is passed on from one generation to the next. Children, in other words, are socialised into a life of poverty. A major problem with Lewis's work is that it is based on detailed

biographical studies of particular families; there is no way of judging how representative the families chosen for the study are. Many poor people are not apathetic and fatalistic, and do participate fully in the life of the community.

Poverty as a structural issue

This approach argues that poverty exists, not because the poor are inadequate or have a culture which traps them in their poverty, but because society as a whole is unequal.

Peter Townsend, for example, begins his conclusion by saying that poverty 'has to be understood not only as an inevitable feature of severe social inequality but also as a particular consequence of actions by the rich to preserve and enhance their wealth and so deny it to others' (Peter Townsend, op. cit., p893).

Poverty, according to this view, can only be understood as part of the whole system of social stratification. Low wages and the inadequacies of the social security system would, according to this view, be blamed for poverty.

Activity 6

a Draw three diagrams to illustrate the different approaches to poverty outlined above.
b Imagine you are Secretary of State for Health and Social Security; outline how you would attempt to deal with the issue of poverty if you believed poverty was caused by:
    1 individual inadequacies **2** the culture of the poor
    3 the structural inequality of the whole society.

The Welfare State

All of us contribute, through taxes, national insurance and rates, to the welfare services provided by central and local government; equally we all benefit from them. We might not use all the services and benefits provided, but there are few people, if any, who do not benefit from the health services, state education, housing benefits, tax relief on mortgage interest or the whole range of social security benefits.

Sociologists are interested in three key questions:
1 What are the aims of the various welfare services? This is not as straightforward a question as first appears, for different

people might well have very different aims. A social worker and her client might well disagree about the purposes of social work, just as not all teachers and parents will agree with the Secretary of State for Education's views on the purposes of schooling.

2 What are the main problems facing the welfare services?

3 Which types of people benefit most from the welfare services?

Activity 7

a Find out from your library how much central and local government are spending on the following in the current financial year;

  1 education 2 health 3 housing 4 social security.

b Briefly outline two major problems currently faced in the areas of education, health, housing and social security.

Extract 10 The State of Welfare

The present nature and problems faced by the welfare services can only be understood by placing them in their historical context.

The conventional wisdom lays down that the welfare state was born with the Beveridge report, Social Insurance and Allied Services, published during the second world war in November 1942. Yet, in fact, the roots of some kind of policy of state assistance to provide minimum standards of life for the casualties of our society go deep into British history, even to Elizabethan times.

But it was William Beveridge's report that gave the idea of a welfare state, and the broad social assumptions that surrounded it, a new ethical coherence, and the dramatic impulse of mass publicity.

Beveridge aimed to blend the old and the new. He sought to fuse the experience of the past – with its mosaic of cooperation between the state and voluntary bodies – with a radical new approach to social engineering. He aimed to slay what his report melodramatically called the 'five giants', defined as Want, Ignorance, Squalor, Idleness and Disease. To this end, he outlined

some major transformations of public policy: a comprehensive system of social insurance for the entire population; flat-rate contributions and benefits, the latter to be granted as of right; child allowances for the maintenance of dependent children by their parents; basic provision of free health and educational services; and a planned strategy for full employment. His scheme would be universal, all-embracing and compulsory. It would provide, in the popular phrase, security 'from the cradle to the grave'.

The welfare state has survived . . . but the problems are undeniable. Beveridge's 'five giants' have a distinctly dated air . . . The current crises are threefold – financial, organisational, and conceptual. Financially, the welfare state has had to contend with a sluggish economy, high unemployment, and a rapid fall in Britain's output and share of world trade since 1970. The monuments to Beveridge – the hospitals, schools, council houses

and social services of the 1940s – are in dilapidated condition, and plagued by cuts in investment.

Again, the very universality of the Beveridge model has given way to a more flexible view of the services required. A more specific, case-orientated approach to welfare, dealing with the precise needs of children, the old, broken families, widows, the disabled, the homeless and the subtly gradated unemployed, is now required, rather than the blanket uniformity of the 1940s. The widespread sale of council houses to working class occupiers suggests a further range of limitations. Finally, the Beveridge report was conceptually shaped by a vision of a society that is disappearing fast. The tensions imposed by the disintegration of the traditional family, by the new mobility for working women and teenagers, by the particular difficulties of ethnic minorities: these present the welfare state with a complex and dangerous inheritance.

Source: 'The State of Welfare', Kenneth O. Morgan, *New Society* for Channel Four, 7 February 1986

GLOSSARY

ethical moral
flat rate all paying the same.
case-orientated a policy aimed at particular groups or individuals in need.

a What five major social problems did Beveridge hope to conquer?
b Explain what is meant by 'universal, all-embracing and compulsory'.
c Why is there pressure for the welfare services to become more 'specific' and 'case-orientated'?
d Examine the main problems caused for the welfare state by the social changes in Britain in the last twenty years.

It is difficult to assess which income groups benefit most from the welfare services, but it is certainly the case that those services, such as free education and the National Health Service, which were introduced largely to reduce inequalities, have not generally succeeded. Middle-class people may have a greater knowledge of, and ability to gain access to, the welfare benefits and services. Further, certain benefits such as tax relief on mortgage interest and the free provision of post-sixteen education are likely to benefit the middle class, although, of course, other benefits will favour primarily low income groups.

GLOSSARY

authoritarianism obedience to a dictatorship.
inhibit prevent
residual left over
collectivist stressing the benefit to all.

Extract 11 Perspectives on Welfare

There are several different views on the role the welfare services should play; broadly, these different views reflect different political values.

In the first perspective, the predominant values are individualism, competition and freedom. State intervention is associated with undesirable tendencies to over-centralisation, authoritarianism and is believed to inhibit competition and restrict individual freedom. Welfare provision is ideally seen as having a residual role: that of providing a safety-net for a small number of people in need.

Within this approach, the government is seen as having a duty to relieve poverty, but this is a necessary evil and provision should be kept to a minimum, both in terms of the scope of assistance and the level of help provided. Most needs can be met on voluntary and private basis.

The second approach can be described as collectivist . . . Equality is believed to be a more important goal than individual freedom and a positive value is set on collective provision and central control. The welfare state, with comprehensive provision of national insurance, health services and education is seen as an important part of a modern industrial society. Where inequality is found to exist, collectivists believe the state has a responsibility to use social policy to bring about reforms. The role of the welfare state extends beyond the relief of individual suffering and the solving of problems to redistribution of access to services such as health and education through universal provision.

The final approach can be broadly defined as Marxist, although there are several strands within a Marxist perspective. From a radical and Marxist point of view, the economic system in Britain, capitalism, contains fundamental and inherent problems of inequality. In this context the role of the welfare state can be seen in a variety of ways. Welfare provision can be characterised as a concession won by working-class people from those in power, a kind of ransom for the continuation of the capitalist system. Alternatively, welfare services are seen as a ploy on the part of those who rule to avert real political and economic change which would take the form of revolution. The welfare state serves to alleviate suffering and reduce inequality to the extent that tensions are removed without any shift in power or redistribution of wealth. With a slightly different emphasis, there is a Marxist critique of the welfare state which sees welfare as helping and maintaining the capitalist system by providing healthy and educated workers at a relatively cheap price. The welfare state functions within capitalism as a form of social control and no real welfare can exist in an inherently unequal society.

Source: *Mastering Social Welfare*, Pat Young, Macmillan, 1985, pp258–259

a Outline, in one sentence and using your own words, the different perspectives presented above.

b Which perspective would each of Britain's main political parties adopt?

c Explain what those who believe in each of the three perspectives would think the role of the state should be in:

    1 social security

    2 housing

    3 health

    4 education.

World Inequality

This chapter has looked at inequality in Britain, but Britain is a rich country, and the vast majority of the world's population are poorer than even the poorest people in Britain. The countries of the world can be divided in different ways: developed and less developed; the rich North and the poor South; or First World (capitalist, industrialised countries), Second World (socialist, industrialised countries), and Third World (poor, less developed countries). None of these distinctions are entirely satisfactory – countries can perhaps be better seen on a continuum ranging from rich to poor, though it is important to bear in mind that in poor countries there may well be significant groups of rich people, just as in rich countries there are, as we have seen, poor people.

Extract 12 Poverty in the Third World

The causes and nature of poverty in the Third World are highly complex and varied; the extracts below give only a flavour of what it is like to be poor in much of Africa, Asia, and Latin America.

1 The populations of North America and Western Europe eat well, consume most of the world's fuel, drive most of the cars, live in generally well serviced homes and usually survive their full three score years and ten. By contrast, the populations of Africa, Asia and Latin America are less fortunate. In most parts of these continents a majority of the population lack balanced diets, reliable drinking water, decent services and adequate incomes. Many cannot read or write, many are sick and malnourished, relatively few live beyond the age of 50 years.

Source: *An Unequal World*, Alan Gilbert, Macmillan, 1985, p1

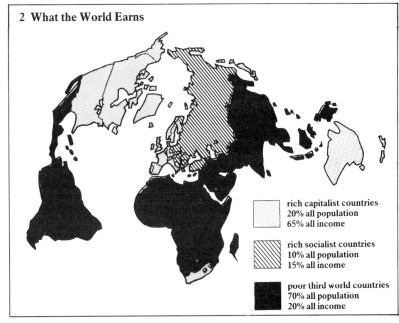

2 What the World Earns

rich capitalist countries
20% all population
65% all income

rich socialist countries
10% all population
15% all income

poor third world countries
70% all population
20% all income

Source: Tony Garrett, 'Society Today', *New Society*, 30 May 1985, pii

3 Three Children who live in Third World Countries

India: Shoba
At 13, fatherless Shoba, from Kamataka in India, earns 25p as 'teawallah' in a local factory. She cooks and cleans for her four brothers and sisters, and puts them to bed before going to night-school to learn to read.

Population *758.9 million*
Children under five *99.2 million*
Under-five mortality rate
158 per 1000 live births
GNP per person *£181.56*

China: Ziping
A two-year-old who lives with his young parents, Ziping is a product of the government's edict that only one child is allowed to each family.

Population *1059.5 million*
Children under five *93.3 million*
Under-five mortality rate
50 per 1000 live births
GNP per person *£216.48*

Ethiopia: Syntayo
Eight-year-old Syntayo survived the Ethiopian famine. She now lives with her parents and four brothers and sister in a mud hut with their few cattle and sheep. Syntayo is lucky to have survived so far.

Population *43.6 million*
Children under five *8.1 million*
Under-five mortality rate
257 per 1000 live births
GNP per person *£76.81*

Source: *TV Times*, 6–12 December 1986, pp26–27

a State four key differences between the lives of most people in Africa, Asia and Latin America and Britain.
b According to the map what is striking about the distribution of wealth in the world?
c 1 In which of the three countries mentioned is a child least likely to reach the age of five?
  2 For this country, complete the following: 'Approximately one child in . . . dies before the age of five'.

Activity 8

Write to the Information Department of two or three Third World charities, asking for information about their work in trying to combat poverty. Always enclose a large stamped addressed envelope, and, if possible, a small donation to cover their costs.
Study the literature you receive carefully, then answer the following questions:
a What are the major causes of poverty in the Third World?
b What policies do you think are most likely to succeed in reducing this poverty? Give reasons for your answer.

Questions and Suggested Projects

Review Questions

1 Outline the types of evidence you would examine when analysing the extent of inequality in Britain today.
2 What do sociologists mean by:
    a absolute poverty
    b relative poverty?
3 Outline, in two or three sentences each, the different approaches to poverty.

Theme-linking Questions

1 How is the educational achievement of children affected by the wealth and income of their parents?
2 Examine how pressure groups concerned with the welfare services try to influence government policy.
3 What welfare services do people of different ages need?
4 What are the relationships between the poverty of much of the Third World and population changes?

Stimulus–response Question

Distribution of Original and Disposable Income (UK percentages)

		bottom fifth	next fifth	middle fifth	next fifth	top fifth	total
				quintile groups of households			
original income	1976	0.8	9.4	18.8	26.6	44.4	100.0
	1981	0.6	8.1	18.0	26.9	46.4	100.0
	1983	0.3	6.7	17.7	27.2	48.0	100.0
	1984	0.3	6.1	17.5	27.5	48.6	100.0
disposable income	1976	7.0	12.6	18.2	24.1	38.1	100.0
	1981	6.7	12.1	17.7	24.1	39.4	100.0
	1983	6.9	11.9	17.6	24.0	39.6	100.0
	1984	6.7	11.7	17.5	24.4	39.7	100.0

Source: *Social Trends 1987*, HMSO, 1987, p17

GLOSSARY

quintile groups groups containing a fifth of the population each.

a How much of the original incomes in 1984 went to the top fifth of the population? (1)
b In which year in the table did the bottom fifth of the population receive their highest proportion of income? (1)
c What overall trend does the table show? (2)
d Explain the difference between the terms 'original' and 'disposable' incomes. (3)

e What are the main reasons for the differences in incomes shown by the table?   (6)

f How can governments attempt to reduce the inequalities in incomes?   (7)

Essays

1 Using examples taken from health, housing and education, examine the extent to which Britain today is an unequal society.

2 **a** What is meant by the term 'Welfare State'?

   b Examine the main problems and issues facing the Welfare State today.

3 'Poverty no longer exists in Britain today.' Discuss. Your answer could include:

absolute and relative poverty

poverty in nineteenth-century Britain

poverty as one aspect of economic inequality

attempts to eliminate poverty

the evidence on differences of income and wealth

health and housing.

Suggested Projects

1 A library study of poverty in one Third World country (see *Activity 8* p.142).

2 A study of how different people define being rich or poor.

3 A study of the take-up rates of different welfare benefits.

4 A comparative study of housing conditions in two very different areas.

5 A questionnaire-based study on attitudes to the rich or poor.

9 Power and Politics

Introduction

Power, the ability to make decisions which affect other people, is a theme which runs through the whole of sociology. Schools, factories and families, for example, can only be fully understood by examining the nature of power within them and who possesses that power.

This chapter looks at the nature of power, and then examines several political issues that sociologists are particularly interested in:
a democracy and totalitarianism
b power in Britain: political parties, pressure groups, the civil service
c voting behaviour.

Even though most people do not take an active interest in politics, few, if any, would deny that the actions of politicians, national and local, have a profound influence on our lives.

Activity 1

Explain, giving examples where possible, the types of decisions politicians make which affect the lives of ordinary people in the following areas:
a education
b health
c housing
d foreign policy and defence
e leisure.

The 'Power and Politics' part of your sociology course will prove to be more interesting, and perhaps even exciting, if you make every effort to find out all you can about current political issues. At the very least, watch a main news programme on television every day – and ask people you know who are politically well informed if there is anything you do not understand.

Activity 2

Find out:

a what constituency you live in, the name of your Member of Parliament, and what party he or she represents;

b which party controls your local authority (if you live in London or one of the six major urban conurbations you will have one local authority; if you live elsewhere you will have two, a county council and a district council, each with its own responsibilities);

c who your local councillors are, and which parties they represent.

It might be interesting to carry out a brief survey of your friends, relatives and neighbours to find out how many know the answers to the above questions.

Power and Authority

Power is the capacity to control the actions of others. It is useful to distinguish different types of power, depending on whether those upon whom the power is being exercised accept it as legitimate, and, if so, why they accept it.

Coercive power rests upon force or the threat of force. Those upon whom the power is being exercised, in other words, do not accept it as justified, but obey out of fear. See pages 21–23 for the use of coercive power in the Warsaw Ghetto.

Power which rests upon coercion is always potentially unstable, and so political leaders have usually attempted to make their power acceptable to those over whom it is exercised.

KEY TERM

authority power which is accepted as justified and legitimate by those over whom it is exercised.

Max Weber (1864–1920) distinguished three ways in which power is legitimated into authority, although in practice actual authority may combine two or three types:

a *charismatic authority* depends upon the extraordinary personality of the leader. People obey the leader, for example, because he or she is seen as superhuman. Historical examples of charismatic leaders range from Christ to Hitler.

b *traditional authority* rests on the belief that those with power are, rightly, continuing long established traditions and customs.

c *legal authority* is based on the acceptance that those who have power have the legal right to exercise it. Unlike charismatic and traditional authority, it is rare for anyone to be given total legal authority; for example, we accept the right of a policeman to stop us fighting in the street, but not to order us to change our hair style.

Activity 3

Explain the basis and extent of the authority of the following:
a teachers
b the Monarch
c the Prime Minister
d the Pope
e judges.

Democracy and Totalitarianism

Just as it is useful to distinguish different types of power and authority, so it is useful to distinguish different types of political system. A common distinction is between democratic and totalitarian systems. Although these are useful terms it must be borne in mind that in practice political systems are rarely, if ever, either completely democratic or completely totalitarian.

Extract 1 The Nature of Democracy

The following extract outlines some of the key characteristics of democracy:

... democracies are characterized institutionally by limitations on governmental action to provide safeguards for individuals and groups, by means for securing the regular, periodic, and peaceful change of their leaders, and by organs of effective popular representation. In attitude, they require tolerance for opposing opinions, flexibility, and willingness for experimentation. Limitation on governmental actions means not only that there are private spheres of life in which government must not interfere, but also that governmental agents, like private persons, must abide by the rules of law and exercise authority only to the degree the law provides. Peaceful changes of representation and of leaders involve a system of elections with some genuine measure of choice between candidates, either at the nomination or the election level.

So that choice may be exercised freely and public policies kept under review, political parties and other associations must have the opportunity openly to analyze issues, criticize governmental actions, and crystallize public sentiment.

Freedom of speech, of association, and of assembly are essential political as well as civil rights.

To make democracy effective, however, requires not only institutions and guarantees, but also attitudes. Respect for the right of the people to assert their point of view, however unpopular or seemingly wrong-headed, is fundamental to the workings of the democratic process of discussion and choice.

Democracy is characterized further by respect for minority and individual rights, by the use of discussion rather than force to settle disputes, by an acceptance of the legitimacy of the system under which the people are governed.

Source: *Government and Politics in the Twentieth Century*, Gwendolen M. Carter and John H. Herz, Thames and Hudson, 1965, pp16–17

a How are political leaders changed in democracies?
b Explain why freedom of speech is important in a democracy.
c Examine the extent to which Britain can be said to be democratic.

Extract 2 The Nature of Totalitarianism

In contrast to the conscious efforts of democracies to maintain diversity, open discussion, freedom of choice among ideas and leaders, and open-mindedness on future programs, totalitarianism is characterized by a persistent drive to enforce unity, by the crushing of open opposition, and by a leadership which claims superior, if not infallible knowledge of how policy should be directed and which exercises power through a self-perpetuating elite. Behind these actions lies an ideology or doctrine which justifies the concentration of power – and whatever restrictions on individual and group liberties this involves – as the means necessary to attain some ultimate and fixed goal or certain end toward which nature or history are said to strive.

Source: *Government and Politics in the Twentieth Century*, Gwendolen M. Carter and John H. Herz, Thames and Hudson, 1965, p18

a Explain what is meant by 'a persistent drive to enforce unity'.
b How do totalitarian governments maintain power?
c What was the 'ultimate and fixed goal' of the Nazi rulers of Germany?

Activity 4

A significant difference between democratic and totalitarian systems lies in the processes whereby young people are socialised into political values and beliefs. Democratic societies allow, within limits, the different agencies of socialisation to present varying and competing values and beliefs, while totalitarian governments maintain a tight control on what values and beliefs are transmitted.

Before answering the questions below, reread the extracts on political conformity, page 25.

a Outline the parts played by families, schools and the media in the process of political socialisation, and how these processes differ between democratic and totalitarian societies.
b What restrictions are there on the presentation of political values and beliefs in the media and in schools in Britain today?

The Resort to Violence

Violence as a means of settling political and economic disputes between nations has a long and tragic history, but it is also common between competing groups *within* societies.

Activity 5

a Which wars are currently taking place *between* countries?
b Which countries currently have groups waging *internal* violence?

Extract 3 **Urban Guerrillas**

Political violence exists in all types of political system. In the extract below, Paul Wilkinson suggests why urban guerrillas are unlikely to be politically successful.

One of the great, possibly decisive, strengths of modern revolutionary movements in Third World countries has been their ability (as, for example, in China, Algeria and Cuba) to establish a firm foundation of popular support among the rural poor. This base is vital to the successful operation of a guerrilla revolution: it ensures, because of its entirely autochthonous character, the vital supply of manpower, aid and succour, and invaluable secure retreats and weapons' dumps. Such guerrilla-mounted operations can take place in perfect camouflage with the tacit or active collaboration of the bulk of the population, right under the noses of the guerrillas' enemies.

The guerrilla strategy, however, is not limited in applicability to economically underdeveloped Third World situations.

There have been many attempts to apply guerrilla strategy and tactics in an urban setting. Urban guerrillas, however, lack the vital security of isolated rural retreats and fastnesses: they have nowhere safe to lick their wounds, to train new recruits or to make contact with external allies. They can, of course, achieve considerable long-term harassment of security forces by terrorization, armed attacks, sabotage and by tricking and evading the police and the military deployed by the regime. These tactics may result in a virtual state of military occupation and partial, recurrent siege, especially where the security forces and the government are inhibited in their response capacity by constitutional, judicial and humanitarian constraints. This gives considerable scope for hit-and-run actions against the authorities. But this does not mean that urban guerrilla activity is an adequate strategy for making a political revolution.

The sacrifice and heroic courage of those who rose in the Warsaw Ghetto against the Nazis was tragic proof that even the most determined and desperate attempt by an urban-based liberation movement could not hold out against the superior technology and firing power of a ruthless occupying force which was prepared to liquidate all who stood in its way.

Source: *Social Movement*, Paul Wilkinson, Macmillan, 1971, pp 38–139

GLOSSARY

autochthonous based on that particular country
fastness a fortress, stronghold

a Why have modern revolutionary movements in Third World countries frequently been successful?
b Would you expect guerrilla-based revolutionary movements to be more common in democratic or totalitarian societies? Explain the reasons for your answer.
c Explain why urban guerrilla movements are unlikely to be successful in advanced, industrial societies.

Activity 6 Political Violence in Northern Ireland

The causes of the violence in Northern Ireland are complex and there are no easy solutions to the divisions in that country. However, especially as Northern Ireland is part of the United Kingdom and its people elect representatives to the House of Commons, it is important that the people of England, Scotland and Wales understand as fully as possible Northern Ireland's difficulties and problems.

a Find out as much as you can about the political situation in Northern Ireland. You could, for example, interview Irish people you know, or ask a history or politics teacher to talk to your group.

b Reread *Extract 1* on Democracy (page 147). Explain why the vast majority of British people regard violent political action in Northern Ireland as politically unjustified and morally wrong.

c On the basis of what you have found out about Northern Ireland, can you suggest any measures which might reduce the political violence?

Power in Britain

Studying how decisions are made

Activity 7

a In groups of four, imagine you have to decide what you will do this evening. Each should argue a (different) case for going to:
  1 a disco
  2 a cinema
  3 a party at a mutual friend's
  4 staying in and doing your sociology homework.

b Write down the decision the group came to. (You must all do the same thing!)

c Explain carefully how the group came to its decision.

d What does this activity tell you about the nature of power and the problems involved in studying how decisions are made?

Your answers to Activity 7 have probably suggested that it is very difficult to identify when, how and by whom decisions are taken. Imagine, for example, being allowed to do participant observation at a meeting of the Cabinet – you would not know what private conversations and deals had taken place beforehand, and you would not know that two or three quiet words from one Cabinet member actually carried more weight than a brilliant, powerful speech from another.

Of course, you would not actually be allowed to observe Cabinet meetings. Indeed, even the written minutes of Cabinet meetings are kept secret for thirty years, and longer if it is considered appropriate. Civil servants who talk publicly about their work risk breaching the Official Secrets Act. It is therefore extraordinarily difficult, and at times impossible, for the sociologist, political scientist or journalist to discover how decisions are made, or who, in practice, has power.

Approaches to power

Partly because of the difficulty of studying who makes decisions, there is no one agreed view on the distribution of power in societies such as Britain. Which of the three approaches below one thinks is most satisfactory will probably depend, in part at least, on one's own political values:

a *Ruling class theory* derives from the work of Karl Marx (see pages 72–73). According to this view, capitalist societies are governed by a ruling class whose political power derives from the ownership of the means of production. The ruling class governs society in its own interests, and its power is ultimately backed by force (i.e. the armed services and police) though this is rarely apparent as the ruling class also controls the institutions (e.g. schools, media) which produce ideas and beliefs. According to those in the Marxist tradition, the ideas and beliefs of the people are those which are in the interests of the ruling class.

b *Elite theory*, like ruling class theory, believes that societies are governed by a small group of people. Marx, however, believed that in a communist society all would participate in government; elite theorists (of whom the two most important are Vilfredo Pareto (1848–1923) and Gaetano Mosca (1858–1941)) believe that all societies at all times must be governed by a small group, simply because few people have the necessary abilities and qualities to govern. According to this view, ordinary people are not capable of making rational decisions, and therefore should be governed by their betters.

c *Pluralism* pictures political decision making in a very different way to ruling class and elite theory. Pluralism sees no one group with overall power, but, rather, a plurality or variety of different groups which compete with each other for the power to influence or make decisions. According to some pluralist writers, governments can be seen as similar to referees, arbitrating between different groups.

Activity 8

The competition between different groups, with different interests, can often be seen clearly in operation at the local level. Imagine you are a local councillor on a planning committee, and a proposal comes before you to adapt a house in your ward into a hostel for the mentally handicapped:

a Which different groups of people are likely to wish to put their opinions on the proposal to you? What differing viewpoints are they likely to have? (If you are doing this activity as a class exercise, it would be useful to divide up into groups representing different interests.)

b How will you make your mind up whether to vote in favour of the proposal or not? Which groups will have most influence over you?

Pluralism therefore sees power as dispersed throughout society, though in practice it is the leaders of groups, such as party leaders, directors of large companies, and trade union officials, who compete for power.

Activity 9

a Explain how the ideas of democracy and totalitarianism can be linked to ruling class, elite and pluralist approaches.

b Explain the three approaches to power to a few friends, relatives or neighbours who are not studying sociology. Ask them which approach seems most satisfactory and why.

KEY TERMS

ruling class those who own the means of production and therefore possess political power.
elite a small group of people who possess influence and power because of their special qualities and skills.
pluralism the view that power is distributed among a variety of competing groups.

Britain's political system

At least once every five years, a general election must be held at which the 650 constituencies (areas with an average of approximately 70,000 voters) elect a Member of Parliament each. MPs sit in the House of Commons and the party leader who has the support of the majority of MPs becomes Prime Minister.

The Prime Minister then appoints the government, about 100 MPs and members of the House of Lords who belong to the Prime Minister's party, and the twenty or so holders of the most important posts form the Cabinet. The Cabinet usually meets weekly, and more frequently if necessary, and it is this group of politicians which it is often thought makes important policy decisions.

However, many political commentators have argued that the Prime Minister has gained in power at the expense of Cabinet colleagues, and that, in practice, many key decisions are taken by the Prime Minister alone, or with a small group of specially chosen ministers, civil servants or advisers.

Activity 10

a Draw a diagram to illustrate the main features of Britain's political system. Include in it general elections, MPs, the House of Commons, the Prime Minister, the government and the Cabinet.
b Using reference books in your school or college library, find out which politicians are in the present Cabinet:
    1 How many had you heard of before your research?
    2 How many women are there?
    3 How many members of ethnic minorities are there?
    4 What is the average age?
c Ask your teacher to recommend a book on British politics. Find out what powers and functions the following have, and summarise in a few lines each;
    1 the House of Commons
    2 the House of Lords
    3 the monarchy
    4 the Cabinet
    5 the Prime Minister.

KEY TERM

political parties people who share a set of political values and attitudes and who join together to try to form, or at least influence, the government so they can put their beliefs into practice.

Political parties

Members of a political party do not, of course, necessarily agree on every issue; indeed, there are often fundamental differences of opinion within the main political parties.

Any group of people can come together to form a political party and put up candidates to fight in elections, but only a small number of parties have a realistic chance of having any of their candidates elected.

Extract 4 *Women and Politics*

The Number of Women MPs					
General Election	Con	Lab	Alliance	Other	Total
1979	8	11	0	0	19
1983	13	10	0	0	23
1987	17	20	2	1	41

Between the general elections of 1983 and 1987 five women were elected in by-elections; one Conservative, two Labour, two Alliance. The reasons for the small proportion of political offices, both national and local, held by women are complex, but the extract below suggests that one of the main reasons why there are so few women MPs is the very nature of the process of selection.

Being politically active to the extent of gaining political office is a time consuming business. As our political system is currently organised the route to political office requires considerable investment of time and energy over a long period.

Institutionalised politics has many features which militate against the success of women within it. The institutional barriers to women's participation in politics are, of course, no longer legal ones. However, to be selected for political candidature, individuals require certain characteristics. People are expected to have what is considered to be 'appropriate' political and employment experience. These informal conditions of eligibility disadvantage women in several ways.

The responsibilities of caring for young children which fall predominantly upon women in our society, mean that even those who are committed to a political career are less able to get involved heavily in politics while children are small.

By the time children are old enough to require less constant care, women are relatively old for embarking on a political career. Women who do enter Parliament are on average older than their male counterparts. In addition, the experience which is regarded by political parties as relevant or appropriate to political office is not common to most women. In the Labour Party, this might mean, for example, a strong trade union involvement (difficult if you are at home looking after young children or an elderly relative). In the Tory Party a successful business career is always useful (few women are company directors or managers). There are several possible routes to becoming an M.P., but in most cases the common experience of the majority of women do not count for very much in the competitive battle for selection to fight safe seats.

The many and varied skills involved in rearing children and household management, and the experience gained by large numbers of women through their member-ship of women's organisations and voluntary work are considered of little relevance, when compared with experience gained from a position in industry or commerce.

Attendance at meetings several evenings a week, plus weekends, is not uncommon for a political hopeful. But even for those without extensive political ambitions, being active at grass roots level is not without its difficulties, particularly for women. Many parties are far from encouraging in their outlook, in holding meetings at times difficult for women to attend and on territory unfamiliar to many women (e.g. the local pub). The 'masculine' atmosphere and excessively competitive style of political institutions is widely recognised and may be a further reason why women prefer alternative forms of political activism. Nowhere is the 'male club' atmosphere more apparent than in Parliament itself. This is clearly evident from the radio broadcasting of the House of Commons debates.

Source: *Women and Power*, Lorraine Culley, Hyperion Press, 1986, pp13–14

GLOSSARY
institutionalised organised
militate against work against

a Why, on average, are women who become MPs older than men?
b What type of experience is useful for someone who wishes to become a Conservative MP?

c What is meant by 'alternative forms of political activism'?

d In what ways can Britain's political institutions be said to be 'masculine'?

e What percentage of MPs elected in 1987 were women?

f Does the above table suggest that the House of Commons is becoming less male-dominated?

Britain's first black or Asian MPs since 1929 were elected in 1987. Three, including one woman, were elected for London constituencies and one for Leicester East, all representing the Labour Party.

Activity 11

a In order to vote wisely as well as to understand Britain's political system you obviously need to be aware of the key differences between the political parties. Find out what the policies of the Conservative, Labour and Alliance (Liberals and Social Democrats) parties are on the following:

    1 unemployment
    2 defence
    3 education
    4 housing
    5 health
    6 taxation.

You could find out by writing to the party headquarters in London, or by inviting a representative of each party to come to talk to your group.

b Apart from the four political parties mentioned above, which other parties put up candidates at the last general election, and which were successful?

KEY TERM

pressure group a group of people who organise together to try to influence political decisions.

Pressure groups

Pressure groups range from large, wealthy national organisations like the Confederation of British Industry and the Trades Union Congress to groups with a handful of members, such as a group of neighbours trying to persuade their local authority to impose a speed restriction on their road.

Pressure groups are unlike parties in two main ways:

a they do not try to obtain power for themselves, but attempt to influence party politicians;

b many members of some pressure groups join for the services provided, rather than because they wish to change government policy. For example, people usually join the Automobile

Association in case their car breaks down, rather than because the AA argues the case for the motorist with the Department of Transport.

A distinction is often made between those pressure groups established to defend their members' interests (such as trade unions), and those which attempt to promote a particular cause or idea (like CND). The first type are often called *interest groups*, the second *cause groups*. In practice, however, the distinction is blurred; many interest groups may also promote a particular cause. Trade unions, for example, organise campaigns on a wide range of issues, not all of direct personal relevance to their members.

Activity 12

a List all the pressure groups the students in your class belong to (also include your teacher).
b Which, if any, of these groups have been successful in changing government policy, either nationally or locally?
c What methods do your pressure groups use to try to influence government policy?

The power and influence of pressure groups varies widely, and the success of each group depends on such factors as:
a size of membership, though probably more important is,
b the dedication and enthusiasm of the members;
c the position in society of its members: the British Medical Association, which represents the interests of doctors, is, for example, in a much more powerful position than Equity, the actors' union;
d the links between the pressure group and politicians and civil servants: some pressure groups, for example, employ MPs to speak on their behalf in the House of Commons;
e how acceptable its demands are to the general public: a group putting forward an idea approved of by the majority of voters is obviously likely to be more successful than one whose beliefs are opposed by most people;
f financial resources available, e.g. for publicity;
g whether there is an opposing group. In the area of smoking and health, for example, ASH (Action on Smoking and Health) is opposed by the Tobacco Advisory Council and FOREST (Freedom Organisation for the Right to Enjoy Smoking Tobacco), both financed by the tobacco industry.

Activity 13

Select a national pressure group which campaigns on an issue which interests you. Find out all you can about it, including how many members it has, its organisation and aims, how it tries to influence government policy, and how successful it has been.

Extract 5 *Pressure Groups and Democracy*

For good or ill, pressure groups are part of modern political democracy. But are they, on balance, helpful or harmful to democracy?

Pressure groups have been successful in providing people with a better life. Old age pensioners have kept their allotments because of pressure group activity. Many disadvantaged groups – the disabled, the mentally handicapped, the homeless – have all benefited from the activities of pressure groups. But do pressure groups represent *all* the interests and ideas in society? For example, the TUC and the CBI represent workers and managers, but who represents the unemployed? The trade union movement and the CBI are wealthy. But those who are unemployed do not have the resources to organise a powerful pressure group.

In other words, groups which represent the most powerful people in society have a great advantage over other groups. Pressure group politics tends to make powerful people even more powerful. The CBI has a staff of 400 full-time employees; the TUC has over 100 employees. The questions arise; do the weaker people in society get left out of pressure group politics? Or if they do take part in pressure group politics, are their interests adequately represented?

Some people are suspicious of pressure groups because much of their work is done in secrecy. These critics do not like the idea of powerful pressure groups and government ministers making deals in private. It is argued that the floor of the House of Commons is where debates should take place, not 'behind closed doors'. Critics of pressure groups feel that pressure group politics has undermined parliamentary democracy in Britain.

Source: *People and Politics in Britain*, Lynton Robins, Tom Brennan & John Sutton, 1985, p83

a State two types of people who have benefited from the activities of pressure groups.

b Why might the poor and underprivileged be further disadvantaged by the activities of pressure groups?

c Why do some people argue that pressure groups are anti-democratic?

d What are the advantages of pressure groups?

The Civil Service

Civil servants work for the government; they are not elected and do not lose their jobs when the government changes. The majority of civil servants work in local and regional offices of such government departments as Health and Social Security and Employment. It is their job to put into practice government policy, but a small number of senior civil servants in government departments in London are actually involved in advising ministers on what that policy shall be.

There has been considerable debate in recent years over how much influence civil servants have, and some political commentators have suggested that they can all too easily dominate a minister, by, for example, restricting the information the minister sees, so that, in effect, it is civil servants, not ministers, who make decisions.

The actual power of civil servants in a government department depends very much on the minister. If a minister is weak and has not a full grasp of the issues, then obviously civil servants are likely to be more powerful. But a strong and determined minister, acting in accordance with Cabinet policy and with prime ministerial approval, will make all key decisions in his or her department.

Voting Behaviour

There are several different types of elections in Britain, including those for representatives to local councils and the European Parliament, but it is at general elections for the House of Commons that the people decide which party they wish to govern the country and who they wish to be prime minister. General elections must be held at least every five years. Unlike many other countries where the length of each parliament is fixed and everyone knows the date of each election in advance, in Britain it is the prime minister who decides when an election shall be held.

People vote for a particular party for a complex variety of reasons. Some voters, for example, automatically vote for the party they have always voted for, while others carefully analyse the various manifestos at each election before coming to a decision.

Activity 14

a Ask a small number of people how they decided to vote at the last general election. What was the basis of their decision?

b Draw up a list of the different types of answers you receive.

c What does your list tell you about the reasons why people vote for particular parties?

Extract 6 *The 1987 General Election*

	VOTES	SEATS		HOUSE OF COMMONS
		gains	losses	
Conservative	13,763,134	12	29	375
Labour	10,033,633	27	6	229
Alliance	7,339,912	3	8	22
Nationalist	540,462	4	2	6
Others	859,111	1	2	18★

Swing from Conservative to Labour nationwide (based on GB vote only) .... 2½ per cent
Turnout .... 75.4 per cent (up 2.7)
Conservative majority over all other parties 101

Share of vote, all UK

	Con	Lab	All	Nat	Other
1983	42.4	27.5	25.4	1.5	3.2
1987	42.3	30.8	22.6	1.7	2.6

Lost deposits at £500 each, Lib 1, SNP 1, Plaid Cymru 25, Others 263
★Includes the Speaker

Source: *The Guardian*, 13 June 1987, p1

a By how much did the Labour Party's share of the vote increase between 1983 and 1987?

b Explain why the Alliance received 22.6 per cent of the total vote, but only 22 out of 650 seats in the House of Commons.

c Give four reasons why approximately one in four of the electorate did not vote.

Throughout the 1950s and 1960s writers on voting behaviour concentrated on analysing the relationships between *social class* and voting. The Labour Party attracted most of its support from the working class, and the Conservative Party from the middle class. This relationship, though central to an understanding of British politics even today, should not be exaggerated. Many working-class people have always voted Conservative (and had they not done so the Labour Party would have won every election), just as a slightly smaller proportion of the middle class have voted Labour. These people, who voted against a commonly accepted view of where their real interests lay, were known as *deviant voters*.

A central theme of studies of voting in the 1970s and 1980s has been that the traditional relationship between class and voting has begun to change.

partisan dealignment the processes whereby fewer voters have a permanent loyalty to one party and the relationships between social class and voting behaviour weaken.

Extract 7 *Partisan Dealignment and Electoral Volatility*

In the following extract, Ivor Crewe describes the forms partisan dealignment has taken and discusses some of its possible causes.

This trend (i.e. partisan dealignment) takes a variety of forms, such as the massive downturn in individual party membership and the emerging dominance of negative rather than positive voting. But the most telling evidence is the declining (although still substantial) number of voters who describe themselves as 'very' or 'fairly' strong party identifiers: in 1964, 82 per cent did; by 1983 the figure had fallen, almost unremittingly, to 64 per cent. Over the same period, the proportion of 'very strong' Conservative or Labour identifiers halved from 40 per cent to 23 per cent.

The various causes of partisan dealignment in Britain are fiercely disputed among academics. But there is general agreement on the importance of three. First, the failures of the 1966–70 Wilson government and the 1970–1974 Heath government sowed the seeds of a lasting disillusion among Labour and then Conservative supporters. Secondly, as television replaced the press as the dominant medium of politics, its adversarial style, born out of an obligation to maintain 'balance', exposed the electorate much more consistently to new points of view. The local one-sided politics of pub and club have been by-passed by television's 'impartial' politics beamed to every sitting room.

Thirdly, changes in the class structure have gradually eroded the social foundations of partisanship. The sharp increase in occupational mobility, the massive entry of women into the labour force, mass unemployment, the spread of house ownership, and the bureaucratisation and unionisation of white collar work mean that about four fifths now belong to 'mixed' class categories. They are working class home-owners, or middle class trade unionists, or the white collar wives of blue collar husbands, or the unemployed live-at-home sons of professional parents. For such voters, class identity is ambivalent, and it is unclear which party best serves their 'class interests' because it is not obvious what their class interests *are*; hence partisanship is weaker.

Whatever the origins of diminished party loyalties, the major consequence is a rise in electoral volatility. Again, this reveals itself in various ways – in the loosening of the two-party grip over the electorate, in a growing instability of the party vote from one election to the next, in the regularity of by-election 'sensations' and in the sharper and more frequent oscillations of the polls between elections.

Source: 'The Campaign Confusion', Ivor Crewe, *New Society*, 8 May 1987, p11

adversarial presenting opposite points of view
ambivalent having different attitudes towards
oscillations variations between extremes

a What does Crewe mean by negative and positive voting?
b Explain how television adopts an 'adversarial style'.
c Why is class identity ambivalent for an increasing number of voters?
d Crewe states that there has been a rise in 'electoral volatility'. What is the evidence for this?

Activity 15

Changes in the social structure are likely to have major consequences for voting behaviour.

a Reread page 77, *Extract 5*. Explain the likely voting patterns associated with:
  1 proletarian traditionalism
  2 deferential traditionalism
  3 privatisation.
b Read the section on the changing occupational structure (pages 239–244). What are the likely implications of these changes for the future electoral prospects of the Conservative and Labour Parties?

Extract 8 The 1987 General Election

The following extracts illustrate the key features of voting in the 1987 General Election. They also tell us a great deal about the nature of British society. Look again at *Extract 6* (page 159) to see the overall result of the election.

The statistics from *The Independent* are based on an ITN/Harris exit survey of 4589 voters who were interviewed as they left the polling stations. The statistics from *The Guardian* are based on a Gallup survey commissioned by BBC Television; 4886 voters were interviewed on the day before or on the day of the election.

a) **Sex and Age**

(Figures in percentages; changes since 1983 in parentheses. Source: ITN/Harris exit poll)	Con	Lab	Lib/SDP	Others
ALL	43.3 (−0.2)	31.6 (+3.3)	23.1 (−2.9)	2.0 (−0.2)
Sex:				
MEN	41 (0)	33 (+3)	23 (−3)	3 (−1)
WOMEN	43 (−1)	31 (+3)	23 (−3)	3 (+1)
Age:				
18-29 YEAR-OLDS	36 (−3)	35 (+3)	26 (+1)	3 (−1)
30-44 YEAR-OLDS	41 (+2)	31 (+3)	26 (−4)	3 (0)
45-64 YEAR-OLDS	44 (0)	31 (+5)	22 (−5)	3 (0)
65+ YEAR-OLDS	47 (+2)	31 (+3)	21 (0)	3 (−2)

Source: *The Independent*, 13 June 1987, p17

b) **Region**

	Con	Lab	Lib/SDP	Others
Region:				
LONDON	46.4 (+2.5)	31.4 (+1.6)	21.5 (−3.2)	0.7 (−0.9)
REST OF SOUTH-EAST	55.8 (+1.2)	16.8 (+0.8)	26.9 (−11.8)	0.5 (−0.2)
SOUTH-WEST	50.5 (−0.8)	16.2 (+1.5)	32.8 (−0.4)	0.5 (−0.3)
EAST ANGLIA	52.0 (+1.1)	21.7 (+1.2)	25.8 (−2.5)	0.5 (+0.2)
EAST MIDLANDS	48.6 (+1.4)	30.1 (+2.1)	21.0 (−3.1)	0.3 (−0.4)
WEST MIDLANDS	45.6 (0.6)	33.3 (+2.1)	20.8 (−2.6)	0.3 (−0.1)
YORKS & HUMBERSIDE	37.5 (−1.2)	40.6 (+5.3)	21.6 (−3.9)	0.3 (−0.2)
NORTH-WEST	38.0 (−2.0)	41.2 (+5.2)	20.6 (−2.8)	0.2 (−0.4)
NORTH	32.0 (−2.3)	47.0 (+7.1)	20.8 (−4.0)	0.2 (−0.9)
SCOTLAND	24.0 (−4.3)	42.4 (+7.3)	19.2 (−5.3)	14.1 (+2.3★)
WALES	29.5 (−1.5)	45.0 (+7.5)	17.9 (−5.3)	7.3 (−0.5★)
				★ Nationalists

Source: *The Independent*, 13 June 1987, p17

The political polarisation between north and south appears to be growing apace. Britain is dividing sharply into two political nations. This process reflects at least in part a longer process of social change in which the south is becoming more middle class more quickly than the north.

But the reflection of this difference in the geographical distribution of party support is magnified by the 'neighbourhood effect'. This simply means that voters' behaviour is influenced not only by their own socio-economic position but also that of their neighbours: thus as the south, for example, becomes more middle class the Conservative vote will rise not simply because there are more members of its class living there, but also because the remaining working-class voters are increasingly likely to vote Conservative.

Source: 'Must Labour Lose', John Curtice, *New Society*, 19 June 1987, p19

c) **The Middle Class**

	University Educated		Public Sector		Private Sector	
	1987 %	1983–87	1987 %	1983–87	1987 %	1983–87
Con	34	−9	44	−4	65	+1
Lab	29	+3	24	–	13	–
Lib/SP	36	+4	31	+4	22	−1

Source: 'A New Class of Politics', Ivor Crewe, *The Guardian*, 15 June 1987, p9

d) The Working Class

| | THE NEW WORKING CLASS | | | | THE TRADITIONAL WORKING CLASS | | | |
	Lives in South	Owner-occupier	Non-union	Works in private sector	Lives in Scotland/ North	Council tenant	Union member	Works in public sector
Con	46	44	40	38	29	25	30	32
Lab	28	32	38	39	57	57	48	49
Lib/SDP	26	24	22	23	15	18	22	19

Source: *The Guardian*, 15 June 1987, p9

e) The Labour Party and the Working Class

My post-mortem survey of the 1983 election concluded that Labour's claim to be the party of the working class was sociologically, if not ideologically, threadbare. The Labour vote remained largely working class; but the working class was no longer largely Labour. The party had come to represent a declining segment of the working class – the traditional working class of the council estates, the public sector, industrial Scotland and the North, and the old industrial unions – while failing to attract the affluent and expanding working class of the new estates and new service economy of the South. It was a party neither of one class nor one nation; it was a regional class party.

The 1987 survey reinforces each of these conclusions. Labour remains the largest party among manual workers (42 per cent), but a minority party, only 6 per cent ahead of the Conservatives. The political gulf between the traditional and new working class remains.

The Conservatives are the first party of manual workers in the South (18 per cent) among owner occupiers (+12 per cent) and non-unionists (+2 per cent) and only 1 per cent behind in the private sector; Labour retains massive leads among the working class of Scotland (+43 per cent) the North (16 per cent), council tenants (+32 per cent), trade unionists (+18 per cent), and the public sector (+17 per cent).

Although the housing gap has slightly narrowed, regional differences have widened further.

In one important sense the picture is even gloomier for Labour this time. Government policies are producing a steady expansion of the new working class, and diminution of the old. Council house sales, privatisation, the decline of manufacturing industry (on which the old unions are based) and the steady population drift to the South have re-structured the working class. The new working class is not only the dominant segment but increasingly dominant. Demography and time are not on Labour's side.

Source: 'A New Class of Politics', Ivor Crewe, *The Guardian*, 15 June 1987, p9

f) The Reasons People Gave for Their Choice of Party

	All	Con	Lab	Lib/ SDP
Q: What is the ONE most important reason for supporting the party you have just voted for?				
The party's policies	50	56	46	48
I usually vote for that party	19	19	25	8
Dislike of another party	13	9	12	23
The party leader	6	8	6	4
The local candidate	5	3	5	10
None of these	5	3	5	7

(Figures in percentages.
Source: ITN/Harris exit poll)

	All	Con	Lab	Lib/SDP
Q: Did you vote for your first-choice party; or did you vote tactically, to defeat another party?				
Voted for party/candidate of first choice	81	88	81	71
Voted tactically	17	11	17	28
Q: When you decided which way to vote, which two issues did you consider most important?				
Unemployment	42	16	66	53
National Health Service	23	7	37	30
Prices/Inflation	20	36	6	10
Nuclear weapons	20	26	14	17
Schools/Education	19	11	22	27
Defence	17	29	4	13
Crime/Law and order	14	18	9	12
Pensions/Welfare benefits	11	6	18	13
Taxation	10	18	2	5
Trade unions	6	10	3	3
Housing/Rates	6	6	6	6
Privatisation	5	8	3	3
Immigration/Race relations	2	3	2	2

Source: *The Independent*, 13 June 1987, p17

a Examine the advantages and disadvantages of using interviews to discover patterns of voting behaviour.

b What is meant by tactical voting?

c What, if any, are the relationships between voting and sex, age and region?

d Explain why middle-class people who work in the public sector are less likely to vote Conservative than those who work in the private sector.

e 'The Labour vote remained largely working class; but the working class was no longer largely Labour.' (*Extract e*) Explain what Crewe means by this statement.

f What are the key differences between the 'new' and the 'traditional' working class?

g What evidence is there in the above extracts for the argument that there is currently a process of partisan dealignment taking place?

h Summarise, in no more than 200 words, what the above data tells you about voting behaviour in the 1987 General Election.

Activity 16

a Collect any information you can find about voting in any local, European, by election or general election which takes place while you are doing your sociology course. Key statistics are published in *The Guardian*, *The Independent* and *The Times* a day or two after elections. Data from opinion polls would also be useful.

b Examine the extent to which data from recent elections and opinion polls confirms or refutes the trends in voting behaviour identified in this chapter.

Questions and Suggested Projects

Review Questions

1 Explain, using examples, the differences between power and authority.
2 Describe the key features of democratic and totalitarian systems of government.
3 Explain the part played by political parties in Britain's system of government.
4 Why are some pressure groups more successful than others?
5 What is meant by:
    a partisan dealignment?
    b electoral volatility?

Theme-linking Questions

1 Examine the relationships between the different types of system of social stratification (i.e. slavery, estate, caste and class) and power.
2 Describe the parts played by pressure groups in the public debates on:
    a education
    b the mass media
    c crime and deviance.
3 Explain how decisions taken by central and local government have influenced your schooling.
4 Why is it difficult to study how political decisions are taken?
5 Explain why the majority of those with political power are men.

Stimulus-response Question

After a thorough survey of the major research on tobacco's links with lung and heart disease and poor general health, James Wilkinson makes a savage indictment of the industry on two fronts; its repeated attempts to obscure the medical evidence and confuse public perceptions of it, and the ruthless war of attrition it has waged against advertising restrictions, largely through sponsorship of sports and the arts. Back-door advertising has been rife, through diversification into other product areas – fashion, holidays, sportswear – while trading on existing brand names or launching new ones. The voluntary agreements with the Department of Health that regulate such promotions have been broached time after time.

But governmental commitment to ending tobacco addiction has never been more than half-hearted. Minutes of a 1954 Cabinet meeting disclosed under the 30-year rule revealed a decision to play down the recently established connection between cigarettes and lung cancer partly because tax revenue was at stake, a factor that, together with business pressures, has dictated policies ever since

The tobacco industry now faces mounting opposition, from the BMA's* campaign to the proliferation of militant anti-smoking groups using direct action to protest against cigarette promotions. It thrives thanks to legality and the respectability that is enhanced by prestige sponsorship and unabated advertising.

Source: 'Running smoke rings round the opposition', Liz Heron, *The Times Education Supplement*, 31 October 1986, p25
(The book by James Wilkinson referred to is *Tobacco: the Truth Behind the Smoke Screen*, Penguin Special, 1986)
*British Medical Association

a What two major criticisms does Wilkinson make of the tobacco industry? (2)

b Why did the Cabinet in 1954 not wish to publicise the link between cigarettes and lung cancer? (1)

c Explain what is meant by the '30-year rule'. (2)

d Explain briefly the part played by the Cabinet in British politics. (4)

e What methods can anti-smoking groups use to put across their point of view? (5)

f The tobacco industry is now opposed by several anti-smoking groups. What advantages and disadvantages does each side possess in this dispute? (6)

Essays

1 Examine the influence of pressure groups in Britain today. Give examples to illustrate your answer.

2 a Explain the different reasons why one person might have power over another.

   b Compare the Marxist and pluralist approaches to power.

3 Examine the relationship between voting behaviour and social class. Your answer could include:

     class and voting in the 1950s and 1960s

     deviant voting

     partisan dealignment

     electoral volatility

     the changing class structure

     other factors, e.g. region, neighbourhood

     political issues, campaigns and leaders.

Suggested Projects

1 A study of two competing pressure groups (See Activity 13).

2 A comparative study of the political attitudes of your fellow students and those of students at a different type of school/college.

3 A historical study of charismatic authority and the circumstances under which it breaks down.

4 A study of a by-election or local election campaign.

5 A participant observation study of how a constituency party selects a prospective parliamentary candidate.

10 Population: Change and Movement

Introduction

Three factors affect the size of a country's population:
a births
b deaths
c migration.

This chapter will therefore look at changes in birth and death rates and migration patterns in Britain, and briefly compare them with population patterns in the Third World.

Sociologists are also interested in *where* people live. The process of urbanisation and the move away from the cities, together with the problems of the inner cities, have been the issues most discussed by sociologists.

Sources of Data

The study of population is one topic where the sociologist or demographer cannot rely on primary research. It is obviously impossible for a sociologist to carry out research, for example, on how many births or deaths there are in Britain each year. Secondary statistics must therefore be used.

In Britain there has been a national census every ten years (except 1941) since 1801. The Census, completed by a member of every household, provides information not just on the numbers of people, their age and sex, but also such issues as employment and educational qualifications.

Activity 1

In strict confidence

1981 Census England

H Form for Private Households

Where boxes are provided please tick the appropriate box (Please use ink or ballpoint pen)

1-3 Include on your census form:

- all the persons who spend Census night 5-6 April 1981 in this household (including anyone who is visiting overnight and anyone who arrives here on the Monday and who has not been included as present on another census form).

- any persons who usually live with your household but who are absent on census night.
  For example, on holiday, in hospital, at school or college. Include them even if you know they are being put on another census form elsewhere.

Write the names in the top row, starting with the head or a joint head of household (BLOCK CAPITALS please)

Include any newly born baby even if still in hospital. If not yet given a name write 'BABY' and the surname.

	1st person	2nd person
Name and surname		
Sex	☐ Male ☐ Female	☐ Male ☐ Female
Date of birth	Day Month Year	Day Month Year

4 Marital status

Please tick the box showing the present marital status.

If separated but not divorced please tick 'Married (1st marriage)' or 'Re-married' as appropriate.

Marital status	**Marital status**
1 ☐ Single	1 ☐ Single
2 ☐ Married (1st marriage)	2 ☐ Married (1st marriage)
3 ☐ Re-married	3 ☐ Re-married
4 ☐ Divorced	4 ☐ Divorced
5 ☐ Widowed	5 ☐ Widowed

5   Relationship in household

Please tick the box which indicates the relationship of each person to the person entered in the first column.

Please write in relationship of *'Other relative'* – for example, father, daughter-in-law, brother-in-law, niece, uncle, cousin, grandchild.

Please write in position in household of *'Unrelated person'* – for example, boarder, housekeeper, friend, flatmate, foster child.

Relationship to 1st person

01 ☐ Husband or wife
02 ☐ Son or daughter
☐ Other relative, please specify
☐ Unrelated, please specify

1981 Census, England, OPCS

a Comment on the above questions on the 1981 Census form. Are they easy to understand? What are the implications of the wording of the questions for the accuracy of Census findings?

b Explain possible circumstances in which people might not give accurate answers about their age and marital status, and relationship in the household, despite it being an offence to give false information.

c Explain why it is useful for governments to know the dates of birth of the population.

d Ask relatives or friends who completed the last Census form how they approached the task. Were they, for example, careful to be as accurate as possible, or did they give little attention to what they were writing?

Every birth, death and marriage has to be registered locally, and such statistics, as well as those on demographic issues such as divorce, abortion and migration, are collected and issued by the government on an annual, and in some cases monthly, basis.

Activity 2

Go to your school or college library and your nearest public library to find the latest population statistics they have. Obtain the latest available statistics on births, deaths and migration. Comment on how easy or difficult it was to find the required information.

Britain's Population: a Brief Historical Outline

At the time of the Domesday Book (1086) the population of England and Wales was probably about two millions. By the end of the seventeenth century it had reached between five and six millions, with a further one million in Scotland. It was in the second half of the eighteenth century that Britain's population began to grow rapidly; the first Census in 1801 recorded a population of 11.9 millions.

Birth rates rose slowly during the eighteenth century, but it was the decline in the death rate which was mainly responsible for population growth. Historians differ on the main causes of this fall in the death rate, but among factors which contributed to increased life expectancy were:

a improved diets, partly due to increased food production resulting from improvements in agriculture;

b better transport which could move food more quickly and more cheaply;

c cheaper and better clothing;

d buildings increasingly made of stone, brick and slate rather than wood and thatch, thus reducing vermin-carried diseases.

KEY TERMS

birth rate the number of live births per thousand population per year. It is calculated by:

$$\frac{\text{total births}}{\text{total population}} \times 1000 = \text{birth rate.}$$

death rate the number of deaths per thousand population per year. It is calculated by:

$$\frac{\text{total deaths}}{\text{total population}} \times 1000 = \text{death rate.}$$

Extract 1 Britain's Population in the Nineteenth Century

It was during the nineteenth century that Britain's population grew most rapidly, as the following Census figures indicate.

	England and Wales	Scotland
1801	8,892,536	1,608,420
1821	12,000,236	2,091,521
1841	15,914,148	2,620,184
1861	20,066,222	3,062,294
1881	25,974,439	3,735,573
1901	32,527,843	4,472,103

Source: *Population*, R. K. Kelsall, Longman, 1979, p16

a What was the population of Great Britain in 1861?

b In which decades did the population of England, Wales and Scotland grow most rapidly?

c Construct a bar chart which illustrates the trends in the above table.

The trends of the late eighteenth century were continued into the nineteenth. Birth rates rose slowly until the mid-1870s, partly because of a significant reduction in the average age at marriage, itself probably caused by the opportunities an increasingly urbanised and industrialised society offered.

Mortality since the mid-nineteenth century

Death rates fell especially from the middle of the nineteenth century. The same factors that caused the fall in the eighteenth century became increasingly important, but additional factors include:

a improvements in public health, especially water supply and sanitation;

b improvements in medical knowledge, though it was not until the twentieth century that these had a marked effect on death rates.

KEY TERM

life expectancy how long, on average, a member of a particular group can expect to live. Life expectancy is usually estimated from birth, but it can be predicted from any age.

Extract 2 Life Expectancy at Birth

	Male	Female
1840	40	42
1870	41	45
1900	44	48
1930	59	63
1960	68	74
1986	71	77

Source: *Britain in Figures*, Alan F Sillitoe, Penguin, 1971, p31, adapted from *OPCS Monitor PP2 86/1*, 1986, p3

a When did the biggest increases in life expectancy take place?

b Draw graphs to illustrate changes in life expectancy for males and females.

c What conclusions can you draw from the shapes of your graphs?

In the eighteenth and nineteenth centuries most people died of infectious and contagious diseases such as smallpox, tuberculosis, whooping cough, influenza and measles. Improved living conditions, diet and medical knowledge mean that few people in Britain today die of such diseases. Instead, most people today die of diseases typically, though by no means solely, associated with old age. The three biggest killers today are heart disease, cancers and respiratory diseases. (See page 130, *Extract 4* for differences in mortality rates according to social class.)

Life expectancy figures must, of course, be interpreted carefully as they are predicting into the future. On the one hand, they tend to underestimate real life expectancy, as they are based on current mortality trends, and improved medicine and living conditions may see an even further reduction in the death rate. On the other hand, life expectancy figures for adults, especially old people, have not seen dramatic improvements. It is infant mortality which has seen the dramatic reduction.

KEY TERM

infant mortality rate the number of deaths of infants before their first birthday per thousand live births.

Extract 3 Infant Mortality Rates in Britain

1851	148
1901	153
1939	53
1955	23
1974	16
1985	9

Source: *Britain in Figures*, Alan F Sillitoe, Penguin, 1971, p33 adapted from *Social Trends*, 1987, HMSO, 1987, Table 1.14

a Out of every hundred babies born in 1985, approximately how many died before their first birthday?
b Explain why the infant mortality rate has fallen so dramatically since the beginning of the twentieth century.

See page 131 *Extract 5* for infant mortality rates and social class.

Extract 4 Death Rates: by Age and Sex

United Kingdom											Rates per thousand population and thousands	
	Age										All ages	Total deaths (000's)
	Under 1[1]	1–4	5–14	15–34	35–44	45–54	55–64	65–74	75–84	85+		
1961												
Males	24.8	1.1	0.4	1.1	2.5	7.5	22.3	55.1	125.0	258.6	12.6	322.0
Females	19.3	0.8	0.3	0.6	1.8	4.5	11.1	31.5	89.1	215.9	11.4	309.8
1971												
Males	20.2	0.8	0.4	1.0	2.4	7.2	20.5	51.4	114.7	235.6	12.2	328.5
Females	15.5	0.6	0.9	0.5	1.6	4.4	10.3	26.8	75.2	189.5	11.1	316.5
1981												
Males	12.7	0.6	0.3	0.9	1.9	6.3	18.1	46.3	106.3	226.6	12.0	329.1
Females	9.5	0.5	0.2	0.4	1.3	3.9	9.8	24.7	66.9	178.4	11.4	328.8
1985												
Males	10.3	0.5	0.3	0.8	1.8	5.6	17.5	45.0	104.8	223.6	12.0	331.6
Females	8.3	0.4	0.2	0.4	1.2	3.4	9.9	24.7	64.7	178.6	11.7	339.1

[1]Rate per 1,000 live births.

Source: adapted from *Social Trends 1987*, HMSO, 1987, Table 1.14

a In 1985 which were the 'safest' ages?

b Between 1961 and 1985 which ages show the greatest reductions in mortality? What reasons can you give for this reduction?

c For every female age category the death rate was lower in 1985 than 1961, and yet the overall female death rate was higher in 1985. Explain these apparently contradictory statistics.

d What are the implications of your answer to **c** for the ways in which death rate statistics should be interpreted?

Activity 3

As the statistics above indicate, death rates are higher for males than females at every age. Examine the possible biological and social reasons for these differences.

Fertility since the 1870s

Couples marrying in the 1860s had, on average, just over six children; couples marrying since the 1920s have had, on average, around two children.

From the 1870s the birth rate began to fall, in the middle classes first, and later in the working classes. Why couples have or do not have children is the result of a complex variety of factors, and it is impossible to accurately assess the relative importance of each factor. The following, however, contributed in some way to the fall in the birth rate after the 1870s:

a according to J. A. Banks (*Prosperity and Parenthood*, Routledge and Kegan Paul, 1954) a major factor is that in the 1870s the incomes of middle-class people failed to keep pace with inflation. In particular, the cost of child care (e.g. nannies and governesses) and private education was rising rapidly. In order to maintain their standard of living and provide their children with a good start in life the obvious solution was to have fewer children.

b in the working class also children increasingly became an economic burden. They were prevented by law from working and the introduction of compulsory education and the progressive raising of the school leaving age, further increased the cost of each child.

c the fall in the infant mortality rate meant parents no longer had to produce extra children as an 'insurance' in case one or more died.

d the decline in the birth rate is in part a *cause* of the greater employment opportunities open to women, but the increased number of women who wish to combine a career with children is clearly likely to want small families.

'I thought I'd told you *months* ago!'

KEY TERM

fertility rate the number of births per thousand women aged 15–44.

e the above factors explain why people might *want* fewer children; the development of contraceptive techniques and their availability have made it easier for people to have no more children than they want.

Since the Second World War, after a 'bulge' in 1946–7 caused by people postponing having babies in the war, the birth rate has fluctuated, partly as a result of the age structure of the population, but it has remained relatively low. A more precise indication of the changing patterns of family size is the fertility rate.

Extract 5 Births in England and Wales since 1951

Live Births: Totals and Rates

England & Wales

	Total live births (000's)	Crude birth rate[1]	General fertility rate[2]	Mean age of mothers at first birth (years)	Total period fertility rate[3]
1951	678	15.5	71.6	25.3	2.14
1956	700	15.7	77.0	25.0	2.35
1961	811	17.6	89.2	24.4	2.77
1964	876	18.5	92.9	24.0	2.93
1966	850	17.7	90.5	23.6	2.75
1971	783	15.9	83.5	23.6	2.37
1976	584	11.8	60.4	24.3	1.71
1977	569	11.5	58.1	24.4	1.66
1981	634	12.8	61.3	24.6	1.80
1983	629	12.7	59.7	24.7	1.76
1985	656	13.1	61.0	24.8	1.78

[1] Total births per 1,000 population of all ages.
[2] Total births per 1,000 women aged 15–44. Includes also births to mothers aged under 15, and 45 or over.
[3] The average number of children which would be born per woman if women experienced the age-specific fertility rates of the period in question throughout their child-bearing life span.

Source: Adapted from *Social Trends 1987*, HMSO, 1987, Table 1.10

a Describe the main changes in the birth and fertility rates since 1951.

b What appears to be the trend in the 1980s for the mean age of mothers at first birth.

c Explain why the general fertility rate is a better indicator of family size than the crude birth rate.

> **Activity 4**
>
> Carry out a brief survey to find out what the students in your sociology group consider to be the ideal family size. Examine the reasons given for their answers.

In short, Britain has moved from being a country with a high birth rate and a high death rate to one today with a low birth rate and a low death rate. It was estimated in 1986 (*OPCS Monitor PP2 86/1*) that the population of England and Wales would grow very slowly until the turn of the century, from 49.9 millions in 1985 to 52.2 millions in 2001, and 53.5 in 2025.

Extract 6 Population by Sex, Age and Marital Status, 1971 & 1985

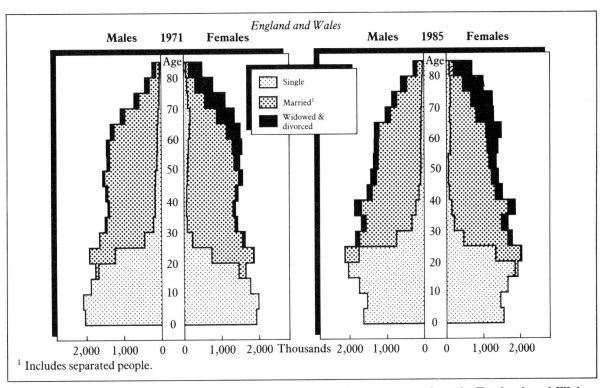

¹ Includes separated people.

Source: *Social Trends 1987*, HMSO, 1987, Table 1.6

a In 1985, how many females were there in England and Wales aged 30–5?

b Describe and explain any differences between males and females in the above diagram.

c Describe how the 1971 and 1985 population 'shapes' differ.

d What is the importance of the information contained in the above diagram?

For statistics on the changing age structure of the population since 1901 see page 125, and for a discussion of the consequences of the changes pages 119–121.

Migration

Internal migration refers to people moving *within* a country, external migration to people moving from one country to another.

Celts, Romans, Saxons, Normans, Dutch, French; Jewish refugees; Irish escaping from poverty; and, more recently, West Indians and Asians, are only a few examples of the immigrants who have made Britain what it is today. However, at the time when Britain's population was expanding most rapidly, between the beginning of the nineteenth century and the outbreak of the Second World War, probably some 20 million Britons emigrated, thus providing a valuable safety valve for the surplus population.

During the 1950s and early 1960s a shortage of labour in Britain and limited opportunities in Commonwealth countries such as India, Pakistan and the islands of the West Indies resulted in what was seen by some people as unacceptable levels of immigration. The Commonwealth Immigrants Act of 1962 restricted entry to Britain, and subsequent legislation in 1968 and 1971 and the 1981 Nationality Act have made it even more difficult to enter Britain to live, with the exception of EEC nationals.

Extract 7 *Recent Migration Patterns in the United Kingdom*

| | Thousands | | |
	Into UK	Out of UK	Balance
1971	200	240	−40
1976	191	210	−19
1981	153	233	−78
1984	201	164	+35
1985	232	174	+58

Source: adapted from *Social Trends 1987*, HMSO, 1987, Table 1.15

a In which year did the number of emigrants most exceed the number of immigrants?

b Explain why net migration fluctuates from year to year.

Raw migration data like the above can be misleading, especially as many people confuse immigration with ethnicity. The agreed international definition of a new resident, as used by the Registrar General, is someone who, having lived abroad for at least 12 months, declares an intention of living in the UK for at least 12 months. A departing resident is the converse. Using this definition, 47% of immigrants into the UK in 1985 were actually British citizens.

Population and Social Policy

The age and sex structure of the population has fundamental implications for health, housing, education and social security policy. Past and current rates, and predictions for the future are used, for example, to estimate the need for hospitals, schools and pensions. Especially important is the proportion of those of working age and those too young or old to work. As we have seen, the proportion of those not working is, for a variety of reasons, increasing.

Activity 5

Explain why, and with what implications, a smaller proportion of working people will have to support a growing proportion of dependent people in the future.

Governments have a great deal of prior knowledge about the need for provision for the elderly; they have less time to estimate the need for educational provision.

Activity 6

Children: by Age Group

England & Wales

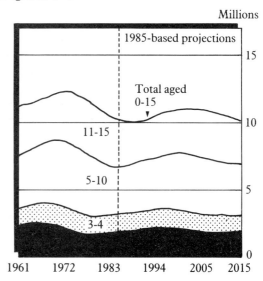

Millions

Source: *Social Trends 1987*, HMSO, 1987, Table 1.4

Imagine you are an adviser to the Secretary of State for Education. Using the information in the above diagram, write a briefing paper outlining the likely need for different types of school between now and 2025.

World Population

If the population of Britain and most other industrialised countries is growing only slowly, this is not true of the world as a whole.

Extract 8 *The Rise in World Population*

	millions	
8000 BC	10	
1400 AD	500	World population is projected to be
1800	900	6.1 billion in 2000, 8.2 billion in
1900	1650	2050, and will probably stabilise at
1985	4800	about 10.2 billion by 2100.

Source: *Social Trends 1987*, HMSO, 1987, p39

a During which period did the world's population increase most rapidly?

b Transfer the above information onto a graph. What does your graph tell you about the advantages of the diagrammatic presentation of statistics?

c Explain how demographers predict future population trends. Why might they be wrong?

The massive increase in the populations of most Third World countries is due to continuing high birth rates and falling death rates. Any increases in food production are all too easily absorbed by the growing population. The consequence is that malnourishment is widespread, and famine a regular occurrence. (See pages 140–142 for poverty in the Third World.)

Activity 7

a Explain why it is frequently difficult for governments of poor countries to persuade people to have fewer children. (It will help you answer this question if you try to look at the world from the point of view of a peasant farmer.)

b Imagine you have been appointed adviser to a community in the Third World with responsibility for persuading the people to have fewer children. Explain how you would set about your task and how you would attempt to overcome the problems you would face.

Urbanisation

In 1801 only 17 per cent of the population of England and Wales lived in towns of more than 20,000. By 1851 over 50 per cent of Britain's population lived in urban areas, and by 1911 80 per cent did.

KEY TERM

urbanisation the process whereby the proportion of the population living in towns and cities increases significantly.

Urban living is often contrasted with rural living, but, as usual in sociology, terms must be used with care. 'Towns' and 'cities' are defined in a variety of different ways, and places cannot be clearly divided into rural or urban. A small commuter village, for example, may in some ways be rural, in other ways urban.

Activity 8

a As a group exercise, complete the following sentences:
  1 A village is . . .
  2 A town is . . .
  3 A city is . . .
(Give examples if you think it will help explain each answer)
b What sociological conclusions can you draw from your group's answers?

Despite the problems of definition, it is clear that a far higher proportion of Britain's population lived in urban areas in 1900 than in 1800. Why? As with external migration there were factors *pushing* people away from the countryside, and other factors *pulling* them to the towns and cities:
a the main push factor was the shortage of employment and poor wages in rural areas; changes in agricultural methods meant fewer workers were needed;
b the main pull factor was the demand by the new factories and mines for labour;
c the nineteenth century, as we have seen, was when Britain's population increased most rapidly; as more and more people moved to the towns and cities and had children this caused the urban areas to grow yet more. Note that, as so often, a major social change, i.e. where people live, is linked to economic changes, i.e. the process of industrialisation.

Activity 9

Produce a brief historical outline of demographic changes in your locality in the last 200 years. (Geography or history teachers will be able to give you suitable sources of information.)

The Move from the Cities

If the nineteenth century was characterised by the growth of towns and cities, more recent years have witnessed a reversal of this trend with a move towards villages and small towns.

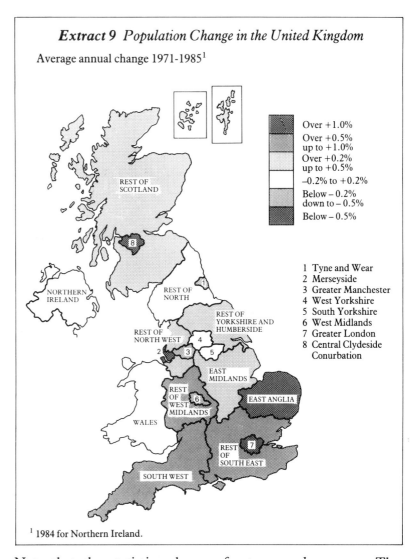

Extract 9 *Population Change in the United Kingdom*

Average annual change 1971-1985[1]

Key:
- Over +1.0%
- Over +0.5% up to +1.0%
- Over +0.2% up to +0.5%
- −0.2% to +0.2%
- Below −0.2% down to −0.5%
- Below −0.5%

1 Tyne and Wear
2 Merseyside
3 Greater Manchester
4 West Yorkshire
5 South Yorkshire
6 West Midlands
7 Greater London
8 Central Clydeside Conurbation

REST OF SCOTLAND

NORTHERN IRELAND

REST OF NORTH

REST OF YORKSHIRE AND HUMBERSIDE

REST OF NORTH WEST

EAST MIDLANDS

REST OF WEST MIDLANDS

EAST ANGLIA

WALES

REST OF SOUTH EAST

SOUTH WEST

[1] 1984 for Northern Ireland.

Source: Adapted from *Social Trends 1987*, HMSO, 1987, p8

Note that the statistics above refer to *annual* averages. The numbered areas are Britain's major urban conurbations.

a Which areas have seen the greatest population increases?

b Which areas have seen the greatest population decreases?

c Explain why different regions of Britain have experienced different demographic changes since 1971.

The reasons for the demographic decline of the cities and large towns include:

a the decline of traditional urban-based manufacturing and its replacement by new industries such as micro-electronics. These newer industries do not need to be near natural resources as the old ones did, and so can choose where to locate;

b increased affluence, which means many people such as the retired can choose where to live;

c improved private and public transport (e.g. commuter services into London), which means workers can commute longer distances. The development of the motorway network is perhaps particularly important here;

d changing public attitudes on where it is most desirable to live.

As the quality of city life is seen to deteriorate because many of the more affluent people are leaving, this is likely to encourage yet more people to leave, and the whole process will be accelerated.

It would be a mistake, however, to see this move from the cities, which in any event is significantly less in the 1980s than in the 1970s, as in any way representing a move away from an urban way of life. Even though people may actually live in the country-side, their lives are not dependent on it. The growth of car ownership in particular means that such 'country-dwellers' can easily use towns and cities for work, shopping, entertainment and education.

Extract 10 *The Inner Cities*

As growing numbers of the more affluent, employed people have left the cities, the poor and unemployed, often members of ethnic minorities, have been left behind. The inner city, in particular, has become a major political issue; Lord Scarman's report on the Brixton disorders of April 1981 attracted wide-spread publicity.

To restore our inner cities to a healthy normality, it is necessary to understand clearly what we mean by the problem of the inner cities. As I argued in my 1981 report, the Brixton disturbances arose from a complex social, political and economic situation that was not special to Brixton, but which exists in many of our inner cities. The core of the problem is this: a decaying urban structure, with its attendant evils of bad-quality and inadequate housing, and a lack of job opportunities, with its inevitable evil of high unemployment. These depressing conditions coexist with the crucial social fact that these areas have a high proportion of ethnic minority groups – blacks and Asians. And these groups believe and feel, with considerable justification, that it is the colour of their skin, and their first or second generation immigrant origins, which count against them in their bid for a fair share in our society. We cannot avoid facing this important racial dimension.

It is certainly possible that if there was full employment, the racial aspect of our inner city problems would not loom large. But once you have deprivation, and once minorities perceive that they are at the end of every queue, then race heats up the furnace of anger to an unbearable temperature. When you have, as we now have in our inner cities, the problems associated with unemployment and its psychological frustrations – idleness, and so on – with the added factor of what is seen to be race prejudice, then the whole social situation becomes that much more bitter, the underlying tension is that much greater, tempers fly more easily.

Source: 'Injustice in the Cities', Lord Scarman, *New Society*, 14 February 1986, p286

a What does Lord Scarman mean by 'decaying urban structure'?

b Why do many inner cities have a higher proportion of members of ethnic minorities?

c If the inner cities became even poorer compared with the rest of Britain, what are the possible consequences?

Activity 10 Living in a Tower Block

During the 1950s and 1960s many city local authorities built high-rise blocks of flats to replace old terraced housing.

a Outline the advantages and disadvantages of living in high-rise flats like the ones in the photograph.

b Such high-rise flats have proved generally unpopular with their residents. What implications does this have for future housing policy?

However, for many people the city *is* an attractive place in which to live. It is nearer work for those who work in the commercial and financial centres such as the City of London, and it does provide unrivalled leisure facilities with its theatres, cinemas, restaurants, concert halls, museums and art galleries. At the same time as some inner city areas have physically decayed, other areas, often only a few hundred yards away, have seen property prices boom as middle-class, mainly young, people have moved in. This process of *gentrification* can be seen, for example, in London's Dockland.

Activity 11

Are any localities in your nearest large town or city under-going a process of gentrification? If so, what are the economic, social and political consequences likely to be?

Activity 12 Rural and Urban Ways of Life

a It is often argued that there are two distinct ways of life, rural and urban. Rural areas, some writers argue, are more close-knit, more personal, more restricting and provide more of a sense of community and belonging. Urban areas, on the other hand, are said to be anonymous, impersonal, unfriendly and allow far more choice of behaviour.
Using your sociological understanding and knowledge, examine the argument that the urban way of life is different from the rural.
b Explain why the terms *urban* and *rural* are of very limited value in any discussion of British society.

Questions and Suggested Projects

Review Questions

1 Define the following terms:
   a birth rate
   b death rate
   c urbanisation.
2 *From memory*, draw two graphs illustrating – in very broad terms – how the birth and death rates have changed in Britain in the last hundred years.
3 Explain why people migrate, both externally and internally.
4 How do governments find out population trends? Why is it important that information about population is easily available?
5 Explain why there has been a move away from cities in recent years.

Theme-linking Questions

1 Examine the relationship between the decline in the birth rate and changing roles within the family.
2 To what extent are changes in birth, death and migration rates and patterns the result of economic changes?
3 Why is there still a close relationship between social class and life expectancy?
4 Examine the extent to which the problems of the inner city are caused by firstly, economic factors, and secondly, ethnic relations.
5 Examine the different leisure patterns characteristic of urban and rural areas.

Stimulus–response Question

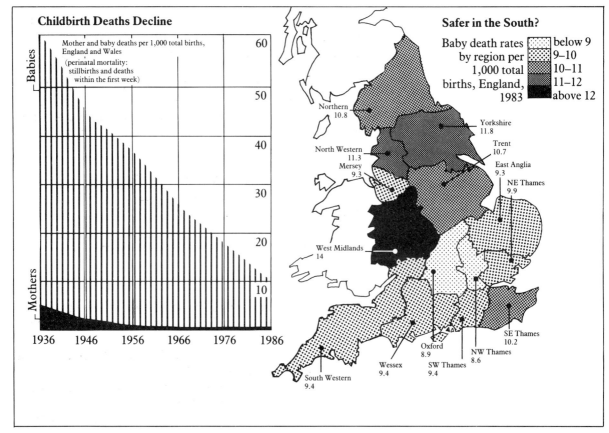

Childbirth Deaths Decline

Mother and baby deaths per 1,000 total births, England and Wales
(perinatal mortality: stillbirths and deaths within the first week)

Safer in the South?

Baby death rates by region per 1,000 total births, England, 1983

below 9
9–10
10–11
11–12
above 12

Northern 10.8
Yorkshire 11.8
North Western 11.3
Trent 10.7
Mersey 9.3
East Anglia 9.3
NE Thames 9.9
West Midlands 14
SE Thames 10.2
Oxford 8.9
NW Thames 8.6
Wessex 9.4
SW Thames 9.4
South Western 9.4

Source: Tony Garrett, *New Society*, 1 August 1986

a What proportion of mothers died during childbirth in 1946? (1)

b Complete the following sentence: 'In 1936 . . . out of 1000 births were stillborn or died within the first week; in 1986 the figure was . . .' (2)

c Which region of Britain had the highest baby death rate in 1986? (1)

d Explain why the differences in baby death rates in the various regions of Britain may actually be largely explained by social class. (3)

e Give four reasons why the infant mortality rate has declined. (4)

f Explain how the infant mortality rate could perhaps be reduced yet further. (4)

g Outline the main reasons why infant mortality rates are much higher in Third World countries than in Britain. (5)

Essays

1 Explain why the birth rate in Britain today is lower than it was 100 years ago.
2 **a** Describe the research methods used to obtain demographic data.
  b Why is it useful for governments to be able to predict future population trends. Give examples to illustrate your answer.
3 Outline and explain recent geographical trends in the distribution of Britain's population. Your answer could include:
  population growth in the south
  the move from the cities
  decline of traditional heavy industry
  growth of high-technology industries
  importance of transport facilities
  the inner cities
  gentrification.

Suggested Projects

1 A study, based on secondary statistics, of recent demographic changes in your locality, and their social and economic consequences.
2 An interview-based study of what the inhabitants of a local tower block think of living there.
3 A study of the value of neighbours and the degree of community identification in two contrasting areas.
4 A methodological study, reusing Census questions on a sample of people, followed by an in-depth interview, to assess the accuracy of people's Census answers.
5 A comparative study, based on secondary data, of the population policies of two contrasting governments.

11 Families

Introduction

This chapter looks at the ways in which families have changed, why most people live in family units, and the types of family that exist in Britain today. Note that the chapter is titled 'Families', rather than 'The Family'; there is no such thing as *the* British family, but instead there is a wide variety of different types.

The importance of families can easily be seen by looking at many other areas of social life; see, for example, the family as an agent of social control (pages 23–24), its role in gender socialisation (pp.85–86), educational achievement (pp.221–224) and child-childhood (pages 110–114).

Apart from the enormous variation in family types, there are two other main reasons why families are particularly difficult for sociologists to study. Firstly, there is a tendency to assume that the types of family that exist in one's own society are natural and desirable. Secondly, families are very private and emotional institutions; doing sociological research in families is therefore fraught with problems.

Activity 1

a Re-read the section on sociological methods (pages 52–60).
b Imagine you have been asked to carry out research into family life in your neighbourhood; what would be the advantages and disadvantages of basing your research on:
    1 questionnaires
    2 unstructured interviews
    3 participant observation?

The Nature and Variety of Families

The family is frequently seen as an inevitable part of society, and as such a desirable framework in which individuals should live.

Extract 1 *The Family: Biology and Culture*

In the following extract Mary Farmer outlines the similarities and differences between the families of humans and those of other species.

For many of us the family constitutes our first experience of social life, and for many also it is the most enduring and permanent social group. It has been maintained by some that the family is essentially a biological unit, centred on the function of reproduction and geared to perpetuating the species. Others have held that its nature is cultural and social, that it *derives* from *society*. Those favouring the biological view argue that the family, regarded as a cohesive group consisting of two parents and their offspring, is not peculiar to man, but is to be found also among a variety of mammals and birds. They maintain that the family is a 'natural' association arising out of the need to care for the young while they are dependent; for human children are produced rather infrequently and in small numbers compared with those of other species and are helpless for a long period, so that continuous care is necessary if enough are to survive to perpetuate the human species. All this may indeed be so, but the human family is peculiar in that it is reinforced by institutions that are indubitably social, and it is the existence of these social institutions, with their embodiment of cultural norms, together with certain cognitive attributes of its members, which principally distinguish the human family from the so-called families of other species.

Source: *The Family*, Mary Farmer, Longman, 1970, p9

GLOSSARY

indubitably without doubt
embodiment expression and putting together
cognitive perceiving and learning

KEY TERMS

nuclear family a family of two generations, parents and children, living together.
extended family a family of more than two generations (i.e. grandparents and/or grandchildren) and/or relatives other than the immediate nuclear family, e.g. aunts and uncles, cousins.

a According to those who argue that the family is essentially a biological unit, what is its main function?
b Summarise, using your own words, the argument that the family is a necessary biological unit.
c Which institutions reinforce and support families?
d Explain the main differences between the families of humans and those of other species.

Activity 2

a Read the following two statements:
   Lyn: 'I'm going to spend a quiet evening at home watching TV with my family.'
   Ken: I'm going to a funeral on Wednesday; weddings and funerals are the only occasions when I see all my family.'
b Explain what Lyn and Ken each mean by the term 'family'.
c What does your answer to b tell you about the term 'family'?

The term 'family' clearly has several different meanings, and sociologists usually distinguish two basic types: nuclear and extended.

However, this division of the family into two types raises almost as many problems as it solves. For example, is a family extended if its members live in separate nuclear households, but spend most of their leisure time together? Further, many middle-aged couples with children have an elderly parent living with them; does this make the family extended? There are, of course, no right answers to such questions, and it is probably most useful to say that some societies emphasise the importance of the nuclear and others the extended family, rather than drawing a sharp distinction between them.

The extended family in modern Britain is best understood as consisting of those close relatives who do not belong to the nuclear family, but we also have a much wider network of relatives – people we may only see at marriages and funerals, if at all, though we may keep regular contact through Christmas and birthday cards.

KEY TERM

kinship system all the people one is related to through blood, marriage and adoption.

Activity 3

a What can be reasonably expected from the different members of one's kinship system varies dramatically between societies, and these expectations also change over time. There are, further, wide variations within society, from family to family, but explain what you think most people in Britain today expect (e.g. financial help, care when sick) from their:
  1 parents
  2 children
  3 grandparents
  4 aunts and uncles
  5 cousins
  6 second cousins.
b At what point in one's kinship system is there a high degree of choice over the nature of the relationship?
c What conclusions can you draw from your answers to the above questions about kinship in Britain today?

Family structure depends to a very great extent on marriage, a relationship which is surrounded by rules. Three such rules are particularly important.

1 How many people one can marry

It is too easy to assume that it is natural for one man and one woman to marry; there are a variety of different patterns throughout the world.

KEY TERMS

monogamy marriage between one woman and one man.
polygamy marriage of one person to two or more of the opposite sex. There are therefore two types of polygamy: polygyny and polyandry.
polygyny marriage between one man and two or more wives, e.g. some Islamic societies.
polyandry marriage between one woman and two or more husbands, e.g. some parts of the Himalayas.

KEY TERM

serial monogamy marriage to more than one person, but only one at any one time.

KEY TERM

endogamous rules require marriage within a particular group.

KEY TERM

exogamous rules prohibit marriage within a particular group.

Even in societies which allow polygamy, simple arithmetic means that the majority of marriages are likely to be monogamous. In polygynous societies, usually only the wealthier men will have more than one wife. On the other hand, polyandry serves to keep the birth rate low and enables more than one man (often brothers) to support one woman and her children; it is therefore usually found among the poorer members of poor societies.

Although it is usual for industrialised societies to practice monogamy, this does not necessarily mean that people have to stay married to the same partner all their lives.

These rules, it must be remembered, refer only to marriage; for example, although marriage to more than one person at once is illegal in Britain, there is nothing in law preventing anyone living with as many people, of whatever sex, as they wish.

2 *Whom one can marry*

All societies restrict whom one can marry, even Britain where there are relatively few legal restrictions. There are two types of rule which restrict marriage partner: endogamous and exogamous rules.

Young people, for example, may be compelled to marry within a particular social class or religious community. The penalites for marrying out of the group could vary from expulsion to minor disapproval. Although for most people in Britain there is, in theory, freedom of choice, in practice most people marry someone from a similar background.

Activity 4

Carry out a survey in your sociology class to find out:
a how many pupils/students hope to marry
b what type of person they expect to marry
c what type of person their parents would disapprove of as a marriage partner.
(If you are an adult student you will need to amend the questions.) What conclusions can you draw from your survey about marriage in Britain today?

The most important exogamous rule is the incest taboo which prohibits marriage (and usually sexual relationships also) between certain close relatives.

Activity 5

a Find out from your library which relatives you are not allowed to marry.

b What biological reasons are often given for the incest taboo?

c How might a sociologist explain the incest taboo? (It will help you answer this question if you imagine what the consequences of incestuous relationships are likely to be.)

KEY TERMS

matrilocal societies married couples live with or near the wife's parents.
patrilocal societies married couples live with or near the husband's parents.
neolocal societies married couples set up their own independent home, away from both sets of parents.

3 *Where married couples live*

Where a married couple set up home has profound implications for their relationships with their wider kin, and it is likely to affect the very quality of marriage itself.

Activity 6

Using the key terms given so far in this chapter, outline the rules surrounding marriage in Britain today.

Extract 2 Ghost Marriage among the Nuer of the Sudan

The wide variety of family and marriage types can be clearly illustrated by the ghost marriage of the Nuer. In Britain, a child's biological father, the genitor, is usually, though not always, also the child's social father, the pater, i.e. the man responsible for the child's upbringing.

Among the Nuer, if a man dies before he has had a chance to marry and beget sons, it is a responsibility of a younger brother of the deceased to 'marry a wife to the dead man', or, as we should put it, to marry a wife in his name and on his behalf. The woman whom the surviving brother espouses in terms of this institution is not *his* wife. She is the wife of the deceased elder brother to whom she is 'married', a person whom she may never even have seen. And her children by her living spouse are not his children, but the children of their dead pater. Nuer would consider it improper for the younger brother of a man who had died unmarried to take a wife for himself before he had discharged this obligation to his elder sibling.

Source: *Other Cultures*, John Beattie, Routledge and Kegan Paul, 1966, p120

a Explain the difference between biological and social parenthood.

b What functions do you think the Nuer ghost marriage performs?

c Under what circumstances may biological and social fatherhood be different in Britain today?

GLOSSARY

espouse marry
sibling brother or sister

Families therefore vary dramatically; the relationships in them are also dynamic. In other words, every family changes over time, if only because of the ageing of its members and the birth of new ones.

Families in Britain; How they have Changed

Until recently, it was widely believed by historians and sociologists that pre-industrial Britain was characterised by extended families, and that with the need for greater social and geographical mobility brought about by industrialisation and urbanisation, these extended families were replaced by much smaller nuclear families.

But industrialisation and urbanisation are not total processes; they do not happen overnight and people who moved to the new towns of industrial Britain in the late eighteenth and early nineteenth centuries did not immediately change all their norms and values. Family life did change, but the changes must not be exaggerated. Recent historical research, for example, has found that in pre-industrial Britain, as today, most people lived in small households and few lived in large extended groupings.

Activity 7

It is impossible to fully understand the social structure of modern Britain and institutions such as the family without a broad and general grasp of the main social and economic changes of the last two hundred years. If you have studied social history you should have a mental picture of the chronology of these changes. To test whether you have such a picture, ask yourself: 'When and where was cotton manufacturing first developed?', and 'When were railways and motor vehicles first introduced?'. 'When was the National Health Service established?' 'When were the two world wars?'

If you do not know the answers to these questions, set yourself the task of learning the broad outlines of Britain's social and economic history of the last two hundred years. You could do this, for example, by:

a asking your teacher or librarian to recommend suitable books or other resources;

b asking students in your sociology class who have studied social history to give brief talks outlining the main social changes in British society.

If sociologists stress the variety of family types in Britain today, historians stress the variety of family types in the past. In particular, most people did not, and do not today, live in pure nuclear families.

Extract 3   *The Nuclear Family as a Minority Type*

There are several reasons why the nuclear family was a minority form in the nineteenth century and still is today, but those reasons have changed.

In the 19th century and indeed right up until the 1930's a common household form was one that included resident domestic servants – an arrangement that has subsequently almost totally disappeared. In the 1930's there were well over 1 million women residential domestic servants. Secondly a common household form in this period was one that included either apprentices or lodgers or boarders. In Camberwell in 1871 for example, 15% of the households contained lodgers. Thirdly, in the middle of the 18th century in Preston there was a 23% likelihood of households containing persons (for example grandparents) outside the nuclear core. Again this is much less likely today.

The reasons why the nuclear family is a minority form today are different. Firstly because of the number of elderly people living alone. In 1981 the proportion of people living alone was 8% – double the 1961 figures. Secondly because of the number of couples whose children have grown up and left home. Thirdly because of the number of one parent families. Between 1961 and 1981 this figure also doubled from 2½% to 5% (applies to single parents with dependent children in G.B.). However despite this recent rise it should be noted, in the longer view, that current levels are still only half of those recorded in the 1851 Census.

Source: 'The Family: Demographic Trends', John Hood–Williams, *Social Science Teacher*, Vol. 14, No. 2, 1985, p44

a What proportion of families with dependent children in 1851 were headed by a single parent?

b Why were grandparents more likely to live with their children in the past than today?

c Complete the following sentence: 'If d . . . and desertion were the main causes of single-parent families in the nineteenth century, the main cause today is d . . .'

d Why are there so few domestic servants today compared with the nineteenth and early twentieth centuries?

Perhaps the most striking change in the structure of families has been the decline in the average number of children per family. (See pages 173–174 for the reasons for this decline.) Two-thirds of married women in the 1870s had five or more children, while today the two-child family is the most common. This decline in family size has had a profound effect on family life, especially perhaps in terms of the amount of care, emotional as well as financial, which can now be given to children by their parents, and it has also been one of the many factors enabling a much greater proportion of married women to work.

If it is dangerous to generalise about the way the structure of families has changed, so different families in the past, as today, performed very different functions for their members. In agricultural societies, however, families typically perform functions that are today carried out by larger, impersonal organisations such as indsutrial companies and the National Health Service. In particular, in rural societies the family is usually the basis of economic organisation; all members of the family, whatever age or sex, can play a useful part in the production and collection of food, and the production of such things as cloth and tools is usually carried out by family units. In industrial societies, on the other hand, the family rarely acts as a unit of production – most people are individually employed outside the home – but the family does still have an important economic function as an agency of consumption.

Activity 8

a Make two lists of items your household consumes, firstly as a family, and secondly as individuals.
b Interview older members of your family to find out what goods used to be bought and owned by families together, but are now bought and owned by individuals.

For most people, the family is still the primary caring agency; when its members are sick, disabled or old it is the family which usually provides the necessary support. Only when families cannot cope (for example, with serious illness) or someone has no immediate family do the welfare services usually step in. What has probably changed is that fewer people today turn to members of their family for financial support when they are sick, unemployed or old. Many people in the past, of course, had no relatives affluent enough to help them in times of financial crisis, but today social security benefits are available to most people.

Talcott Parsons (1902–1979), an American sociologist who emphasised the positive and beneficial side of family life, claimed that the family has two basic functions:
a the primary socialisation of children;
b the stabilisation of the personalities of adult members of the family.

Many critics of the family have claimed that it frequently does not perform either function particularly well! Although the family is still a key agency of socialisation, especially primary, it is now faced with often competing influences such as education, the mass media and peer groups, and this makes conflict between parents and children more likely. The second of Parson's functions refers to the provision of affection and emotional support. Young people are exhorted to marry for love, and sex and companionship in marriage are stressed. Suffice it to say here that families vary from those which offer lifelong emotional support and love to those where wife- and child-battering are considered normal, everyday behaviour.

Families in Britain Today

Activity 9

a Write down the types of family (e.g. single-parent with two children, married couple) in the six houses or flats nearest your home.
b Compare your answers with your fellow students; what conclusions can you draw from your answers?
(If you do not know who lives in the six nearest houses or flats, what conclusions can you draw from your lack of knowledge?)

Even though there is a wide variety of family types at any one time, it is important to remember that over time a very high proportion of people will go through certain common stages.

Extract 4 *The Family Life Cycle*

A simplified family life cycle might involve the following stages:

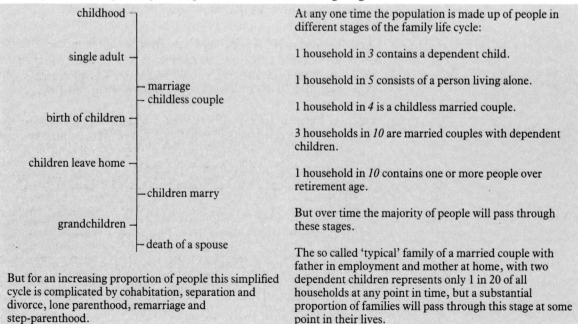

childhood
single adult
— marriage
— childless couple
birth of children
children leave home
— children marry
grandchildren
— death of a spouse

But for an increasing proportion of people this simplified cycle is complicated by cohabitation, separation and divorce, lone parenthood, remarriage and step-parenthood.

At any one time the population is made up of people in different stages of the family life cycle:

1 household in *3* contains a dependent child.

1 household in *5* consists of a person living alone.

1 household in *4* is a childless married couple.

3 households in *10* are married couples with dependent children.

1 household in *10* contains one or more people over retirement age.

But over time the majority of people will pass through these stages.

The so called 'typical' family of a married couple with father in employment and mother at home, with two dependent children represents only 1 in 20 of all households at any point in time, but a substantial proportion of families will pass through this stage at some point in their lives.

Source: *The Family Today Fact Sheet 1*, Family Policy Studies Centre, 1985, p3

a According to the above diagram, what three stages are likely to come between childbirth and the birth of one's own children?
b Explain what is meant by the term 'dependent children'.
c Why must the above diagram be interpreted carefully?

Extract 5 Changing Views on the Family

If there were many different types of family in the past, a commonly held belief used to be that the most desirable type of family involved lifelong marriage to one partner and children. But Robert and Rhona Rapoport conclude their study of British families today by stating:

> . . . families in Britain today are in a transition from coping in a society in which there was a single overriding norm of what family life should be like to a society in which a plurality of norms are recognised as legitimate and, indeed, desirable.

Source: *Families in Britain*, ed. by R. N. Rapoport, M. P. Fogarty and R. Rapoport, Routledge and Kegan Paul, 1982, p476

a Explain the meaning of 'a plurality of norms are recognised as legitimate'.
b What are the arguments for and against the view expressed in the above extract?

Extract 6 Families by Type

The breakdown of the nuclear family of two parents and children should not be exaggerated. Over three-quarters of children under 16 live with their married natural parents. The diagram below shows those families with children in 1985.

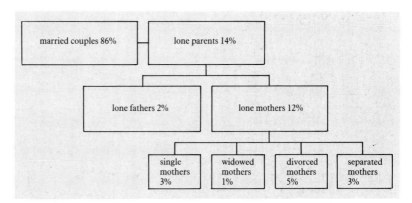

Source: adapted from *The Family Today Fact Sheet 1*, Family Policy Studies Centre, 1985, p5; and *OPCS Monitor GHS 86/1*, September 1986

a What proportion of families with children were headed by lone fathers?

b What is the commonest cause of lone motherhood?

c Explain why there are many more lone mothers looking after children than lone fathers.

Approximately a quarter of the people getting married in 1986 had been married before, and over one in eight marriages were between a divorced woman and a divorced man. With the rise in divorce rates more children are growing up with one natural parent and one step-parent. For example, in 1983 7% of children under 18 lived with their natural mother and stepfather. Many of these second marriages, of course, produce children, who will live alongside the children of the husband and wife's first marriages.

Reconstituted families may well face practical problems and difficulties with relationships. Practical problems may include housing and issues of maintenance of and access to children. In terms of relationships, there are relatively clear and widely understood norms on how, for example, parents should behave towards children, and sisters towards brothers. The norms governing behaviour between, for example, step-parents and step-children, and step-siblings, are, on the other hand, far from clear and this uncertainty may well give rise to tension and conflict within the family.

It is sometimes argued that couples are increasingly cohabiting rather than living together. However, the 1982 General Household Survey found little evidence that cohabitation is replacing marriage; only one in 25 women aged 18–49 was cohabiting. What has changed is that living together before marriage is much more common; in the early 1980s about one-third of women under 35 lived with their future husband before marriage, and the figure rose to two-thirds where one or both partners had been divorced.

Activity 10

Carry out a brief survey among young, unmarried people to find out their attitudes towards cohabitation before marriage. Then ask retired people their views on the same subject. Does your survey suggest there are changing attitudes towards cohabitation?

Nuclear, single-parent and reconstituted families, as well as the growing number of people living alone, do not, of course, usually live totally separately from the members of their extended families. Studies, especially of traditional working-class communities, have shown that members of the extended family frequently give each other mutual practical support (e.g. financial help, baby-sitting, shopping) as well as providing close personal relationships. Research carried out by Peter Willmott and Michael Young in Bethnal Green in the 1950s (*Family and Kinship in East London*, 1957) found that in this traditional working-class community the key figures were the older women who maintained close contact with their married daughters. But many of the younger couples and their children moved away to a new council estate. Although contact with kin was maintained through regular visits, the members of the extended family could no longer provide each other with day-to-day practical support, and the nuclear unit correspondingly gained in importance.

Although most people in Britain maintain links with at least some members of their extended family, the precise nature of the relationships they form depends partly on choice and partly on geographical proximity.

Extract 7 *Asian Families in Britain*

Source: 'Conflict, Continuity and Change, Second-generation South Asians', Catherine Ballard, in *Minority Families in Britain*, ed. by Verity Saifullah Khan, Macmillan, 1979, pp111, 112, 114, 128

The families of ethnic minorities in Britain provide further evidence that we cannot talk of *the* British family. The differences between family life in Bangladesh, India, Pakistan and Britain are described in the extract below, but, as Catherine Ballard points out, the problems these differences cause should not be exaggerated.

Most second-generation Asians in Britain are being brought up by parents whose own upbringing was in rural India, Pakistan and Bangladesh. In the sub-continent households are often large and several adults share the responsibility for making decisions affecting the family, for running the household and family economy and for caring for the children. Within the village each household is part of a tightly knit community of close kinsmen. Social change is slow in rural areas and, at least until recently, there has been no expectation of the need for significant differences in behaviour from one generation to the next. The experience of adults is directly relevant to their children. Boys are trained to run the family farm or to practise their hereditary craft and girls learn the domestic skills expected of a good wife and mother. They learn through gradually increasing participation in the work of the household and by their early teens they play a significant part in the domestic economy. The toys which they play with in childhood are miniatures of the tools and utensils which adults use or natural materials available in the village and the surrounding fields. For most children education is the acquisition through very formal teaching of basic skills in reading, writing and arithmetic. Relationships within the family are affectionate but hierarchical; great emphasis is placed on respect for elders, on restraint in relations between the sexes and on maintaining the honour and good name of the family.

Asian households in Britain may often be smaller than those in the villages of the sub-continent, because very often only a section of the family has settled in Britain. As time passes however, and as some grow up, marry and have children of their own, the household begins to increase in size. Many families make great efforts to remain together, but the small size of most British houses often makes it necessary to establish several residential and domestic units, although the ties between them may remain very close. It is still common for young couples to spend the first few years of their married life living with the boy's parents, and invariably one son and his wife and children will continue to live with them, even if others move out. It is extremely rare to find elderly people living on their own. Households where two brothers and their families live together are also by no means unusual. Chain migration, where early settlers called relatives to join them, has ensured that almost every family has an extensive network of kinsmen living in Britain.

English family life is puzzling and threatening to many Asian parents. It seems insecure and cold and there appear to be little respect for the older generation. Marriages break up, old people go into homes and children into care for what seem to be the flimsiest of reasons, and sexual licence is visible everywhere. Such behaviour is inhumane and outrageous by Asian standards.

The second generation participate in the British educational system and they are exposed to the values of their British peers. A gulf between them and their parents is inevitable, but it is usually neither so wide nor so clear-cut as outsiders may assume. Intense socialisation in the family and the community means that most young Asians value the supportiveness, economic co-operation and clear morality which their families provide. They generally treat the elders of the family with respect and recognise that maintaining the family's good name is in the interests of all its members. They may disagree very strongly with their parents over specific issues and may envy the freedom and independence of British teenagers, but many young Asians feel strongly that too much freedom leads to confusion and unhappiness. They are critical of the casualness of British attitudes to family responsibility and educational success and believe that obligations should be taken seriously:

I have to behave differently at home than I do at college, like I can't dress in really fashionable clothes and of course I can't smoke. But I don't want to because I'm proud of my family and being Indian, and I don't want to give that up. I don't mind taking orders from my brother, in fact it's right that I should. He's paying for my education and he trusts me to do well for the sake of the family.
(*Dentistry student*)

The notion that young Asians are likely to 'suffer from culture conflict' is a gross oversimplification of a wide range of complex personal experiences. It assumes a straightforward clash, a tug-of-war, between East and West, traditional and modern, rural and urban, repression and freedom, resulting in an unbridgeable gulf between the generations. In reality, young Asians are not faced with an either/or situation. They have difficult dilemmas to resolve and in resolving them they work towards their own synthesis of Asian and British values.

GLOSSARY

hierarchical some ranked above
others
synthesis combination

a Explain why the experiences of adults in Asian villages are of
direct relevance to children.
b Why are Asian households in Britain likely to be different to
those in Asia?
c Why does a 'gulf' frequently emerge between Asian parents in
Britain and their children?
d Explain why it is misleading to exaggerate this gulf or 'culture
conflict'.

Marriage

Marriage is the central relationship in most families. Nine out of
ten people marry at some point in their lives. Compared with the
nineteenth century the average age at marriage has fallen,
although it has been increasing in recent years. The average age
at marriage for spinsters in 1986 was 24.1, for bachelors 26.3
(*OPCS Monitor FN2 87/1*).

Activity 11

a Explain why the average age at marriage has increased
over recent years.
b Explain why, on average, women get married younger
than men.

KEY TERM

conjugal roles roles, within
marriage, of husband and wife.

Sociologists, however, are not just interested in how many
people marry, and at what age; the actual nature of relationships
between husbands and wives has been an important topic of
research in recent years.

Some sociologists have argued that modern marriage has become
more egalitarian, with husband and wife sharing responsibilities
today in a way that was unheard of in Victorian Britain. Other
sociologists, however, have claimed that there is still a great deal
of inequality in many marriages.

KEY TERMS

joint conjugal roles husband and wife share domestic responsibilities and leisure activities.
segregated conjugal roles husband and wife have different domestic responsibilities, with the husband taking little part in bringing up children; leisure activities are also likely to be separate.

Activity 12

Real marriages, of course, are not totally segregated or totally joint, but they do differ significantly in terms of how equal they are.
a Classify the marriages of people you know well according to how joint or segregated you think they are.
b Explain the basis on which you made your classification.
c Do you think the terms 'segregated' and 'joint conjugal roles' can help us understand actual marriages?

Relationships between husbands and wives have been affected by a wide variety of social and economic factors, including:
a Increased life expectancy and the decline in average family size. These two factors have resulted in most married couples having a long period together after their last child has left home; this may cause problems of personal adjustment for couples who have seen their marriage mainly in terms of bringing up their children.
b Increased geographical and social mobility. These have served to separate many married couples from their other relatives.
c The increase in the proportion of married women who work. Many married women work part-time and it is still rare for a father to give up his job to look after young children, but clearly the power of a wife within marriage may well increase if she is, even partially, economically independent.
d Most homes are much more pleasant and comfortable places than they used to be. Further, the home itself now provides many leisure facilities, of which television is, in terms of hours spent, by far the most important.

In a frequently quoted study, *The Symmetrical Family*, (Penguin, 1973), Michael Young and Peter Willmott suggest, on the basis of their survey findings, that the family is becoming increasingly symmetrical. According to Young and Willmott, the main characteristics of this new type of family are:
a equality of husband and wife in marriage;
b the nuclear family has grown in importance at the expense of the extended;
c the nuclear family has become more home-centred and privatised.
But the research methods of Young and Willmott were highly suspect; their research was based on a questionnaire of 113 questions, and it is extremely difficult, if not impossible, to find out how people perform intimate family roles by this (or any other!) method (see page 56).

Extract 8 Equality in Marriage

Ann Oakley's study of women's attitudes to housework, *The Sociology of Housework*, comes to very different conclusions. Oakley found patterns of husbands' participation in domestic chores differentiated by class; middle-class husbands were more likely to participate than working-class husbands, and this, at least, ties in with Young and Willmott's finding that middle-class marriages are more likely to be symmetrical. Interestingly, the working-class wives in Oakley's survey expressed much less dissatisfaction with the housewife role than middle-class wives did. But, most fundamentally, Oakley points out that discussions of equality in marriage frequently beg the question of what is meant by equality.

In only a small number of marriages is the husband notably domesticated, and even where this happens, a fundamental separation remains: home and children are the woman's primary responsibility. Doubt is cast on the view that marriage is an egalitarian relationship. The important question is: what is meant by equality? Psychological intimacy between husband and wife, an intermingling of their social worlds, and a more equitable distribution of power in marriage are undoubtedly areas in which marriage in general has changed. But the importance of women's enduring role as housewives and as the main rearers of children continues. Inequality in this area is often overlooked, and sociologists surveying marriage are no exception to the general rule. They bring to their data their own values about the place of men and women in the home, values which repeat the popular theme of gender differences.

GLOSSARY

equitable fair

Source: *The Sociology of Housework*, Ann Oakley, Martin Robertson, 1974, pp164–165

a What does Oakley mean by:
  1 'psychological intimacy'
  2 'intermingling of their social worlds'?
b Explain how sociologists 'bring to their own data their own values' and how this influences their views on equality in marriage.
c In what ways does Oakley suggest marriages are not equal?

Activity 13

Write one paragraph supporting, and one opposing, the view that marriages in Britain today are egalitarian. What sociological conclusions can you draw from your two paragraphs?

Divorce

England and Wales has one of the highest divorce rates in Europe. Divorce statistics, however, must be interpreted very carefully as they refer only to marriages which have been legally terminated, not those where the partners have separated. In view of the difficulty and expense of obtaining a divorce until recently, it seems likely that more married couples in the past separated without legally ending their marriage through divorce.

Extract 9 *Divorce in England and Wales*

	Decrees made absolute
1906–10	3,118
1926–30	16,789
1946–50	199,507
1971	74,437
1972	119,025
1980	148,301
1984	144,501
1985	160,300
1986	153,903

Source: adapted from *Marriage and Divorce Statistics*, 1980, OPCS (in 'The Family: Demographic Trends', John Hoad-Williams, *Social Science Teacher*, Vol. 14, No. 1, p5), *OPCS Monitor FM2 86/2*, 1986, p.3, *OPCS Monitor FN2 87/2*, 1987, p3

a Approximately how many divorces were there each year between 1906 and 1910?
b When was there a massive increase in the number of divorces?
c Using the above statistics, produce a graph or diagram to illustrate how divorce has increased.

It is very dangerous to predict the future, as social and economic circumstances can change dramatically, but if present trends continue probably about one marriage in three will end in divorce.

'Their marriage is going through rather a sticky patch at the moment.'

So why has divorce increased? One obvious answer is that far more people are getting married, but there are other important legal, demographic, social and marital factors which have pushed the divorce rate up.

Legal Factors

Changes in the law to a great extent reflect changing social attitudes, but progressive easing of the divorce laws has certainly enabled many couples to legally terminate their marriage who in previous generations would have either just separated or lived unhappily until one partner died.

Before 1857 a special Act of Parliament was required for divorce; not surprisingly divorce was rare and only available to the rich. Between 1857 and 1937 divorce was usually only available on the grounds of adultery; until 1923 a husband could obtain a divorce on the grounds of his wife's adultery, but a wife had to prove cruelty in addition to adultery. In 1923 the law was made the same for both sexes. In 1937 desertion and prolonged insanity were added as grounds for divorce, and in 1949 legal aid was introduced for divorce, thus abolishing the financial barriers which had previously existed.

The most dramatic changes to the law on divorce came with the Divorce Law Reform Act of 1969 (which came into effect in 1971). This Act makes the 'irretrievable breakdown of marriage' the sole ground for divorce; if the marriage has broken down irretrievably, a divorce will be granted. Irretrievable breakdown can be proved in a variety of ways:
a adultery
b unreasonable behaviour
c two years separation, with both partners wanting a divorce
d five years separation, if only one partner wants a divorce
e two years desertion.

The law was eased further with the 1984 Matrimonial and Family Proceedings Act which allows husbands and wives to ask for a divorce after one year of marriage instead of the previous three.

Demographic factors

People have been marrying younger (until recently) and, more importantly, living longer than previous generations, thus increasing the likelihood of marriages ending in divorce rather than death.

Social factors

Several changes in society have tended to push the divorce rate up, two of which are perhaps particularly important. Firstly, the stigma attaching to divorce has all but disappeared; this is partly a *consequence* of the increasing number of divorces, but has made it yet easier for couples to divorce. Secondly, the improved economic position of women, especially the increase in the proportion of wives who work, has made it easier for them to obtain a divorce and live independently afterwards. It is interesting to note that in 1986, 72% of decrees made absolute were granted to women.

Marital factors

Paradoxically, it may be the very emphasis placed on marriage today which is responsible for the rise in the divorce rate. Love, affection and sexual satisfaction are fragile things, and if they can no longer be obtained within a marriage, husband and wife may think there is little point continuing with it.

It is not, of course, just husbands and wives who are affected by divorce:

Divorcing couples by number of children, 1986

	%
no children under 16	44
1 child under 16	24
2 children under 16	23
3 or more children under 16	9

adapted from *OPCS Monitor FM2 87/2*

The divorce rate cannot be used as evidence that marriage is a declining institution, for a high proportion of divorced people subsequently remarry. In 1986, for example, 307,806 people were divorced, while 163,365 divorced people remarried (*OPCS Monitors FM2 87/1* and *87/2*).

Activity 14

a Find out (for example, from *Social Trends*) divorce statistics for the years since 1986.
b Explain why a high rate of divorce does not necessarily prove marriage is unpopular.
c What are the possible consequences of divorce for:
   1 wives **2** husbands **3** children?

Alternatives to the Family

Families are rarely seen as neutral. Many people see the social problems of our time as caused by the decline of the family: high divorce rates, single parenthood, illegitimacy and extra-marital sex, it is argued, are the causes of juvenile delinquency, vandalism, pornography, AIDs and the rising crime rate. The solution, for people who argue along these lines, is to strengthen the family unit.

An opposing view claims that, far from being the solution to our problems, families are actually the cause of many of them. Critics of the family argue that it encourages people to become solely concerned with their own small group and not the wider society. As well as potentially making people selfish, some psychologists and psychiatrists also believe that the intense emotional relationships of the nuclear family are potentially very dangerous, and can all too easily lead to emotional disorders and illnesses such as schizophrenia.

The truth about families, of course, is that some are warm, caring and supportive while others are emotionally cold and produce children with severe personality disorders. Unfortunately, we know very little about how many families are in each category or, indeed, what factors make for 'good' or 'bad' families.

One problem is that of defining family, a term which is frequently confused with household.

KEY TERM

household the people who share a home.

For most people, the household consists of some, though not all, members of their family, but for a significant number of people family and household are not the same. People living alone or young people sharing a flat, for example, have families they do not live with. Further, many people live in non-family residential institutions such as children's homes, hospitals, monasteries and convents, barracks and prisons.

An aim of many of the critics of the family has been to establish voluntary households not based on family relationships. Such communes were introduced in the Soviet Union and China after their revolutions in 1917 and 1949 respectively, but they were short-lived. The best-known examples of communes are the kibbutzim (singular: kibbutz) of Israel.

KEY TERM

kibbutz a communal, usually agricultural, settlement in Israel.

The kibbutzim, lived in by less than 5% of the population of Israel, were introduced in order to break away from the hier-archical and patriarchal Jewish family. Kibbutzim vary a great deal, but generally they aim to protect children from all-powerful, emotionally possessive mothering. In the early days at least, children were brought up and slept communally, were looked after by special nurses in an impartial and impersonal way, and spent only an hour or two each evening with their parents. However, many kibbutzim now allow children to spend more time and sleep with their parents, and the nuclear unit generally has become more important in the day-to-day life of kibbutzim members.

In a controversial study, *The Children of the Dream* (Thames and Hudson, 1969), Bruno Bettelheim pointed to the advantages and disadvantages of the kibbutzim for the rearing of children. There appears to be little cruelty or neglect and most children grow up to be caring and stable adults. On the other hand, Bettelheim argues, there is little scope for individuality or creativity, and kibbutzim produce children who find deep, intimate personal relationships difficult.

While the Israeli kibbutzim have survived, communes in Britain are characterised by their temporary nature. In particular, few communes survive from one generation to the next. The key distinguishing features of communes are that all individuals share, and that children are seen as children of the group. Of more importance in Britain are collective households which consist of separate nuclear households sharing some facilities and activities.

Activity 15

What are the advantages and disadvantages of living in a:
a nuclear family
b commune
c collective household?

Questions and Suggested Projects

Review Questions

1 Explain why it is difficult to study families.
2 Explain the meaning of:
    a extended and nuclear families
    b monogamy and polygamy
    c reconstituted families
    d segregated and joint conjugal roles.
3 Why is it misleading to talk of *the* British family?
4 Outline the main changes in British families in the twentieth century.

Theme-linking Questions

1 Examine how families have been affected by changing attitudes towards childhood.
2 Explain how occupation may affect family life.
3 'The changing position of women in society is, in part, a cause, and in part, a consequence, of changes in the family.' Explain this statement, and examine its implications for how societies change.
4 Explain how the following terms can help us understand families:
    a culture
    b role
    c norm
    d socialisation.
5 What contribution do families make to the maintenance of social order?

Stimulus–response Question

Some Family Indicators in Europe	Ireland	United Kingdom	France	Belgium	Netherlands	Luxembourg	Denmark	West Germany	Italy	Greece
average age of woman at birth of first child	24.9	25.0	25.0	24.5	25.7	n/a	24.8	25.2	24.9	23.3
one parent families as a percentage of all families	5.6	11.9	10.2	9.8	10.7	13.3	12.0	9.1	9.4	n/a
illegitimate births per 100 live births	5.4	12.5	12.7	3.4	4.8	7.1	35.8	7.9	4.3	1.6

The figures are for 1981 or the latest year available except for females in employment where the figures are for 1982

Source: *The Family Today*, Family Policy Studies Centre 1985, p9

    a In which country in the above table is the average age of women at the birth of their first child highest? (1)
    b Out of every 100 births in Denmark, how many are outside marriage? (1)

c Which of the three indicators in the above table varies least? (1)

d Give three reasons why families might be headed by a lone parent. (3)

e Explain why illegitimacy rates tell us nothing about family type. (3)

f What personal and social factors influence when women have their first child. (5)

g Explain the effects of the decline in the birth rate in the last hundred years on family life. (6)

Essays

1 Describe and examine the success of alternatives to the family.

2 a What functions do families perform in Britain today?

   b Examine the arguments for and against the view that the family is declining in importance.

3 Examine the causes and consequences of the rise in the divorce rate in post-war Britain. Your answer could include:

   legal changes
   increased life expectancy
   changes in the meaning of marriage
   effects on children
   increase in lone parenthood
   remarriage.

Suggested Projects

1 A library study of family life in a different society.

2 A study of what your fellow students expect from marriage.

3 A study comparing the attitudes of different generations towards cohabitation or lone parenthood.

4 A study of the various voluntary agencies concerned with family life, e.g. Marriage Guidance Council, NSPCC.

5 A participant observation study of family life in a religious group, e.g. Mormons, Jehovah's Witnesses.

12 Education

Introduction

Apart from the family, you probably have more personal knowledge of education than any other topic in sociology. The sociological study of education should help you locate your own educational experiences in a wider social context.

This chapter is concerned with three major issues:
a how and why the educational system has changed
b which children succeed at school
c the importance of education for society.

For a discussion of the part schools and colleges play in maintaining social control, see pages 24–27.

Activity 1

a Ask your fellow students to complete the following sentence: 'The things I want to get from school or college are . . .'
b Ask your teachers to complete the following sentence: 'The things I want my students to obtain from their schooling are . . .
c Compare the answers of the students with those of the teachers. What does this comparison tell you about the nature of education?

Extract 1 Formal, Informal and Non-formal Education

Learning does not just take place in schools and colleges; indeed, we are learning, or being educated, all the time, and sociologists often distinguish between types of education.

Formal Education: The hierarchically structured, chronologically graded 'educational system', running from primary school through the university and including, in addition to general academic studies, a variety of specialised programmes and institutions for full-time technical and professional training.	*Informal Education:* the truly lifelong process whereby every individual acquires attitudes, values, skills and knowledge from daily experience and the educative influences and resources in his or her environment – from family and neighbours, from work and play, from the market place, the library and the mass media.	*Non-formal Education:* any organised educational activity outside the established formal system – whether operating separately or as an important feature of some broader activity – that is intended to serve identifiable learning clienteles and learning objectives.

Source: *New Paths to Learning for Rural Children and Youth*, P. H. Coombs *et al.*, International Council for Educational Development, 1973. Quoted in *Non-formal Education and Development*, Tim Simkins, Manchester Monographs, 1977, pp10–11

GLOSSARY

hierarchically structured organised into different grades.
chronologically graded based on age.

a Explain how the formal educational system is 'chronologically graded'.
b What alternative sociological term could be used for 'informal education'?
c Explain how a TV programme could be either formal or informal education.
d What opportunites for non-formal education are there in your community? What advantages might non-formal education have compared with formal?

Chapters 1 and 2 have examined informal education; this chapter will look at formal education, though it must always be borne in mind that we are likely to undergo considerable non-formal education in adult life. The effects of formal education depend to a very great extent on how it is organised; it is essential, therefore, to be aware of the main changes in the educational system.

Education in England and Wales: a Brief Historical Outline

Before the Second World War

Until the twentieth century it was rare for anyone to challenge the view that children should be educated in accordance with their social class and their sex. Children were to be educated to fit them for their position in life. The idea of equality of opportunity has dominated much recent change in education, but it was not always so.

Education was made compulsory in 1880; before then how much education a child received depended almost totally on the class of his or her parents. Many middle-class children went to the increasing number of independent schools; for working-class children there was a wide variety of educational provision – some went to church schools during the week, some went to Sunday schools only, some to 'schools' run by neighbours who could not even read or write themselves, and others received no formal education at all. Hardly any working-class children received an education above the most basic.

From 1880, even though education was compulsory – at first to 10 but raised to 14 by 1918 – middle-class and working-class children rarely attended the same schools. Most working-class children attended *elementary schools*, where they learned the 'three Rs' (reading, writing and arithmetic) and frequently little else apart from religion. The better off children attended fee-paying *secondary* or *grammar schools*, or even *independent schools*. A small number of elementary school children were able to transfer to the secondary school by passing the scholarship examination at the age of 11, but necessary expenditure on uniform, books and materials prevented many bright working-class children from poor homes from doing so. Secondary/grammar and independent schools were the route to the best jobs; their pupils studied classics and, increasingly, sciences, as well as those subjects taught in elementary schools.

Activity 2

a Interview a small number of people who went to school before the Second World War. Ask them:
   1 what type of school they went to
   2 what subjects they studied
   3 what the facilities (e.g. class size, equipment) were like
   4 what sorts of relationships they had with their teachers
   5 what types of jobs they were expected to enter
b What, on the basis of your interviews and your own experiences of the educational system, appear to be the main differences between schools before the Second World War and today?

The tripartite system

The pre-Second World War system of education clearly wasted the abilities of many working-class children whose parents could not afford to pay for a secondary education. The war itself acted as a catalyst for social change, and the educational system (apart from the private sector) was transformed by the Education Act of 1944 (often known as the 'Butler Act' after R. A. Butler, the Minister of Education at that time).

The basic principle of the 1944 Education Act was that all children should receive an education appropriate to their age, abilities and aptitudes. All children were to attend primary schools from five to 11, and, although the Act did not make it compulsory, nearly all local authorities decided to examine children at 10 or 11, and then allocate them to what was considered an appropriate type of secondary school.

KEY TERM

tripartite system the system of secondary education which existed in most areas after the 1944 Education Act, consisting of grammar, secondary technical and secondary modern schools.

The *grammar schools* were meant to take those children who were academically gifted, the *technical schools* those who were technically capable and the *secondary modern schools* those who possessed practical skills. The system rested on the belief that there were three different types of children; the 11+ examination would show which type of education would suit each child.

Activity 3

a The three types of schools were meant to have 'parity of esteem' (equal status). Explain why, in practice, grammar schools were seen as the highest status schools.
b Comment sociologically on the view that there are three different types of child and that a test at 10 or 11 can accurately assess a child's abilities and aptitudes.

Few local authorities built technical schools, and so, in practice, there was usually a bipartite rather than a tripartite system. But, above all, it was the aim of equality of opportunity which was not met; although all children in a local authority area took the same 11+ exam, working-class children seemed to have little, if any, more chance of attending a grammar school than before the 1944 Act.

The tripartite system was originally seen as providing, for the first time, equal opportunities for all children. But even many middle-class parents found their children going to secondary modern schools, and they, as well as an increasing number of teachers and politicians, began to question the whole basis of the tripartite system:
a the number of grammar school places varied widely from area to area; whether a child went to a grammar school therefore depended to a great extent on where his or her parents lived;
b especially during the 'bulge' in the number of 10–11 year-olds during the late 1950s, an increasing number of middle-class

parents found their children not being selected for grammar schools (where places were always limited);

c many children selected for grammar schools at 11 later did not succeed; conversely, many children selected for secondary modern schools did well. This cast doubt on the whole validity of deciding a child's educational future at the age of 10 or 11;

d the majority of children, about 70%, attended secondary modern schools, the schools for 'failures'. There were thus many dissatisfied parents!

The consequence of this growing dissatisfaction with the tripartite system – based above all on the belief that, like the pre-war system, it was unfair and wasted much of the country's potential talent – was the growing pressure for a system of secondary schooling not based on selection.

Comprehensive schools

Although there are still grammar schools in some parts of England and Wales, over 90% of secondary school children in the state system now attend *comprehensive schools*.

There had been a very small number of comprehensive schools from the late 1940s, but it was in the 1970s that most local education authorities changed their systems of secondary education from tripartite to comprehensive. However, it can be argued that many comprehensive schools do not take children of all abilities:

a some comprehensive schools co-exist with grammar schools which 'cream off' the 'most able' pupils;

b the Assisted Places Scheme, introduced in 1981, provides a scholarship (based on parental income) to enable 'able' children to attend private schools;

c many physically and mentally disabled children attend special schools.

Activity 4

Whether mentally disabled children should attend comprehensive or special schools is currently a controversial issue.

a List the advantages and disadvantages of educating mentally disabled children in comprehensive schools alongside other children.

b Which argument do you think is the stronger. On what basis did you make up your mind?

---

d most comprehensive schools are neighbourhood schools, i.e. they take children from one particular locality. Because housing tends to be socially segregated (e.g. working-class council estates, middle-class commuter villages), comprehensive schools are likely to take children of one particular social class or even, in some areas, one particular ethnic group.

Not all comprehensive systems, of course, are the same. Some put all 11–18 year-olds together in the same school, some have two separate schools, one for 11–14 year olds, and another for older children. Increasingly common, however, are systems where children attend a comprehensive school from 11 or 12 to 16, and those who wish to continue their education transfer to a college which specialises in education for 16–19 year-olds.

Activity 5

If possible using your own personal experiences, assess the advantages and disadvantages of 16–19 year-olds being educated in colleges rather than schools.

Many schools, especially grammar schools, in the tripartite system had been single sex; most local authorities, as they changed to comprehensive schools, also changed to *co-educational* education (i.e. boys and girls attending the same schools).

Extract 2 Three Different Views on Comprehensive Schools

It is ideas, especially perhaps those of politicians and teachers, about the purpose of comprehensive schools which largely determine how they are organised and what is taught to whom. Stephen Ball here identifies three very different views.

1 *The meritocratic view* rests on the notion of 'equality of opportunity'. The idea is that everyone should start with an equal chance to succeed. Much the same thinking originally lay behind the tripartite system, but here it is associated with everyone going to the same school. Once inside the school the most academically able will be identified over time and be provided with the most appropriate courses to exploit and suit their talents. The survival of the cleverest. Other pupils will be catered for according to their talents to ensure that everyone has the opportunity to realise their full potential, but it is taken for granted that differences, not to say inequalities, will emerge over time. Such schools would typically be streamed or set, and offer a differentiated curriculum, but primarily they are concerned with the pursuit of academic goals. Little account is taken here of social inequalities that may arise from class or cultural differences originating from outside the school.

2 *The integrative view* assumes that by providing one school for all, with social classes mixed together, greater tolerance and social harmony will result and class tensions will abate. It is not necessarily assumed that social classes will disappear but rather that they will be more tolerant of one another. Here the goals for the comprehensive school are primarily social rather than academic, schooling is to be employed as a form of social engineering, to change society.

3 *The egalitarian view* is the most radical and pays greatest attention to changes in the process of schooling. What is stressed here is equality of outcome rather than equality of opportunity. Streaming would be abolished, a common curriculum established, and the barriers between school and the outside world reduced. Pupils would be treated as of equal worth, with greatest resources devoted to those who find school most difficult.

Source: *Education*, Stephen Ball, Longman, 1986, p24

a In what ways is the meritocratic view similar to the ideas which led to the establishment of the tripartite system?

b What assumptions about social class does the integrative view make?

c Explain the differences between *equality of opportunity* and *equality of outcome*.

d Outline the implications of each view for what happens in schools.

Changes in the curriculum

Until recent years, the public debate about education was mainly concerned with how it should be organised. Should there, for example, be comprehensive schools, and, if so, should they stream their pupils? Increasingly, however, politicians, teachers, parents and employers have become more concerned with the curriculum, i.e. what skills and knowledge children are taught and learn at school.

There are several elements in this concern with the curriculum – including a growing belief that many less able children were not receiving an appropriate eduction – but probably the major driving force behind curricular change has been the belief that education should be made more relevant for the world of work. Many of the new vocational educational initiatives have been financed not by the local education authorities or the Department of Education and Science, but by the Manpower Services Commission.

Activity 6 New Education and Training Initiatives

Among the new schemes/courses are:
a YTS
b TVEI
c CPVE.
Interview two or three students/trainees on each scheme or course, and produce a brief summary of the purpose and content of each.

Other important recent curricular changes include:
a the replacement of GCE O level and CSE examinations by a single examination, the GCSE;
b the introduction of Advanced Supplementary (AS) levels;
c the expansion of alternative courses to GCSE and A level. Many such courses, examined by the City and Guilds or BTEC, are assessed largely on coursework, and they are usually more vocationally oriented, usually including work experience.

Activity 7

Among new educational proposals in recent years have been
  city technical colleges
  a national core curriculum
  testing for all children at 7, 11 and 14
  the freedom for schools to withdraw from local
  authority control and to be funded directly by the
  Department of Education and Science.
Explain:
a how far these proposals have been implemented
b the arguments for and against each proposal.

Private schools

Approximately 6% of children do not attend state schools. There
are many different types of private school, but, somewhat con-
fusingly, the most prestigious (e.g. Eton, Winchester, Harrow),
usually boarding schools, are called *public schools*.

There is considerable political disagreement about private
schools. Many socialists would like to abolish them, arguing that
they give some children an unfair start in life, mainly through
smaller classes and better facilities, and that comprehensive
schools would benefit from having those middle-class children
currently being educated privately. On the other hand, supporters
of private schools would argue that parents should be able to
educate their children as they wish, and that to abolish them
would be an infringement of individual liberty.

Higher education

Since the Second World War, and especially since the mid-
1960s, there has been a big increase in the number and proportion
of young people receiving higher education, usually defined as
education to a post-A level standard. The proportion of young
people going on to university, polytechnic or college of higher
education is still, however, lower in Britain than most other
advanced industrial societies.

Activity 8 Primary Schools

Sociology textbooks frequently make no mention of primary schools, and generally primary education has not proved to be politically controversial.

a Why do you think politicians, teachers, parents and employers have shown more concern and anxiety about secondary than primary education?

b In what ways *have* primary schools changed in the last thirty years? (It might be useful to talk to people of different ages to find out how their primary schooling differed, or, ideally, a teacher who has taught for many years in primary schools.)

Educational Achievement

It is likely that you are reading this book because you want to pass an examination; it is equally likely you want to pass the examination not for its own sake but because you need the qualification for employment purposes. Success at school or college is therefore of profound importance for a student's employment prospects which will in turn affect such things as health, standard of living, housing as well as job satisfaction.

But educational success is not necessarily the same as passing examinations. Pupils, teachers and parents might well have other educational aims, such as gaining in confidence, learning how to cope with personal relationships and developing athletic skills. For a child in a special school, educational achievement might be being able to shop or travel on a bus alone.

However, examination pass rates are easy to measure and compare, and they are a key determinant of a pupil's future life, and so most sociologists studying educational achievement base their research on differential success rates.

Activity 9

One of the most widely taken examinations in Britain is the driving test.

a What are the key similarities and differences between the way your driving skills are learned and examined and the way your sociological skills are learned and examined?

b Why do most people pass the driving test, even if more than one attempt might be necessary?

Extract 3 *The Increase in the Number of the Qualified*

School Leavers – Highest Qualification: by Sex, 1976/77 and 1984/85

Great Britain	*Percentages and thousands*			
	Boys		*Girls*	
	1976/77	*1984/85*	*1976/77*	*1984/85*
Percentage with:				
2 or more 'A' levels/ 3 or				
more 'H' grades	*14.0*	*15.3*	*11.8*	*14.1*
1 'A' level/ 1 or 2 'H' grades	*3.7*	*3.5*	*4.1*	*4.4*
5 or more 'O' levels/grades:				
A – C grades[2]	*8.1*	*9.7*	*9.9*	*11.8*
1-4 'O' levels/grades:				
A – C grades[2]	*24.9*	*24.5*	*28.1*	*29.1*
1 or more 'O' levels/grades:				
D or E grades, or CSE				
grades 2–5	*30.9*	*34.3*	*29.6*	*30.9*
No GCE/SCE or CSE grades	*18.4*	*12.8*	*16.4*	*9.8*
Total school leavers				
(=100%) (thousands)	*431*	*441*	*411*	*425*

[2] includes CSE grade 1.   **H grades** – Scottish Higher examinations

Source: *Social Trends 1987*, HMSO, 1987, Table 3.13

Percentage of English School Leavers with no Graded Result at O level or CSE

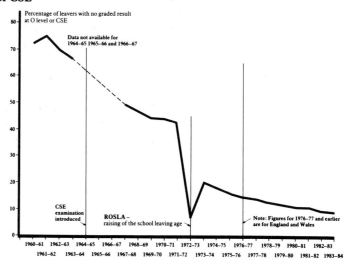

Source: *DES Statistical Bulletin 12/86*, 1986, p5

a What proportion of English school leavers had not even one CSE Grade 5 in 1970?

b What proportion of British school leavers had no GCE or CSE grades in 1984–85?

c Why did far more children obtain qualifications when the school leaving age was raised?

d It is often argued that educational standards in recent years have declined. Do the above statistics support this view?

e Explain why the proportion of school leavers with no qualifications has declined, and what the implications of this are.

But if more children have obtained qualifications, sociologists have been concerned with the reasons why some types of children achieve more than others. Above all, middle-class children are more likely to be successful than children from working-class backgrounds. Note the *more likely* in the preceding sentence – it must not be forgotten that many middle-class children do badly at school, and many working-class children well.

In the nineteenth century it was easy to explain away the greater achievements of mdidle-class children – they were simply believed to be born more intelligent! However, although few would deny that individual children are born with different abilities, there is no reliable scientific evidence that shows that children of certain *groups* (e.g. classes, sexes or ethnic groups) are born more intelligent than others. If one child does better than another at school this could be due to different inherited abilities, different attitudes or different educational experiences, but if one class, gender or ethnic group does better than another then this must be due, not to inheritance, but to *social* factors. (See pages 1–6 for a discussion of heredity and environment). Sociological explanations of why some types of children succeed more than others can be broken down into two main categories, those which emphasise the child's family and class backgrounds, and those which emphasise what happens in schools.

The home, social class and educational achievement

There is a great deal of evidence that shows that working-class children are less likely to succeed in the educational system in terms of examination pass and staying on rates.

Extract 4 *16–24 year-olds in Full-time Education, by Social Class*

16–19 year-olds in Full-time Education by Socio-economic Group of Father

Professional	Employers/ managers	Inter- mediate	Skilled manual	Semi and unskilled manual
percentage				
72	48	45	29	27

Source: *General Household Survey, 1984.* Quoted in *New Society,* 6 February 1987, p11

Students[1] Attending University or College: by Socio-economic Group of Father[2], 1984

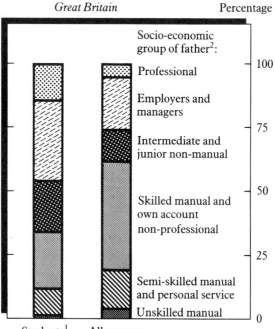

Great Britain   Percentage

Students[1] aged 18–24   All persons aged 18–24

[1] Full time and sandwich course students aged 18–24, studying at universities, polytechnics, or colleges of further education (including colleges of education in Scotland and N. Ireland).

[2] People whose fathers were members of the armed forces, full-time students, or had never worked are excluded from the sample.

Source: *General Household Survey, 1984.* Quoted by Tony Garrett in *New Society,* 6 February 1987, p11

a What proportion of 16–19 year-olds with skilled manual fathers were in full-time education in 1984?
b Complete the following sentence; 'Approximately . . . % of 18–24 year-olds in 1984 had professional fathers; approximately . . . % of full-time students of the same age had professional fathers.'
c Outline, in two or three sentences, the main conclusions that can be drawn from the above statistics.
d Explain why it might be misleading to base statistics on social class and education on the occupational position of the student's *father*.

'I don't know! Sometimes I wonder if even your father isn't brighter than you.'

If working-class children do less well educationally than middle-class children then it might seem obvious to look to their background for an explanation. An enormous amount of research was carried out on this topic, especially in the 1950s and 1960s, which pointed to several family and social class factors as being important:

a middle-class parents were said to be more interested in their children's education and offered more encouragement;
b middle-class parents were found to be more knowledgeable about the educational system and therefore better able to help their children;
c middle-class children had better living conditions (e.g. they were more likely to have a room for study) and more financial support (especially important for staying on after 16);
d middle-class children were brought up to see things in the long term and could therefore see the point of school and homework; working-class children saw things in the short term and tended therefore to see school, especially those aspects of it they didn't enjoy, as a waste of time;
e the language (e.g. structure of sentences, vocabulary) of middle-class children was more in tune with that of the teacher than that of working-class children whose linguistic skills were much more restricted.

What all these explanations have in common is that they explain the relative failure of working-class children in terms of their home background. Note how the school itself is omitted and not seen as a key factor in educational achievement.

A common sociological error, often made in the studies which emphasised children's home background, is to assume that because two things *vary* together one must necessarily *cause* the other.

Activity 10

a It is quite probable that children who have regular foreign holidays are more successful at school than other children. Using the terms correlation and causation, explain how a research finding along such lines could be misinterpreted.

b How could the answer you gave for **a** above be applied to those studies which explain low working class achievement in terms of home background?

However, middle-class children *are* likely to possess several advantages, and many working-class children several disadvantages, in the English and Welsh educational systems. Perhaps particularly important is whether parents and children can see the 'point' of school and know how to benefit from it. This, of course, does not just depend on the values of the home but also on the values of the school.

Extract 5 *The Values of the School*

If a child is to succeed at school it is important that he or she accepts, or at least conforms to, the values of the school (or, rather, the teachers). Cathy Bird *et al.* argue that several value assumptions can be identified in schools, notably:

that education, in the form of schooling, is beneficial to children, in terms of developing their intellectual abilities, and broadening their social and cultural horizons;

that all children should attend school regularly, until the statutory school leaving age, and for longer if they can benefit from so doing;

that during their school years, pupils will benefit from giving a considerable degree of priority to school work and attainment, as opposed to alternative domestic, work or leisure pursuits;

that any child who is deprived of his full complement of statutory education is likely to be personally less fulfilled, and socially and economically less well-equipped for adult life.

Source: *Disaffected Pupils*, Cathy Bird, Rosemary Chessum, John Furlong and Daphne Johnson, Brunel University, 1980, p18

a Explain what is meant by 'broadening their social and cultural horizons'.
b Explain how these value assumptions make it easier for some children to succeed at school than others.
c Can you think of any alternative values that schools could have which might be to the benefit of different types of children?

'Don't kid yourself about rearing a childhood prodigy, Dad . . . It's just you who's thick.'

The school and educational achievement

The school may therefore be structured in such a way that middle-class children can more easily benefit from it. There are several important studies of British schools, and most conclude that schools *do* matter. How well a child does at school depends, in other words, not just on home background and parents but on teachers and the way the curriculum is organised.

Extract 6 The Junior School Project

This research was based on a longitudinal study of 2000 London children from the age of seven to 11; children in 50 schools were studied and the results compared.

The Report found 12 factors which significantly helped produce a successful school ('success' was judged on the basis of several factors such as reading and maths scores):

1 purposeful leadership of the staff by the head
2 involvement of the deputy head
3 involvement of teachers
4 consistency among teachers
5 a structured day
6 intellectually challenging teachers
7 a work-centred environment
8 a limited focus within sessions
9 maximum communication between teachers and pupils
10 thorough record keeping
11 parental involvement
12 a positive ethos, e.g. in the effective schools there was less emphasis on punishment and criticism and more on rewarding pupils and praise.

Source: adapted from *The Junior School Project*, Inner London Education Authority, 1986

a Explain, giving examples to illustrate your answer, why consistency among teachers is important.
b Using your own school experiences as a guide, explain which of the above 12 factors are the most important and why.

Activity 11

Imagine you have just been appointed head of a comprehensive school which has a poor reputation in the community. Staff morale is low, the pupils appear bored and apathetic, and examination results are poor. Explain how you would set about improving the school and the difficulties you would face.

Extract 7   *The Importance of the Teacher*

Increasingly, sociologists have become interested in what happens in the classroom, and, in particular, the key role teachers play in creating eductional success or failure.

An early influential study by Rosenthal and Jacobson (1968) applied the notion of the self-fulfilling prophecy to the ways in which children came to fail differentially. After a (claimed but criticised) equalising for intelligence, teachers were given what they were told were the IQ scores for particular children, but were in fact randomised scores. The measured IQ of children came to resemble what the teachers had been told to expect, more than their 'real' IQs. The teachers, this suggests, were consciously or unconsciously modifying their behaviour in relation to children they associated with particular scores, with the consequence that the children 'failed' or 'succeeded' in the light of a 'prophecy', and the teacher's expectations based on that. The study has been extensively criticised for poor methods, and has not been replicated successfully despite attempts to do so. But it did encourage the examination of the detailed processes of the assessment of ability in the classroom and school. Success or failure depends, as much as anything, on delicate and drawn-out processes of negotiation and interaction between staff and pupil, teaching colleagues, teachers and pupils, administrators, and so on, on the basis of variable but persistently used conceptions of ability employed by those 'educational decision-makers'. Thus conceptions like 'bright', 'articulate', 'co-opera-tive', formed early in a child's school career by particular teachers or informal consensus, can be linked to middle-class membership and familiarity with formal occasions, and to cues like styles of dress, cleanliness and politeness, and can then operate to produce teachers' judgements of those qualities, as a continuing matter. Practices of reporting, and bureaucratic dossiers, can be used to create pictures of children which can reflect such inputs, and reputations, once created, can be difficult, or impossible, to live down. If (possibly defensive and aggressive) children react to such processes by suspending interest and co-operation, the effect becomes self-fulfilling.

Source: 'Education: Sucess and Failure', Dianne Phillips, in *Applied Sociological Perspectives*, ed. by R. J. Anderson & W. W. Sharrock, George Allen and Unwin, 1984, pp75–76

a Explain how the teachers Rosenthal and Jacobson studied might have treated pupils differently just because they *thought* they were clever.
b Why might middle-class children be more likely to be labelled 'bright', 'articulate' and 'co-operative'?
c Explain why it might be difficult to 'live down' a bad school report.

KEY TERM

self-fulfilling prophecy the process whereby someone is given a particular label (e.g. delinquent, clever) and comes to behave according to that label.

Partly because several children might receive a similar label and partly because some children might share similar out of school experiences, it is common for peer groups to develop which are hostile to the values of the teachers. Because streaming into classes of different ability levels carries with it a message of approval or disapproval (e.g. 4A=bright, 4D=stupid) it is likely anti-school sub-cultures will develop in the lower streams. Status can usually be obtained in such anti-school sub-cultures by breaking the rules of the school. Membership of such a group will of course, make educational failure even more likely.

A key process in schools therefore is the way children are labelled, both by teachers and by their peers. See pages 41–42 for a discussion of the labelling approach to crime.

Source: 'Reactions to Labelling', David Hargreaves, in *The Process of Schooling*, ed. by Martyn Hammersley & Peter Woods, Routledge and Kegan Paul, 1976, pp201–202

Extract 8 *Reactions to Labelling*

Pupils do not, however, automatically accept all the labels applied by teachers. David Hargreaves here outlines four of the factors which might influence whether a pupil accepts a particular label.

1 The frequency of the labelling

A pupil who is called a 'chatterbox' or a 'trouble-maker' on one or two occasions is not likely to accept this label as part of his identity, even though he may accept the label as legitimate within the specific context in which it is applied. We are all 'called names' many times by many different people without any deep or long-term effects. But if one particular label is repeatedly applied by a variety of teachers in a wide variety of situations, then at minimum the pupil will be under no illusions with regard to the teachers' conception of him, and part of the groundwork for the acceptance of the label by the pupil has been laid.

2 The extent to which the pupil sees the teacher as a 'significant other' whose opinion counts

If the pupil cares about the teacher's opinion of him, then he is more likely to accept the legitimacy of the teacher's label, whether it is a 'conformist' or 'deviant' label. In the case of the (middle-class?) pupil who values the teacher's opinion, his *early* acceptance of the legitimacy of the deviant label may actually help to insulate the pupil from acquiring a deviant identity and from committing further acts of deviance, since he will alter his conduct so that the teacher no longer has grounds for applying the deviant label to him. Here the teacher's intention in performing the labelling, namely social control, is realized. In the case of the pupil (working-class?) who sets a lower value on the teacher's opinion, he may be able to discount the deviant label in its early application ('I don't care what he thinks'), thus avoiding the need to reform his conduct. Here the teacher's attempt at social control by labelling fails. However, this pupil may be constrained to accept the label at a much later stage when the application of the deviant label has become frequent

and a matter of routine. What can be discounted in the short-term may prove to be more pervasively troublesome in the long term.

3 The extent to which others support the label

Sometimes a single teacher finds a pupil 'difficult' or a 'problem', but none of his colleagues shares the view that this pupil is in any way deviant. At other times all the teachers to whom a pupil is exposed will agree that the pupil merits a deviant label. We may call these two types, respectively, 'idiosyncratic' and 'consensual' deviants. It is certain that idiosyncratic deviants do exist in schools. They tend to remain hidden because teachers learn to recognize that the grumbling about a pupil whom nobody else finds 'difficult' will be taken by colleagues as a reflection on the teacher's competence rather than as evidence of pupil misconduct. The informal gossip and eternal discussions about pupils in staffrooms facilitate the development of a consensus about deviant pupils. One learns which pupils to grumble about in staffrooms. The consensus appears to be greater than it is, in part because those teachers who do not find the pupil 'difficult' tend to keep silent lest their overt denial that they find the pupil 'difficult' be interpreted by others as a form of boasting. One important consequence of the emergence of consensual deviants is that a teacher may acquire a preconception that a pupil is deviant, based on staff gossip, *before* he has actually taught a pupil.

The extent of the acceptance of the label by other adults in the pupil's environment may also be important. If the pupil's parents and neighbours also apply the label which is consensual among the teachers, then the pupil will be under greater pressure to accept its legitimacy. Here again the middle-class pupil may be at an

advantage. First, because of their greater interest in their child's schooling, parents are more likely to discover that the pupil is being labelled as deviant; and second, they are likely to investigate the events leading up to the labelling and make a considered judgment upon it. If the parents think that the labelling was justified, they will censure the child as well and seek to ensure that he commits no further deviant conduct. They will reinforce the teacher's social control attempts. If they think the labelling was unjustified, they will help the pupil to neutralize the labelling with such comments as: 'Well, the teacher was probably angry and upset and didn't really mean it. Just make sure that you keep out of trouble.' In extreme cases, such parents might make an official complaint against the school. The working-class parent on the other hand may hear of such events less frequently and make a generalized response rather than investigating the details. A response such as: 'I'm not surprised – your dad and your older brother were just like that at school, always up to some mischief', when the pupil feels that the labelling was unjustified, or a response such as: 'Never mind what the teachers say, love, I never liked them either', when the pupil knows that the labelling was justified, may help to undermine the teachers' labelling as attempts at social control.

4 The public nature of the labelling

When a pupil is labelled before a large public, such as in the school assembly or in front of a large class, the psychological effect is likely to be more severe than when the labelling takes place in a private setting such as an interview with the teacher at the end of a lesson. It is the same as the difference between an appearance in court and a confrontation with a policeman on the street-corner.

a Summarise, in your own words and in one sentence each, the four factors which affect whether a pupil accepts a particular label.

b Why and how might teachers use labels as a means of social control? Why might this tactic be more successful for middle-class pupils?

c Explain how 'consensus' deviants are created.

d How might labelling processes in schools combine with other factors to make it more likely that working-class children will be unsuccessful at school?

'My teacher said that if I don't try harder at school I'll end up like you.'

Activity 12

Produce a scatter diagram to indicate all the factors which contribute towards the greater educational achievement of middle-class children.

Gender and educational achievement

The relative performance of boys and girls in the educational system has been examined in detail in recent years, but it can only be understood in the context of the wider social differences between men and women. It would therefore be useful here to re-read Chapter 5, concentrating on gender-role socialisation.

The educational performance of girls has improved considerably in recent years, and, in many ways, they are now more successful than boys. Since 1974, for example, girls have obtained more GCE 'O' level A–C grades, even though there are more boys in the relevant age group.

However, although girls and boys now achieve broadly similar levels of overall success, they achieve it in different subjects, and the extent to which subjects and courses are gender-specific increases the higher up the educational system one goes.

Extract 9 *Gender and O & A Levels*

In the graphs below 1.0 means that there are an equal number of passes for girls and boys; 0.95 indicates real equality as there are more boys than girls in the appropriate age groups.

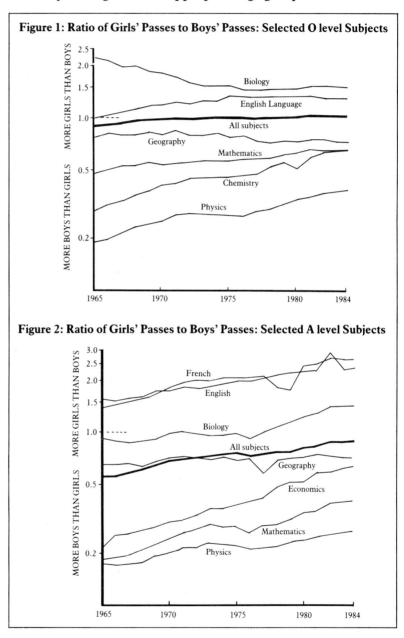

Figure 1: Ratio of Girls' Passes to Boys' Passes: Selected O level Subjects

Figure 2: Ratio of Girls' Passes to Boys' Passes: Selected A level Subjects

Source: *Times Educational Supplement*, 14 February 1986, p21

a At O level which subject is:
    1 most **2** least
gender specific?

b At A level which subject was passed by more boys in 1965, but in the 1980s by more girls?

c For every 100 boys who passed A level maths in 1980 how many girls did?

d What explanations can you give for the fact that subjects appear to have become less gender-specific at O level but not at A level? What effects, if any, do you think the introduction of GCSE will have on subject choice?

I WANT A DOLL!

Extract 10 *Gender and University*

Gender differences are significant in further education, where often whole courses (e.g. engineering, secretarial, hairdressing) have students of only one sex, and in higher education.

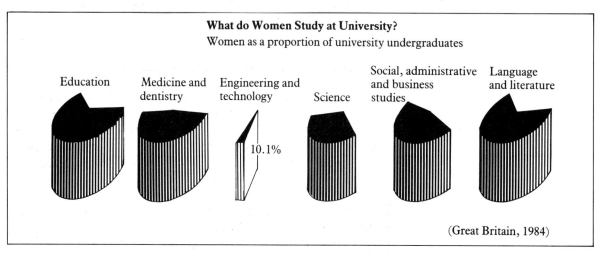

What do Women Study at University?
Women as a proportion of university undergraduates

Education   Medicine and dentistry   Engineering and technology   Science   Social, administrative and business studies   Language and literature

10.1%

(Great Britain, 1984)

Source: University Grants Committee. Quoted by Tony Garrett in *New Society*, 26 September 1986

a What are the least gender-specific types of course at university?
b Which of the six types of course do you think has increased its proportion of women most in the last 20 years?
c Explain why so few girls study engineering and technology at university.

Although girls have improved their examination success rates relative to boys in recent years, studies of schools and colleges have shown that boys and girls experience classroom life in different ways. The *hidden curriculum* (see page 26) is often presented so that pupils internalise gender-specific values and patterns of behaviour. Michelle Stanworth (*Gender and Schooling*, Hutchinson, 1983), for example, found that boys were more likely to:
a join in class discussions
b ask for the teacher's help
c receive the teacher's time and attention
d be asked questions by teachers
e be praised, and criticised, by teachers.

Activity 13

a Using participant observation as your method, try to identify any ways in which girls and boys are treated, and behave, differently in classes at your school or college. You could, for example, look for:
    1 the number of times boys and girls speak
    2 who is asked more questions
    3 who is given which tasks.
b What conclusions can you draw from your study?
c Explain the advantages and disadvantages of using participant observation for this type of research.

Ethnicity and educational achievement

As with gender, one can only begin to understand the educational experiences of different ethnic groups by understanding the overall positions of such groups in society. You should therefore reread Chapter 6, concentrating on the extent of racism and racial discrimination in Britain, and the employment experiences of members of ethnic minorities.

There is no simple relationship between ethnicity and educational achievement. Children born in India and Pakistan, or with parents born there, do about as well as white children, while West Indian and Bangladeshi children are less succesful. The Swann Report (*Education for All*, 1985), produced after five years' study of the education of ethnic minority children, found, for example, that while 4% of Asian and white children in the areas they studied went on to university only 1% of West Indians did. Similarly, at A level 5% of West Indians obtained one or more passes compared with 13% of Asian and white school leavers.

So why do West Indian children do less well at school? As with social class differences, two types of explanations can be put forward, one emphasising the home and social class background, the other emphasising the school, although, again as with class, it is the interrelationships between the two which are perhaps particularly important.

West Indians are in a disadvantaged position in British society, and discrimination in employment and housing adds an extra element of deprivation. The explanations of why working-class children are relatively unsuccessful can therefore be used to explain the relative failure of West Indian children, adding in an extra factor for racial discrimination.

But the Swann Report, like other research in this area, found that schools are organised and children taught in such a way that ethnic minority children are placed at a disadvantage. This aspect of the hidden curriculum may operate in a variety of ways:
a teachers may have racial stereotypes, e.g. they may believe West Indian children are naturally gifted at sport and thus encourage them in this area at the expense of academic progress;
b the curriculum itself may be ethnocentric (see page 7); black writers and West Indian history may be ignored with the world seen very much from a 'white' point of view;
c the small number of teachers of ethnic minority groups may suggest to black children that school is a place organised and run by white people.

Activity 14

a Analyse subjects you have studied or are currently studying to see if there are any elements of ethnocentrism or racism in the syllabuses or books used.
b Ask your teachers if the local education authority has an equal opportunities policy for members of different ethnic groups. If there is one, what are the attitudes of the teachers towards it, and how successful has it been?

The reasons for the different educational experiences of the various ethnic groups in Britain are clearly highly complex. It is, for example, difficult to explain the relative success of Asian children without discussing their family backgrounds, as Asian people in Britain suffer as much discrimination as West Indians. Although schools can play a significant part in reducing educational inequality, ethnicity will probably only become irrelevant in education when it is irrelevant in the rest of society.

The Importance of Education

Education has long been a major issue of public and political concern; most parents are keen for their children to do well at school, and most children themselves want to pass as many examinations as possible.

Educational qualifications are used by employers as a means of selection; GCSEs and A levels rarely, if ever, guarantee a job, but the lack of appropriate qualifications usually prevents young people from even being considered for the best-paid and most interesting jobs. Although examinations have not become easier to pass, because of the expansion of secondary, further and higher education since the Second World War, employers have been able to demand higher and higher levels of qualifications.

KEY TERM

qualification spiral the process whereby qualifications are obtained by more and more people; employers are therefore able to demand increasingly higher levels of examination passes. This in turn encourages people to try to obtain yet higher levels of qualification.

Activity 15

a Find out, either by asking people in each job or by interviewing a careers adviser, how the entrance requirements for the following jobs have changed over the last twenty years:
    1 nursing
    2 police
    3 teaching
    4 librarianship.
b What are the implications of these changes?

In their concentration on educational qualifications, and how educational achievement varies from group to group, sociologists have perhaps tended to take for granted or even ignore that school is a place where important skills are learned.

Extract 11 *Literacy and Numeracy*

Two of the key skills learned at school are literacy and numeracy. Society is organised in such a way that being illiterate or innumerate poses massive problems. Research by Mary Hamilton, published in 1987, suggests illiteracy and innumeracy are far from uncommon.

Of the 12,5000 people, more than 1,600 – nearly one in eight – said they had trouble reading, writing, or adding up.

More than half the teenagers questioned (52 per cent) could not understand a simple fire notice, while 44 per cent could not read and understand a bus timetable. One in four (25 per cent) had difficulty filling in a simple application form correctly, while 23 per cent could not add up the cost of a simple café meal. More than one in four (26 per cent) could not work out 10 per cent of £2. A similar pattern is reflected in the adults' answers.

Source: *Times Educational Supplement*, 6 February 1987

'Remember me, Mr Simpkins? I'm the little lad you gave hell to in 3C.'

a Explain why, despite compulsory education to the age of 16, so many people in Britain appear to have difficulty reading, writing and counting.
b Illiteracy in particular is often seen as something to be ashamed of. How do people disguise their illiteracy from others?
c Outline how being illiterate would affect the quality of your life.

Largely because such a large proportion of children leave school without having developed their abilities to anything like their true potential, alternatives to the current state system of education have occasionally been suggested. These alternatives include private, progressive schools which try to foster co-operation rather than competition, and a small number of parents who educate their children at home. For the vast majority of children, however, the state system of education will continue to be the only possible provider of qualifications and many of the skills without which living in an advanced industrial society is difficult.

Activity 16

It is not illegal for parents to educate their own children at home provided they can provide a full-time education suitable for the child's age, ability and aptitude. Assuming a 'suitable' education could be provided at home, what would be the advantages and disadvantages of a child not attending school?

Questions and Suggested Projects

Review Questions

1 Explain the differences between formal and informal education.
2 Why were the tripartite and comprehensive systems of secondary education introduced?
3 What problems do comprehensive schools face?
4 In what ways does a child's home background influence educational achievement?
5 Explain what is meant by the *qualification spiral* and why qualifications are now so important.
6 Outline the relationships between educational achievement and:
    a gender
    b ethnicity.

Theme-linking Questions

1 Explain what sociological methods you would use if you were asked to study relationships in a class at school. What would be the disadvantages of your chosen methods?
2 Explain why education has become a major political issue.
3 How have what are seen as the requirements of industry and commerce affected schools and colleges in recent years?
4 How important is the education system in maintaining class divisions in Britain today?
5 How do teachers attempt to maintain social control in schools?

Stimulus–response Question

'Basically you're not bad. It's just that everybody expects you to be bad, and that makes you bad.'

a What two important sociological terms could be used to describe the processes in the above cartoon? (4)
b Explain how a parallel could be drawn between the psychiatrist and wolf, and a good teacher and his or her pupil. (4)

c Why, and with what consequences, do children treated in a similar way by teachers often form anti-school peer groups? (5)
d What factors, other than school, influence educational achievement?   (7)

Essays

1 Describe and give the reasons for the main changes in the educational system in the last twenty years.
2 a What is meant by the *hidden curriculum*?
  b Explain how the educational performance of girls and members of ethnic minority groups may be affected by the hidden curriculum.
3 Examine how the school can affect a child's educational performance. Your answer could include:
      resources and facilities
      the curriculum
      teacher behaviour and attitudes
      labelling and the self-fulfilling prophecy
      streaming
      peer groups.

Suggested Projects

1 A study of local YTS schemes to examine whether they are gender-specific.
2 A participant observation study of one particular class to observe the different attitudes of the students and how these affect educational performance.
3 A study of a local adult illiteracy campaign and the difficulties it faces.
4 A study of GCSE subject choices in your school or college; on what basis do students decide which subjects to study?
5 A study comparing what parents and children think are the most important purposes of schooling.

13

Work, Unemployment and Leisure

Introduction

Previous chapters have suggested how a person's occupation affects other areas of life such as educational achievement and health; this chapter will concentrate on the nature of work itself. The following issues will be looked at:

a the meaning of work
b how the occupational structure has changed
c the new technology and its effects
d the experience of work
e industrial relations
f unemployment
g leisure and how it is affected by work.

The Meaning of Work

Activity 1

a As a group exercise, complete the following sentences:
   1 'Work is . . .'
   2 'Leisure is . . .'
b Produce a list of your answers, if possible grouping them into different categories.
c What conclusions can you draw from your answers?

Your answers to Activity 1 have probably shown that work and employment are not necessarily the same thing, and that some people define work in a much broader way than others.

Extract 1 *A Two-dimensional Time and Activity Scheme*

In the diagram below, Stanley Parker attempts to categorise all our daily activities in terms of whether they relate to work or not, and how much choice we have over whether to perform them or not.

		ACTIVITY		
		Constraint		*Freedom*
TIME	*Work*	Work (employment)	Work obligations (connected with employment)	'Leisure in work'
	Non-work	Physiological needs	Non-work obligations	Leisure

Source: *The Future of Work and Leisure*, Stanley Parker, Paladin, 1972, p28

a Give an example each of:
    1 'leisure in work'
    2 physiological needs
    3 work obligations
    4 non-work obligations.
(It may help you answer this question if you think of your daily activities.)
b The diagram assumes that people are in employment. How would the diagram have to be adapted in order to deal with the circumstances of people not in paid employment?
c Does Parker's typology appear to you a satisfactory way of categorising activities? If not, why?

Activity 2

Explain how the activity of gardening could be seen by the person doing it as:
a paid employment
b voluntary work
c a non-work obligation
d leisure.

Throughout this chapter we shall concentrate on paid employment and occupation, though it should be borne in mind that many of the issues (e.g. alienation, new technology) can also be applied to activities such as voluntary work and housework.

The Changing Occupational Structure

In 1830 over 70% of Britain's labour force worked in agriculture; in 1985 only 2.7% did. Between 1961 and 1981 the number of workers employed in non-manual jobs increased by 48% while the number of unskilled manual workers declined by 35% and skilled by 20%. These statistics indicate clearly the two major changes that have taken place in Britain's economic and occupational structure; firstly, from an agriculture- to a manufacturing-based economy, which took place in the late eighteenth and early nineteenth centuries, and secondly, the current shift towards employment based on services such as banking, teaching and retailing.

It is customary to distinguish three sectors of the occupational structure: primary, secondary and tertiary.

When most people worked in the primary sector, there was relatively little specialisation of task; for the most part workers performed similar activities, as demanded by the seasons and the weather. With industrialisation, however, came greater specialisation.

However, before industrialisation, there had been highly skilled, specialist craft workers, such as hand-loom weavers and blacksmiths. Although some crafts did continue, and have survived to this day, many could not compete, in terms of cost and quantity of production, against machines.

KEY TERMS

primary sector agriculture and mining.
secondary sector manufacturing.
tertiary sector services, e.g. banking and retailing.

KEY TERM

division of labour specialisation of work roles, i.e. different workers perform different tasks.

KEY TERM

mechanisation the process whereby hand labour is replaced by machines operated by workers.

Activity 3

a List four types of machine invented or developed in Britain between 1750 and 1850.
b Briefly explain the social and economic effects of these machines.

Before World War Two over half of Britain's work force was employed in manufacturing; today the proportion is less than a quarter and nearly all experts predict the figure will decline further.

Extract 2 *Changes in Type and Location of Employment*

It is not just that certain types of jobs have grown and others declined; also important is where these jobs are.

Changes in Employment 1951–1981 (thousands)

	inner cities	outer cities	smaller cities and larger towns	small towns and rural areas	Great Britain
manufacturing					
1951–1961	−143	+84	−21	+453	+374
1961–1971	−428	−217	−93	+489	−255
1971–1981	−447	−480	−311	−717	−1929
private services					
1951–1961	+192	+110	+128	+154	+944
1961–1971	−297	+92	−7	+535	+318
1971–1981	−105	+170	+91	+805	+958
public services					
1951–1961	+13	+54	+38	+200	+302
1961–1971	+25	+170	+110	+502	+807
1971–1981	−78	+102	+53	+456	+488
total employment					
1951–1961	+43	+231	+140	+1060	+1490
1961–1971	−643	+19	+54	+1022	+320
1971–1981	−538	−236	−150	+404	−590

Source: Tony Garrett, *New Society*, 25 October 1985

a By how much did manufacturing jobs in Britain decline between 1971 and 1981?
b Give an example each of a private and a public service.
c What relationships does the above table suggest exist between type of area and type of employment? Which areas have benefited from this relationship?
d Briefly summarise the main trends indicated by the above table.

Extract 3 *People in Employment*

The two diagrams below illustrate, firstly, the change in the proportion of workers in each type of job between 1979 and 1985, and, secondly, those industries where most people are employed.

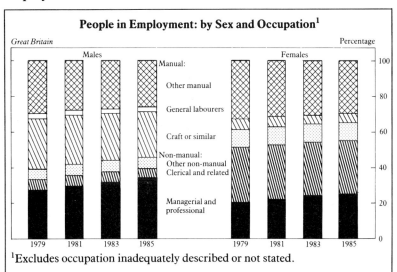

People in Employment: by Sex and Occupation[1]

Great Britain   Percentage

Males   Females

Manual:
Other manual
General labourers
Craft or similar
Non-manual:
Other non-manual
Clerical and related
Managerial and professional

1979 1981 1983 1985   1979 1981 1983 1985

[1]Excludes occupation inadequately described or not stated.

Source: *Labour Force Surveys*, Department of Employment. Quoted in *Social Trends 1987*, HMSO, 1987, p75

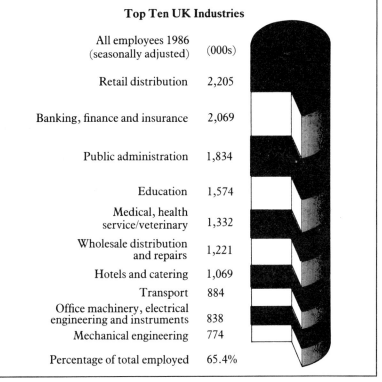

Top Ten UK Industries

All employees 1986 (seasonally adjusted)	(000s)
Retail distribution	2,205
Banking, finance and insurance	2,069
Public administration	1,834
Education	1,574
Medical, health service/veterinary	1,332
Wholesale distribution and repairs	1,221
Hotels and catering	1,069
Transport	884
Office machinery, electrical engineering and instruments	838
Mechanical engineering	774
Percentage of total employed	65.4%

Source: *Employment Gazette*, Department of Employment, Table 1.2. Quoted in *New Society*, 12 December 1986

a What proportion of females in 1985 worked in a craft occupation?

b How many people worked in the hotel and catering industry in 1986?

c Briefly summarise the changes in the occupational structure between 1979 and 1985.

d Imagine you are a careers adviser; on the basis of the information above what advice would you give to young people?

The striking change in recent years therefore has been the growth of the services sector (e.g. banking, retailing, education and catering) and the decline of the manufacturing sector. The reasons for this decline in the secondary sector are complex, but include the decline in Britain's competitive position in industries such as car manfuacture and ship-building, and automation, which is reducing the need for large numbers of workers to control machines.

KEY TERM

automation the use of automatic equipment to control either production or processes.

Activity 4

Briefly explain, in your own words, the differences between mechanisation and automation, and give an example of each.

'Take the lift to the sixth floor, Mr Frensham. The computer will meet you there.'

KEY TERM

dual labour market an occupational structure, said by some economists and sociologists to exist in Britain today, which offers very different rewards to two very different types of job.

A current theme in the sociology of work is that there are increasingly two types of employment, which differ significantly in the rewards they offer. The first type of job, known as those belonging to the primary market or the core, offers security, high pay and good promotion prospects. The second type of job, known as those belonging to the secondary market or the periphery, offers little security, low pay and little, if any, prospect of promotion, and is, in addition, often part-time.

Activity 5

List three examples each of jobs that derive from the primary market, or core, and the secondary market, or periphery.

Extract 4 Jobs and Careers

John Westergaard argues that the traditional distinction between non-manual and manual workers is now of little value. Instead, he uses the idea of the dual labour market to distinguish two broad categories of people who experience work, and thus the other areas of their lives, in very different ways.

The larger group are those whose lives are confined within the resources and horizons of routine *jobs*. This is work which, even if skilled, involves neither autonomy nor authority on the job; allows little discretion or variety; carries with it no increments in pay and few chances of promotion to better things after the early years; leads often to hardship in old age; and is relatively vulnerable to redundancy in recession.

The other group are those whose lives centre on *careers*. This is work – now or within realistic prospect – of a significantly different kind: it promises regular increments in pay to take income well above job wage-levels after the early years; offers visible opportunity, though no certainty of promotion beyond that; carries some authority even at subordinate levels, while allowing discretion and variety in the application of skills or experience; demands (and tends to elicit) more commitment than goes with merely working for a wage; offers security in retirement; and, while not immune from the risk of redundancy, is much less exposed to it than routine work and provides better resources to cope with it should it happen.

The distinction is rough. It blurs at the edges and glibly neglects graduations and variations on either side. But it makes a good deal better sense than the old 'manual/non-manual' dichotomy for identifying those crucial differences in circumstances among the bulk of the population – differences likely to affect material interests and socio-political outlook.

Source: 'Class of '84', John Westergaard, *New Socialist*, No. 15, January/February 1984, pp31–32

GLOSSARY
autonomy personal freedom
dichotomy division into two

a State three advantages people with careers have over those with jobs.
b Give two examples each of a 'career' and a 'job'.
c What does Westergaard mean by saying that differences between job and career are likely to affect 'material interests and socio-political outlook'?
d Explain how Westergaard's distinction between job and career can be linked to the idea of a dual labour market.

Activity 6

a Using information from your local newspaper and/or Jobcentre, find out the main types of job available in your area.
b Explain what types of industry most vacancies are in, and whether the jobs are full- or part-time.
c By interviewing older people, find out the main sources of employment in your area 20 years ago.
d Write a paragraph explaining how patterns of employment in your area have changed in the last 20 years.

The decline in the secondary and the growth of the tertiary sector have been the most important change in employment patterns in recent years, but for many people the nature of employment is changing in other ways too.

A shorter working life
The actual number of years spent in full-time paid employment is declining. At the beginning entry into employment is delayed by youth unemployment and training schemes, and at the end more men and women are retiring before the statutory retiring age.

Part-time working
In 1986 21% of jobs were part-time, the majority of them held by women. The proportion of part-time jobs is expected to increase further.

Self-employment
Approximately one in 10 of the work force is self-employed, a figure which has been growing in recent years and is expected to carry on doing so. One of the major reasons for this growth is the increasing trend among large companies to sub-contract specialist services.

Home-working
This in itself is not a new phenomenon. Home-working has long provided paid employment, nearly always for women and usually very badly paid, in such industries as clothing and toy-making. More recently, however, developments in computers and information technology have enabled a different type of worker, much better paid, to work at home.

Activity 7

Imagine you are employed as a writer of computer software and your employer says that, if you wish, you can work at home. What factors will influence your decision?

All the statistics and trends referred to so far in this chapter are based on those jobs that people report to official bodies such as the Inland Revenue and the Department of Employment. There are, of course, jobs which people get paid for which are not officially reported. Obviously, no one knows how much this *black economy* is worth or how many people work in it, but it does appear to be of some importance, especially in such areas as house maintenance and the provision of domestic services.

The New Technology

The new technologies of communication, information processing and micro-electronics are affecting not only the types of employees required but the very nature of the work performed by an increasing number of people.

Extract 5   *Printing; an Example of New Technology*

The printing industry provides one of the most dramatic and best publicised cases of the effects of the new technology.

Traditional methods of newspaper production are cumbersome and inefficient. A story passes from journalist to subeditor to typesetter. The 'linotype' machine operated by the typesetter produces 'slugs' of lead type, a line at a time. A 'galley' of the story is printed from the type, and checked and corrected by a proof reader. The lines of metal type are then corrected, and a number of stories are made up into a page, by a compositor. A mould is made from this page, and from this, in turn, the printing plates are made. The content of the paper undergoes at least eight processes, involving six different groups of workers. Some of the content is retyped four times as it moves along the chain of operations. At each stage errors are introduced. Correcting them often only produces new errors at the next stage.

The new technology streamlines and simplifies the production process. The journalist writes the story using a word-processor, and files it in the store of the newspaper's computer. This can be done in the newspaper's office, or direct from court, football stadium or hotel bedroom, using the public telephone system. The subeditor can consult a directory, maintained by the computer itself, of those stories which have been filed. He can then retrieve, on the screen, the stories which he wants, and these are edited using the powerful controls of the word-processor. Once the stories for a particular page have been selected, the layout of the page can be designed on the screen. Finally a computer system 'photosets' the page onto film, which is then used to produce the printing plate.

In this new system, there are fewer opportunities for errors to be introduced. One individual, the journalist concerned, is more directly responsible for the correctness of the 'copy', the written text, of a story.

The gains of computerisation for newspaper management are quite clear. A keyboard operator using the traditional linotype typesetting machine produces around 6,000 letters an hour. Modern computerised typesetting produces 3,000 lines a minute, and in some cases with fewer errors. Using the traditional 'hot metal' technology, a typical quality newspaper needs five hours' work from between 100 and 200 production staff, to prepare an edition for the presses. The new 'cold-type' techniques, which are much quicker, require only a quarter of that number of staff.

Source: *Society and the New Technology*, Kenneth Ruthven, Cambridge University Press, 1983, p26

a In what ways is new technology likely to improve the quality of printing?

b Who is likely to benefit from the introduction of new printing technology?

c Explain why the printing unions have often been opposed to the introduction of new technology, and why there has been considerable conflict in the newspaper printing industry in recent years.

Activity 8

Retailing provides another obvious example of an occupation which is being affected by new technology.
a Describe and explain the technological differences between a traditional small grocer's shop and a large hyper- or supermarket.
b Explain the effects these technological changes in shops are having on shop assistants and customers.
c How could shopping be affected yet further by technological changes in the future?

It is not just that some jobs disappear with new technology, but that many jobs that remain become less skilled. In particular, as in printing, some highly skilled, craft occupations are giving way to less skilled jobs.

'Williams is adapting well to increased automation.'

Deskilling potentially reduces the bargaining power of the worker as well as job satisfaction; less skilled workers who can be trained quickly can be easily replaced. But if some jobs become deskilled, then the skill requirements of others increase.

KEY TERM

deskilling the process whereby the amount of skill needed to do a particular job is reduced through technological change.

KEY TERM

reskilling the process whereby workers learn new skills required by technological change.

Activity 9

Explain how what you have learnt at school and/or college has been influenced by what are believed to be the skill requirements of the types of jobs you are likely to have in the future.

Extract 6 *The New Technology and Job Satisfaction*

People derive a great deal from their work; the effects of new technology on work satisfaction is therefore an issue of great importance. As the extract below illustrates, there are widely differing opinions on the effects of new technology.

Many jobs are dreary and unsatisfying, repetitive and exhausting. The most that can be said for them is that they provide an income. It is jobs such as these, on the assembly line, or in unpleasant and dangerous conditions, that are likely to be automated.

For most people, however, a job is far more than just a source of income. Many people take pride in doing their job well, and get satisfaction from using their special skills and abilities. Jobs are also a source of social status; skilled workers are usually more highly regarded than unskilled. And the workplace provides people with social opportunities to meet people, to make friends, to form part of a community. The unemployed are denied the possibility of these benefits; indeed, unemployment undermines self-respect, and attracts social disapproval. The 'deskilled' suffer a loss, if not of income, of status and job satisfaction.

The danger is that the new technology, while removing unsatisfying jobs on the assembly line, or in the paint shop, may create them elsewhere by deskilling previously satisfying jobs. Printing is an example of this process already in action. And by forcing up the level of unemployment, thus denying people the monetary and social rewards of participation in work, the new technology may create and exacerbate social problems.

The evidence on deskilling is far from clear. In the electronic future, for example, pessimists talk of offices where people sit at screens all day, keying in words as fast as they can, like battery hens. They argue that the pursuit of higher productivity will end the informal social life of the office. They suggest that the new technology will be used to squeeze out the minutes and hours of labour power lost in these moments of personal contact. The optimists argue that the new technology will, on the contrary, take over the repetitive work of the office (such as routine clerical tasks, and copytyping), leaving workers free to do more varied work, and exercise greater initiative.

Source: *Society and the New Technology*, Kenneth Ruthven, Cambridge University Press, 1983, pp32–33

GLOSSARY

exacerbate make worse.

a Which types of jobs are most likely to be automated?
b What are the social consequences of deskilling likely to be?
c Briefly outline the two opposing arguments about the likely effects of new technology on office work. What types of evidence would you need in order to come to a balanced judgement on this question?

'You know what I miss? Paper aeroplanes.'

Activity 10

a Interview someone you know who has been in the same job for at least 10 years; find out how the nature of their job has changed since they began work, and how this change has affected the satisfaction they derive from work.

b Compare your interviewee's replies with those obtained by your fellow students. Which types of jobs have changed most?

The Experience of Work

As the previous section on the new technology has suggested, sociologists (unlike economists, who are primarily concerned with issues such as production, profit and wages) have been mainly interested in the social and economic consequences of work for worker themselves and the attitudes people have towards their work. Different workers, of course, want very different things from their work, and the very thing that attracts some people to a job might well repel others. Some workers, for example, might thrive in a job which gives them plenty of autonomy and independence, while other people might find such a job far too stressful.

Activity 11

a Carry out a brief survey in your sociology group to find out what your fellow students want from a job. Organise the answers into different categories.
b What conclusions can you draw from your survey about what people want from work?

There have been many studies, usually based on interviews and questionnaires, on work satisfaction, and, although it must always be borne in mind that different people want different things from work, certain general themes have emerged as making work satisfying to a high proportion of workers. Stanley Parker (*The Future of Work and Leisure*, Paladin, 1971, pp44–47) identifies these as:
1 creating something
2 using skill
3 working whole-heartedly
4 using initiative and having responsibility
5 mixing with people
6 working with people.

Similarly, Parker (ibid., pp47–49) identifies several themes of work dissatisfaction:
1 doing repetitive work
2 making only a small part of something
3 doing useless tasks
4 feeling a sense of insecurity
5 being too closely supervised.

Activity 12

Using the above themes of work satisfaction and dissatisfaction, assess your attitudes towards a part-time job you have had or still have.

Extract 7 Karl Marx on Alienation

A recurrent theme in the sociology of work is that many workers derive little satisfaction or meaning from work, and, indeed, are alienated from it. Karl Marx claimed that the very nature of the capitalist organisation of industry would produce this alienation.

In what does this alienation of labour consist? First that the work is *external* to the worker, that it is not a part of his nature, that consequently he does not fulfil himself in his work but denies himself, has a feeling of misery, not of well-being, does not develop freely a physical and mental energy, but is physically exhausted and mentally debased. The worker therefore feels himself at home only during his leisure, whereas at work he feels homeless. His work is not voluntary but imposed, *forced labour*. It is not the satisfaction of a need, but only a *means* for satisfying other needs. Its alien character is clearly shown by the fact that as soon as there is no physical or other compulsion it is avoided like the plague. Finally, the alienated character of work for the worker appears in the fact that it is not his work but work for someone else, that in work he does not belong to himself but to another person.

Source: *Selected Writings in Sociology and Social Philosophy*, Karl Marx, ed. by T. B. Bottomore and Maximilien Rubel, Penguin, 1963, pp177–178

a What does Marx mean when he says 'work is external to the worker'?
b What 'other needs' does work satisfy?
c How could work be organised in a non-capitalist way? Would this solve the problem of worker alienation?

While Marx stressed that the ownership and control of the means of production was the basis of the alienation of the worker, he also said that the increasingly specialised division of labour and mechanisation would further reduce the worker's job satisfaction. These latter arguments have been developed by several writers who have suggested that it is not the capitalist nature of society but the very nature of some occupations which results in alienation.

In a frequently quoted study of American workers in the chemical, printing, textiles and car industries, Robert Blauner (*Alienation and Freedom*, University of Chicago Press, 1964) claims that it is the nature of technology itself which can produce alienation. The craft printers Blauner studied could use their

alienation a feeling of being
emotionally separated from an
aspect of life – usually used to refer to
a feeling of a lack of involvement in
work.

initiative in a highly skilled job, working closely with other people, and producing a product they were proud of. The assembly-line car workers, on the other hand, had virtually no control over their work, they carried out routine and repetitive tasks, largely isolated from other workers. On the basis of his research, Blauner suggests there are four dimensions of alienation:

1 powerlessness: the worker has little or no control over his or her work;
2 meaninglessness: a lack of any purpose in work;
3 isolation: little or no solidarity with other workers or identification with the company;
4 self-estrangement: this comes close to Marx's view of alienation and refers to a general lack of involvement in work, a failure to realise one's potential as a human being, and a lack of self-worth.

Extract 8   *Working for Ford*

Blauner suggests that working on an assembly line is the most alienating of jobs. Huw Beynon, in a study of Ford's Halewood plant in Liverpool, vividly describes, often in the words of the workers themselves, what it is like to work on an assembly line.

Working in a car plant involves coming to terms with the assembly line. 'The line never stops', you are told. The assembly plant itself is huge and on two levels, with the paint shop on the one floor and the trim and final assembly departments below. The car shell is painted in the paint shop and passed by lift and conveyor to the first station of the trim assembly department. From this point the body shell is carried up and down the 500-yard length of the plant until it is finally driven off, tested, and stored in the car park . . .

Most people survive their period of probation and become fully fledged assembly-line operatives. They all found the experience painful and had established means of coping with it. They 'blanked out their minds', perfected 'mental blackouts' or thought about crossword puzzles . . . 'It's the most boring job in the world. It's the same thing over and over again. There's no change in it, it wears you out. It makes you awful tired. It slows your thinking right down. There's no need to think. It's just a formality. You just carry on. You just endure it for the money. That's what we're paid for – to endure the boredom of it.'

Source: *Working for Ford*, Huw Beynon, Penguin, 1973, pp109, 117, 118

a Briefly describe the type of task an assembly-line worker carries out.
b How do workers cope with the pressures of the assembly-line?
c Henry Ford I said 'I have not been able to discover that repetitive labour injures a man in any way'. (ibid., p108). Does sociological evidence support Ford's claim?
d Examine the consequences of new technology for the manufacture of cars, patterns of employment and work satisfaction.

KEY TERMS

expressive orientation to work an outlook which expects work itself to be satisfying and meaningful.
instrumental orientation to work an outlook which sees work not as providing satisfaction in itself, but as important in providing the financial means which allows the worker to enjoy life *outside* work.

Other research, especially on semi- and unskilled manual workers, but also on routine white-collar workers, has suggested that it is not just the nature of the job itself which determines the degree of satisfaction a worker obtains from work, but also the attitudes and expectations a worker brings to work. Obviously, different people have very different expectations from work, but an unskilled worker with no qualifications is likely to have very different expectations from a professional worker.

Research by John Goldthorpe and David Lockwood (*The Affluent Worker: Industrial Attitudes and Behaviour*, Cambridge University Press, 1968) has shown how the majority of semi- and unskilled manual workers expect little from work and so work primarily for instrumental reasons. The family was the central life interest for most of the workers Goldthorpe and Lockwood studied, and, although they certainly did not enjoy work, their jobs were judged mainly in terms of the financial rewards they offered. Indeed, many workers *chose* unsatisfying and boring jobs because of the relatively high rewards they offered.

In reality, workers' orientations and attitudes to work are highly complex and varied, and are influenced both by the nature of the job itself and the attitudes the worker brings to work from outside. Further attitudes are not static – the job which is interesting and enjoyable on Tuesday morning might well be tedious and boring on Friday afternoon.

Industrial Relations

All types of workers, from unskilled to the highest managerial and professional, adopt various occupational strategies or methods in order to improve their economic position, power and status. Workers acting alone are relatively powerless and so they have frequently combined together to form trade unions and professional associations. Similarly, different employers in the same industry have often joined together to form organisations in order to negotiate collectively with trade unions. But employers and employees are not free to act and negotiate totally how they wish. For example, the Trade Union Act of 1984 makes trade unions' legal immunity for industrial action conditional on the prior holding of a secret strike ballot; on the other hand, the Health and Safety Act of 1974 states that employers must provide a healthy and safe environment. The extent to which governments should seek to influence relations between employers and employees has been an issue of considerable controversy in recent years.

Extract 9 *Trade Unions: Numbers and Membership*

	Number of unions	Total membership (thousands)	Percentage change in membership since previous year
		United Kingdom	
1975	470	12,026	
1976	473	12,386	+3.0
1977	481	12,846	+3.7
1978	462	13,112	+2.1
1979	453	13,289	+1.3
1980	438	12,947	−2.6
1981	414	12,106	−6.5
1982	408	11,593	−4.2
1983	394	11,337	−2.2
1984	371	11,086	−2.2

Source: Adapted from *Social Trends 1987*, HMSO, 1987, Table 11.8

a How many fewer trade unions were there in 1984 than 1975?
b By how much did union membership decline between the peak year and 1984?
c Explain why the number of people in trade unions has declined.
d The main reason why there are fewer trade unions today is that many have combined with others to form large unions. What are the advantages of such mergers?

Trade unions were originally formed by manual workers but as the occupational structure has changed, trade unions representing workers in the tertiary sector (e.g. teachers, bank clerks) have become more important, while those in the primary (especially mining) and secondary sectors have lost most members. The growth in white-collar unions also reflects changes in the work situation of many clerical workers (e.g. working in large offices for bureaucratic organisations rather than working with the boss in a small family firm), and the view of many non-manual groups that they have suffered a relative decline in status and pay in recent years. See page 78 *Extract 6* for changes in non-manual work, and the consequences of these changes for Britain's system of social stratification.

Trade unions adopt various strategies in order to improve the pay and conditions of their members; the most common, of course, is negotiation with an employer. Usually only when this negotiation breaks down do workers turn to industrial action.

Extract 10 *Industrial Disputes*

The chart below indicates the number of working days lost through industrial disputes in the United Kingdom.

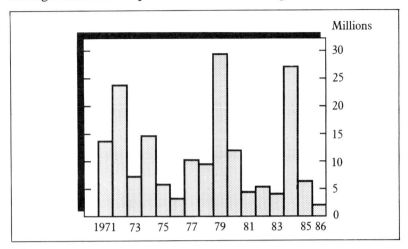

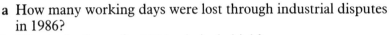

Source: Adapted from *Social Trends 1987*, HMSO, 1987, Table 4.20 and *Employment Gazette*, Department of Employment, March 1987, p543

a How many working days were lost through industrial disputes in 1986?
b Why is the figure for 1984 relatively high?
c Some industries have more strikes than others. What reasons can you give for these differences?

Individuals or small groups of workers who are dissatisfied at work may take less organised action such as absenteeism or industrial sabotage. Such action, unlike organised trade-union action, is unlikely to do anything to solve the cause of the dissatisfaction.

'Aha! Trying to buy us off with huge salaries and great working conditions, huh?'

Activity 13

a By asking workers you know, find out the name of one trade union for:
    1 teachers
    2 coal miners
    3 clerical workers
    4 shop workers
    5 bus drivers.
b What benefits do workers gain from belonging to trade unions?
c What criticisms can be made of trade unions in Britain today? Are these criticisms justified?

Unemployment

Not everyone who wishes to work can do so, and unemployment has become today, as it was in the 1920s and 1930s an issue of major political, social and economic importance. It is impossible to estimate exactly how many people are unemployed, partly because the methods the Department of Employment uses for collecting statistics on and defining unemployment have changed on several occasions, and so the statistics below should be interpreted as indicating general trends and differences between groups rather than exact numbers.

Extract 11   Unemployment Rate: Annual Average

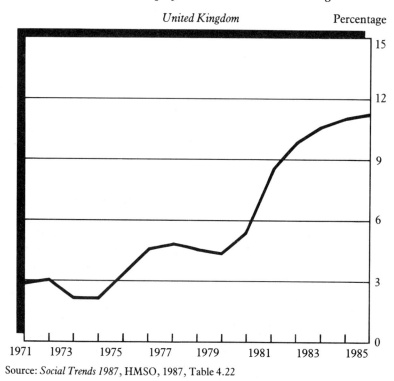

United Kingdom   Percentage

Source: *Social Trends 1987*, HMSO, 1987, Table 4.22

a What proportion of the work force was unemployed in 1985?
b By how much did the unemployment rate rise between 1971 and 1985?

Activity 14

In groups of three or four, draw up lists of the different reasons put forward to explain why the unemployment rate has risen in recent years. Which explanations seem to you to be most satisfactory?

Extract 12 *Unemployment by Social Class*

An individual's chances of being unemployed depend on several factors, one of the most important being social class.

Those without a Job and Actively Seeking Work as a Proportion of those Economically Active (Great Britain)			
previous social class	spring 1979	spring 1985	change
		percentage	
1 professional etc.	★	1.5	★
2 intermediate	1.6	3.5	+1.9
3 skilled	3.0	6.7	+3.7
4 partly skilled	5.2	9.6	+4.4
5 unskilled	8.2	12.7	+4.5

Source: *New Society*, 6 February 1987, p11

★No meaningful rate can be computed for this group because of the sampling error that would be involved.

a In 1985, which types of workers had the highest and which the lowest unemployment rates?

b What explanations can you give for the differences in the above table?

Extract 13 *Who is Most Likely to be Unemployed?*

Source: 'Unemployment and Poverty', Adrian Sinfield and Neil Fraser, in *The Thatcher Revolution*, Modern Studies Association, 1986, pp41–42

The extract below summarises a variety of factors that influence the likelihood of being unemployed. See p.101 *Extract 4* for statistics on ethnic origin and unemployment.

Unemployment is not distributed equally across the work force: those living in some areas have always been much more vulnerable than others. The variation in unemployment by region is still considerable although it has been reduced in the recent recession.

Northern Ireland continues to bear the heaviest burden and the North and North-west of England, Wales and Scotland continue to fare worse than London and the South – a pattern which first emerged in the inter-war years and has persisted since. The main change is in the West Midlands, which was experiencing severe labour shortages during the 1950s with the boom in the car industry. Its collapse, combined with the more general recession in manufacturing, resulted in a very sharp increase in jobless rates.

However there may be marked variations within areas as large as these. The whole of Scotland, for example, had a rate of 16.4 per cent in January 1986. The regions however ranged from the Shetland Islands 6.8 per cent, Grampian 8.6 per cent, and Borders 10.2 per cent to Highland 17.8 per cent, Strathclyde 19.4 per cent, and Western Isles 19.9 per cent. 16 of the 60 local travel-to-work areas in Scotland published by the Department of Employment had rates of 20 per cent or over and these included 5 of the 8 areas given for Highland and 6 of the 12 in Strathclyde.

The risk of unemployment also varies by many other factors including class, race, age and sex. Those at both the end and the beginning of their working lives experience well above average rates of unemployment. At least 1 in 10 of the currently unemployed are young people who have not had a job since leaving school despite the availability of Youth Training and other schemes specially directed towards school-leavers. Black and other ethnic minority workers are also particularly vulnerable as discrimination and disadvantage increase their difficulties. The impact on women has been concealed by the method of counting the unemployed which results in an undercount of those not likely to be eligible for benefits, and this group includes very many married women.

a Which region of Britain has the highest unemployment rate?

b According to the extract, why is it misleading to discuss unemployment in terms of large regions?

c Explain why those at the beginning and end of their working lives are most likely to experience unemployment.

Extract 14 Unemployment: by Duration

It is not just the fact of unemployment that is important, but also how long that unemployment lasts.

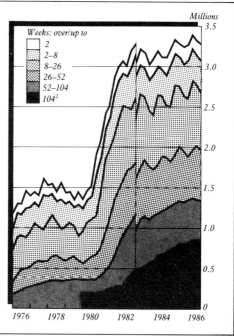

United Kingdom[1]

Weeks: over/up to
- 2
- 2–8
- 8–26
- 26–52
- 52–104
- 104[2]

[1] *Figures up to October 1982 relate to the registered unemployed.*
From October 1982 the figures are on the new basis (claimants).
From April 1983 some men aged 60 or over did not have to sign on at an Unemployment Benefit Office to receive the higher rate of supplementary benefit and national insurance credits. Between March and August 1983 the number affected was 162 thousand, of whom about 125 thousand were in the over 52 weeks category.
[2] *Dates are only available from October 1979.*

Source: *Social Trends 1987*, HMSO, 1987, Table 4.23

a How many workers had been out of work for two years or more in 1986?

b Why do the statistics for all groups decline in October 1982?

Extract 15 The Financial Consequences of Unemployment

There seems to be a double handicap for the less skilled – a greater risk of becoming unemployed and a small chance, once unemployed of finding work again. The double handicap is made worse because the less skilled are generally lower paid and so less protected against the loss of earnings. Studies have shown that they are less likely to have savings and receive smaller redundancy payments, if any. Both statutory and private schemes usually relate their payments to previous earnings AND to length of service, and the lower skilled and lower paid a job the shorter time it is likely to last.

Source: 'Unemployment and Poverty', Adrian Sinfield and Neil Fraser, in *The Thatcher Revolution*, Modern Studies Association, 1986, p43

a What is redundancy pay usually based on?

b What other factors are likely to cause less skilled workers to be especially badly off if unemployed for a long period?

Activity 15

Carry out a brief survey among your fellow students on how they would feel if they could not find employment on leaving school or college.

Extract 16 The Effects of Unemployment

Work is so central to most people's lives that it would be surprising if the lack of it did not have a profound effect on the lives of the unemployed. Geoffrey Beattie, in a study of Sheffield in the 1980s, here points to the psychological effects of unemployment.

What's so bad about unemployment these days? After all, don't the unemployed live in conditions not even dreamed of by social reformers in Victorian times? A comfortable existence, an easy life. No need to get up in the morning, no need to get your hands dirty; TV, video nasties (at a pound a night). So what's wrong with all this? The answer seems to be – quite a lot. The obvious physical harm of the first industrial revolution has been replaced by the more insidious harm of the second (the microchip revolution). Two psychologists from Sheffield University, Paul Jackson and Peter Warr (1983), studied in some detail a large sample of unemployed men. They found that a fifth of the sample experienced psychological deterioration since losing their job. (A few individuals' psychological health, however, improved with unemployemnt.) The deterioration included anxiety, depression, insomnia, irritability, lack of confidence, inability to concentrate and general nervousness.

Peter Warr suggested in 1983 that there are nine features of the unemployed person's role which may bring about reduced psychological wellbeing. First, and most obvious, is the reduced income. Warr reports that two-thirds of his sample of unemployed working-class men had an income half or less of their income when employed. This is a bitter blow to a generation reared on materialism and brought up on a diet of glossy adverts and constant incitements to buy, change, keep ahead. The second potentially damaging feature of unemployment is that with work gone and income reduced, the variety in a person's life becomes restricted. There is more inactivity, sleeping during the day, sitting around watching TV or the video. Work also provides goals. In unemployment there are fewer goals and a smaller scope for important decision-making (there is more scope for trivial decision-making like what time to get up in the morning). Many jobs, even apparently mundane ones, allow the practice of certain skills; unemployment allows the practice of few

skills. With unemployment there is an increase in what Warr calls 'psychologically threatening activities', such as making applications in the knowledge that they will probably end in rejection. There is also a good deal of insecurity about the future in the unemployed and reduced contact with other people. Work got you out of the house, and you may not have liked your workmates but you were at least afforded some degree of human contact with them. Unemployment can and does isolate people. And finally there is the individual's self-concept, in our society often tightly bound up with his or her position in paid employment.

The general psychological impact of unemployment is clearly deleterious but it is not equally so for every person. As always, some suffer more than others. Research has shown that those with the highest 'employment commitment', i.e. those who really do want a job, suffer the most distress.

Source: *Survivors of Steel City*, Geoffrie Beattie, Chatto and Windus, 1986, pp18, 19

GLOSSARY

insidious treacherous and subtle.
materialism emphasis on material possessions, e.g. cars, new kitchens.
deleterious harmful.

a What does Beattie mean by the 'more insidious harm' of the second industrial revolution?
b How can unemployment isolate people?
c Which types of people are most likely to be harmed by the experience of unemployment?

d Explain how unemployment may affect an individual's self-concept or image.

Leisure

Occupation will determine how much time and money is available for leisure, and, to some extent, the type of leisure activities pursued. It is therefore not surprising that sociologists have often studied leisure in terms of its relationship to occupation. However, over half of Britain's population does not have paid employment, and, irrespective of occupation, people do have considerable freedom in how to spend their leisure time.

Extract 17 How People Spend their Time

Time Use in a Typical Week: by Economic Status, 1985

Great Britain						Hours
	Full-time employees[1]		Part-time employees[1]			
	Males	Females	Males	Females	Housewives	Retired people
Weekly hours spent on:						
Employment and travel[2]	45.0	40.8	24.3	22.2		
Essential activities[3]	33.1	45.1	48.8	61.3	76.6	49.8
Sleep	56.4	57.5	56.6	57.0	59.2	60.2
Free time	33.5	24.6	38.5	27.5	32.2	58.0
Free time per weekday	2.6	2.1	4.5	3.1	4.2	7.9
Free time per weekend day	10.2	7.2	7.8	5.9	5.6	9.1

[1] Excludes the self-employed.
[2] Travel to and from place of work.
[3] Essential domestic work and personal care. This includes cooking, essential shopping, child care, eating meals, washing, and getting up and going to bed.

Source: *Social Trends 1987*, HMSO, 1987, Table 10.1

a How many daily hours free time, on average, did a woman with a full-time job have in 1985?

b Who has more free time, men or women? What explanations can you give for the differences in free time?

c Explain why 'essential activities' and 'free time' will be seen in different ways by different people. Give examples to illustrate your answer.

Activity 16

a Carry out a brief survey on how a small sample of people spend their leisure time.

b Ask the people you study if there are any other leisure activities they would participate in if they had the time or money.

c What conclusions can you draw from your survey about the relationships between work and leisure?

Extract 18 *What People Spend their Money on*

How people spend the money they have left over after they have paid for essentials like housing, heating and food is a useful indicator of the importance attached to different leisure activities.

Household Expenditure on Selected Leisure Items: by Economic Activity of Head of Household, 1985

United Kingdom						£s and percentages
		Economic activity of head of household				
		Employee out of a job		Retired or unoccupied		
	Employed	For up to 1 year	For over 1 year	Under pension age	Pension age or over	All households
Average weekly household expenditure on (£s):						
Alcoholic drink consumed away from home	7.82	6.47	4.38	4.58	1.73	5.76
Meals consumed out[1]	4.99	1.80	1.47	2.06	1.39	3.54
Books, newspapers, magazines, etc.	3.02	2.11	1.77	2.13	1.97	2.59
Television, radio, and musical instruments	5.34	4.14	2.69	3.14	2.16	4.17
Purchase of materials for home repairs, etc	3.97	3.47	1.10	0.99	2.13	3.09
Holidays	6.73	1.46	1.80	1.66	3.17	4.98
Hobbies	0.13	–	0.00	0.04	0.03	0:08
Cinema admissions	0.12	0.10	0.10	0.06	0.02	0.09
Dance admissions	0.16	0.13	0.09	0.11	0.03	0.12
Theatre, concert, etc admissions	0.33	0.06	0.05	0.11	0.10	0.23
Subscriptions and admission charges to participant sports	0.89	0.52	0.19	0.39	0.18	0.62
Football match admissions	0.12	0.07	0.05	0.03	0.01	0.08
Admissions to other spectator sports	0.04	0.07	0.01	0.02	0.01	0.03
Sports goods (excluding clothes)	0.48	0.06	0.16	0.15	0.04	0.31
Other entertainment	0.42	0.24	0.16	0.18	0.08	0.30
Total weekly expenditure on above	34.56	20.70	14.02	15.66	13.04	25.98
Expenditure on above items as a percentage of total household expenditure	*16.8*	*16.1*	*14.9*	*12.8*	*14.3*	*16.0*

[1] Eaten on the premises, excluding state school meals and workplace meals.

Source: *Social Trends 1987*, HMSO, 1987, Table 10.15

a Which two items do employed people spend most on?

b Which item shows the biggest difference between the employed and other groups?

c The average household headed by an employed person in 1985 spent £7.82 on alcohol consumed away from home. Why must this statistic be interpreted carefully?

d Why does expenditure not tell us how much time people spend on particular activities?

Activity 17

For many people leisure activities are centred on the home.
a Draw up a list of popular home-centred leisure activities.
b Explain why there has been an increase in home-based leisure.

Extract 19 The Links between Work and Leisure

Stanley Parker has argued that there are three types of relationship between work and leisure; extension, opposition and neutrality.

Briefly, the *extension* pattern consists of having leisure activities which are often similar in content to one's working activities and of making no sharp distinction between what is considered as work and what as leisure. With the *opposition* pattern leisure activities are deliberately unlike work and there is a sharp distinction between what is work and what is leisure. Finally, the *neutrality* pattern consists of having leisure activities which are generally different from work but not deliberately so, and of appreciating the difference between work and leisure without always defining the one as the absence of the other.

With the extension pattern there is a similarity between at least some work and leisure activities and a lack of demarcation made between what is called work and what is called leisure. Having work as a central life interest is part of the definition of the extension pattern.

The key aspects of the opposition pattern are the intentional dissimilarity of work and leisure and the strong demarcation between the two spheres. The extreme cases of this pattern are those who hate their work so much that any reminder of it in their off-duty time is unpleasant. But paradoxically such people do not in one sense get away from work at all: so deeply are they marked by the hated experience of work that they measure the delights of leisure according to how much unlike work they are.

The crucial difference between extension and opposition on the one hand and neutrality on the other is that the former denote respectively a positive and negative *attachment* to work, while the latter denotes a *detachment* from work that is, in Berger's phase, neither fulfilment nor oppression. In the cases of extension and opposition, the imprint left by work on leisure is relatively marked, in either a positive or a negative way. But people showing the neutrality pattern are neither so engrossed in their work that they want to carry it over into non-work time nor so damaged by it that they develop a hostile or love-hate relation to it. Instead, work leaves them comparatively unmarked and free to carry over into leisure the non-involvement and passivity which characterizes their attitude to work. In other words, detachment from any real responsibility for and interest in work leads to detachment from any creative and constructive leisure pursuits. Although some individuals are able to break out of this vicious circle, the tendency is to sit back and wait to be entertained. Since entertainment is more 'fun' than work, people with the neutrality pattern are likely to find their central life interest outside the work sphere.

Source: *The Future of Work and Leisure*, Stanley Parker, Paladin, 1972, pp103, 104, 105

a Briefly explain, in your own words, the three patterns of work–leisure relationships identified by Parker.

b Give an example of each type of relationship.

c Which pattern would you expect to increase in the future? What are the implications of this for people's leisure activities?

'He's a glutton for work – that's as close as he ever gets to a holiday.'

Although work does influence leisure, this influence should not be exaggerated. All teachers, for example, do roughly the same job, but they have very different leisure patterns. Further, an emphasis, as in Parker's typology, on occupation, fails to take into account those people not in paid employment.

Leisure is of key importance in the lives of most people. It can provide relaxation, friendship, intellectual, emotional and physical excitement and feelings of worth and belonging that might be difficult to find elsewhere. How we spend our leisure time is restricted by money and time, health and where we live, but these limitations should not be allowed to hide the considerable freedom most people have in deciding how to spend their free time.

Activity 18

On the basis of this chapter, and other reading you have done, outline how you expect work and leisure to change in the next 50 years.

Questions and Suggested Projects

Review Questions

1 Explain why it is difficult to define the terms *work* and *leisure*.
2 What is the evidence for the emergence of a dual-labour market?
3 Outline the main changes in the occupational structure in recent years.
4 What are the main factors that influence job satisfaction?
5 Explain the meaning of:
    a alienation **b** deskilling and reskilling
    c an instrumental attitude to work.
6 What are the main causes and consequences of employment?

Theme-linking Questions

1 Examine the relationships between leisure and:
    a age **b** gender.
2 What effects may unemployment have on family life?
3 Examine the links between Britain's changing occupational structure and the system of social stratification.
4 Examine how the development of new technology is affecting men and women in their working and leisure lives.
5 If you wished to study work satisfaction in a factory or office, explain the advantages and disadvantages of:
    a participant observation **b** unstructured interviews
    c questionnaires.

Stimulus–response Question

Great Britain	Average Weekly Hours of Full-time Employees[1], April 1985					
	Males			Females		
	Manual	Non-manual	All employees	Manual	Non-manual	All employees
Percentage of each group with total weekly hours in the range:						
34 or under	*0.4*	*5.6*	*2.7*	*7.8*	*10.9*	*10.2*
Over 34 but not over 36	*1.7*	*17.8*	*8.8*	*9.1*	*23.1*	*19.9*
Over 36 but not over 40	*43.0*	*56.8*	*49.1*	*62.0*	*59.4*	*60.0*
Over 40 but not over 44	*16.1*	*9.3*	*13.1*	*10.5*	*4.1*	*5.6*
Over 44 but not over 48	*15.0*	*5.1*	*10.6*	*5.5*	*1.4*	*2.4*
Over 48 but not over 50	*5.4*	*1.5*	*3.7*	*1.6*	*0.3*	*0.6*
Over 50	*18.4*	*3.8*	*11.9*	*3.5*	*0.7*	*1.3*
Sample size (= 100%) (thousands)	40	32	71	8	27	35
Average weekly hours						
Normal basic hours	39.1	37.0	38.2	38.0	36.1	36.5
Overtime hours	5.4	1.6	3.7	1.5	0.5	0.8
Total weekly hours	44.5	38.6	41.9	39.5	36.6	37.3

[1] Hours of full-time employees on adult rates whose pay for the survey pay-period was not affected by absence and for whom normal basic hours were reported. Total weekly hours are the sum of normal basic hours and paid overtime hours.

Source: *Social Trends 1987*, HMSO, 1987, Table 4.16

a What proportion of female manual workers worked over 50 hours per week in April 1985? (1)

b What was the average number of hours worked per week by all
employees? (1)

c Why is it misleading to base hours of work on paid work at the
place of employment? (3)

d Which group, on average, worked longer hours, manual or
non-manual workers, according to the above table? (1)

e Explain why many workers do overtime when there is high
unemployment? (2)

f State four work benefits non-manual workers are more likely
to have than manual workers. (4)

g Explain why the proportion of workers working part-time has
increased in recent years. (3)

h Outline the main occupational differences that exist in Britain
today between males and females. (5)

Essays

1 'What we do in our leisure time is determined primarily by our
work.' Examine the arguments for and against this view.

2 **a** Explain the main changes that have taken place in the
number and size of trade unions in recent years.

b Outline the different occupational strategies workers can
use to improve their pay and conditions.

3 Examine the likely effects on the patterns and nature of work
of new technology. Your answer could include:
    expanding and declining occupations
    effects on the levels of employment and unemployment
    deskilling and reskilling
    work satisfaction
    working at home
    examples such as office work, retailing and printing.

Suggested Projects

1 An interview-based study asking personnel officers of local
firms what qualities they look for in applicants for jobs.

2 A study of industrial relations in a local factory.

3 A study, based on secondary sources, of the changing employment patterns in your area.

4 A study of how one occupation has changed over recent years
and how the workers have adapted to these changes.

5 A questionnaire-based study of what additional leisure facilities
people in your area would like to see provided.

Index

Longman Group UK Limited
*Longman House, Burnt Mill, Harlow, Essex, CM20 2JE, England
and Associated Companies throughout the World.*

© Longman Group UK Limited 1988

First published 1988
ISBN 0 582 00289 3

Edited by Stenton Associates
Design by Ken Vail Graphic Design
Typeset by Goodfellow & Egan (Phototypesetting) Ltd

Set in Plantin Medium
Printed in Great Britain at The Bath Press, Avon